An Oil and Gas Journal Book

The Natural Gas Industry

Monopoly and Competition

in Field Markets

by Edward J. Neuner

UNIVERSITY OF OKLAHOMA PRESS : NORMAN

By Edward J. Neuner

Financial Analysis of TVA Power Distributors. Knoxville, 1950.
The Natural Gas Industry: Monopoly and Competition in Field Markets. Norman, 1960.

The publication of this work has been aided by a grant
from the Ford Foundation.

To My Wife

Preface

FEW PUBLIC ECONOMIC POLICIES have engendered more controversy in recent years than the federal regulation of natural gas production. Not only are private interests of gas producers affected by the prospect of a utility-type control of gas field prices, but large regional economic interests are also involved—to a point where "consuming" states have been pitted against "producing" states in the political arena. To support their position, the proponents of regulation have vigorously asserted the existence of monopoly; the opponents of control have been no less vocal in denying this charge. But the facts of the situation have by no means been made clear, and the task of social choice has not been facilitated.

The objective of this study is to provide factual and analytical materials needed for a rational policy decision and to offer a policy judgment on the monopoly issue in natural gas production. The fulfillment of this aim is sought by an investigation of natural gas field markets over the period of 1945–53, during which time the major postwar expansion of the industry took place.

To facilitate presentation, the book is divided into three parts: Part I develops basic factual information about concentration, field price levels, and field market practices; Part II explores market behavior in the gas field through a systematic examination of market transactions; Part III undertakes to evaluate the case for and against gas field monopoly. All who are primarily interested in an evaluation will find that Part III can be read as an independent unit, although it is based essentially upon the facts and analyses of the two sections which precede it.

Acknowledgment is gratefully extended to the many persons whose assistance made completion of this work possible. In particular, the aid and encouragement given by Professor James C. Bonbright, Columbia University, are warmly appreciated. Finally, any errors and all conclusions in this study are entirely the author's responsibility.

EDWARD J. NEUNER

San Diego, California
March 21, 1960

Contents

ix

Tables

xi

Figures

xv

Maps

Introduction

UNTIL RECENTLY, the most immediate issue in the controversy about federal regulation of natural gas producers was that of jurisdiction. This question, dealing with the extent of the Federal Power Commission's authority under the Natural Gas Act of 1938, had been a matter of dispute for almost fifteen years, during which time direct regulation of gas producers was suspended. But the question of jurisdiction was largely settled by the Phillips decision, handed down by the Supreme Court in 1954.[1] In essence, that decision held that the existing statutory language of the Natural Gas Act of 1938 makes all interstate sales of natural gas for resale, including those sales made in the gas field by independent or non-pipe-line producers, subject to the Federal Power Commission's jurisdiction. As a consequence of this interpretation, interest and attention have shifted to the question of whether or not federal regulation of natural gas field prices is a sound public policy.

This is not to assert that the policy question was ignored or slighted during the struggle over jurisdiction. It was certainly the desire of those denying the existence of FPC jurisdiction under the terms of the Act to avoid the substantive consequences of control. And both the regulatory agency and the Supreme Court must have realized that their interpretation of statutory language constituted an immediate policy choice. Nevertheless, in a jurisdictional dispute, administrative and judicial authorities were unable to deal directly with the central issues of public policy.

At the same time, legislative policy-making efforts during the course of the jurisdictional struggle were weakened by un-

[1] *Phillips Petroleum Company* v. *State of Wisconsin et al.*, 347 U. S. 672 (1954).

xvii

certainty concerning the meaning of existing law. In a closely divided Congress, the thought that judicial reading of the Act would resolve a vexing controversy about public policy undoubtedly diminished the pressure for legislative action. With the Phillips decision, the final testing of jurisdictional limits appears to have been made, and contention on this matter has been brought to an end. Barring unlikely reversals of judicial position, further action to exempt natural gas producers from federal regulation must come from a Congressional amendment to the Act.

Under these circumstances, and in view of continued efforts to secure gas producer exemption, an investigation of the basis for field market regulation would greatly aid a public policy decision. But, to mark the limits of such a study, it is desirable to bring into sharper focus the various issues in the natural gas policy dispute, two of which have been identified as primary. They provide the rationale for accepting or rejecting public control.

The first of these two issues relates to the question of monopoly. If such a condition were brought to light, it would undoubtedly provide the most readily accepted justification for gas producer regulation. Formulated precisely, the monopoly issue may be stated as follows:

Has there been, or is there likely to be, such a degree of concentration in the ownership of natural gas reserves or of monopolistic market control in the field sales of natural gas that competitive forces are, or will be, insufficient to prevent the exploitation of ultimate consumers, thus requiring the public regulation of natural gas field prices?

While the importance of the monopoly question is almost self-evident, a second basic issue is involved in the regulation of natural gas production. Although it has not always been clearly articulated, there are many indications that it is a basic issue dividing the opposing camps in the natural gas controversy and that it is a source of fundamental disagreement with respect to the proper course of public action. This second issue may be stated as follows:

Introduction

Assuming adequate, workable competition in the gas field and thus setting aside the monopoly issue, shall the scarcity returns or economic rents which arise with an increasing demand for the relatively fixed supply of a depleting natural resource accrue to the private owners of gas reserves or be subject to social appropriation for the benefit of either consumers or the general public?

The significance of the scarcity return issue resides in its potential as a rationale for control. Even if no monopoly condition exists in natural gas production, a decision to seek the social appropriation of scarcity returns would justify a utility-type regulation of natural gas field prices. This is true since one of the effects of a cost-oriented system of utility regulation is to transfer scarcity returns to consumers in the form of lower prices.

But utility price controls applied to natural gas production in order to achieve consumer appropriation of scarcity returns opens up a new area of public economic intervention. It departs radically from existing public policy with respect to the distribution of incomes arising from natural resource ownership. As such, the scarcity return issue is basic and controversial.

Despite the fact that the scarcity return issue poses an entirely separate policy problem, it has been obscured by mixture with the monopoly question—so much so that rational decision-making has been impaired. Alternative public policy choices depend upon a clear-cut separation of these two issues. For example, it might be decided that, since no monopoly condition exists in natural gas production, no regulation of that industry is justified, notwithstanding the presence of large scarcity returns. On the other hand, regulation to appropriate scarcity returns might be considered in the public interest, even in the absence of monopoly.

While this book does not treat the scarcity return issue at length, its detailed investigation of the problem of field market monopoly blocks out boldly the public policy decisions which have to be made. Thus the answer to the monopoly question will determine for many legislators the proper policy choice. For others, the settlement of this question will bring into sharpest focus the issue of whether or not scarcity returns arising from natural gas production should be subjected to a special form of social appropriation.

The Natural Gas Industry

Monopoly and Competition in Field Markets

PART I

Concentration, Field Prices, and Market Practices

A BASIC ELEMENT in the case for direct public regulation of natural gas field prices has been the asserted existence of a monopoly condition, not mitigable by any other means. While much information dealing with natural gas field markets is available in Congressional and other public records, it has not been properly organized or fully analyzed to determine its bearing on the gas monopoly question. Preparation of such a factual foundation, therefore, is a necessary first step.

One important and frequently disputed factual area has been the degree of concentration in natural gas field markets. Its pertinence to the question of gas field monopoly is apparent, since markets characterized by excessive seller concentration negate one of the basic prerequisites for effective competition, namely, numerous sellers providing many alternatives to buyers. By facilitating seller communication, such concentration makes possible many forms of seller co-operation, intended to diminish the rigors of competition.

Whether or not market structures in the gas field are conducive to the exercise of monopolistic market power becomes, therefore, a matter of some significance. A full investigation of the subject necessitates a measurement of concentration in the ownership of gas reserves, as well as in the field sales of gas, within both large regional markets and smaller submarkets.

However, in spite of their evidential importance, the facts of market structure and concentration may not be enough to support a case for or against public regulation. Social judgments relative to the public control of private industry are unusually circumspect, and a high concentration level may be insufficient to justify price-fixing regulations unless monopoly behavior and

3

results can be demonstrated. Furthermore, monopolistic market conditions can develop as the outcome of seller collusion, regardless of concentration levels. Such collusion may take the form of open and direct price-rigging actions by communicating sellers. Or it could be nothing more than a tacit adherence to marketing practices which give rise indirectly to noncompetitive price results.

In dealing with the question of gas producer monopoly, therefore, an examination of market structures does not suffice; an investigation of market behavior is also necessary. But the possibility of such an investigation depends heavily upon the availability of information concerning price movements, seller actions, and buyer responses, as well as marketing practices and other factors affecting prices. In short, an analysis of seller market behavior in the gas field requires detailed information concerning individual price-forming transactions.

Fortunately, a large body of data containing such information is available in the form of natural gas purchase agreements. Consisting of 723 natural gas purchase contracts negotiated in the southwestern United States between gas producers and interstate pipe lines during the period from 1944 through 1953, these data provide the informational foundation for much of this study.

CHAPTER I

Field Market Concentration

One INVESTIGATIVE APPROACH to the problem of natural gas monopoly is to determine the degree of concentration in natural gas field markets, since it is generally agreed that such seller concentration is evidence of the potentialities, at least, for monopolistic market control. A correct and proper determination of concentration levels in natural gas field markets, however, is a task not without its own special problems. Among these, and a matter of some importance, is the relative significance of the two principal measures of concentration, namely concentration in the ownership of gas reserves and concentration in the field sales of natural gas.

The objective sought by measuring concentration levels is to ascertain the potentialities for a manipulative seller control of total output or supply. In most industries, total output—except for inventory fluctuations—is reflected in sales and is highly correlated with the capacity of existing operative plant facilities. It may also be assumed that, in normal periods, the ratio of sales to the capacity of their respective plants is relatively uniform for different producers. Under these circumstances, concentration in sales becomes an accurate indicator of the degree of seller control over output, the productive capacity behind it, and thus the possibility of a monopolistic control over supply.

However, any inferences of monopoly derived from such a sales concentration measure are valid only for short-run supply—output forthcoming during the period of time required for any sizable increase in industry productive capacity. If the construction of additional productive plants by new firms were readily possible, the market power based on concentrated seller control would soon be dissipated. Perpetuation of dominance requires effective restraints upon entry.

One such restraint is derived from the mere existence of seller concentration, since new and relatively small firms would be at a considerable disadvantage in the struggle for markets and would therefore be impeded in efforts to enter the industry. Increases in productive capacity are also retarded whenever the users of an industry's output have such small individual demands for the products that they cannot economically construct their own producing facilities. In many industries, then, the effective restraints upon new entrants are sufficiently strong to make concentration in current sales a useful test of market power, even with respect to long-run supply.

In the case of natural gas production, however, sales concentration, while of considerable value as an indicator of current and short-run seller dominance in the gas field, is much less useful as a means of measuring the potential for long-term market control. Instead, the greatest reliance in this industry must be placed upon the degree of concentration in ownership of natural gas reserves. Although the short-run availability of gas supplies is dependent upon the existing plant, such as wells and gathering lines in developed gas fields, these facilities are not difficult to enlarge, and a concentrated control over such a plant would not, by itself, result in significant market power with respect to pipe-line buyers. Pipe-line purchasers, having large supply needs and possessing the necessary financial means, could readily undertake the construction of new producing facilities, if access to gas reserves were otherwise available. Consequently, any large and sustained market power in natural gas production depends upon control of gas reserves, for these reserves are the factor limiting entry and determining the long-run expansion of field gas supplies.

A. Concentration in Natural Gas Reserves

The general and long-run potential for monopolistic control in natural gas production is closely connected with the ownership of gas reserves. Thus a tabulation of such ownership, with some breakdown between gas reserves already committed by long-term contracts and those not yet dedicated, is vital for an assessment of the gas monopoly issue. Unfortunately, with the exception of gas reserve holdings of interstate pipe lines subject to Federal Power Commission jurisdiction, information pertaining to the ownership of gas reserves has not been available to the extent desirable as part of the public record. During Congressional consideration of the Harris-Fulbright bill, the deficiencies in reserve ownership data were noted and, in one instance, criticized.[1] Despite the incomplete coverage, many useful inferences and conclusions can be derived from available data.

The bulk of reserve ownership information consists of data secured by the Federal Power Commission in response to Congressional request. The federal agency tried to ascertain gas

Table 1

OWNERSHIP OF NATURAL GAS RESERVES

IN THE UNITED STATES, 1953*

Reserve-Ownership Rank	PRODUCER	Reserves TCF
1	Humble Oil & Refining Co.	16.0
2	Phillips Petroleum Co.	13.2
3	The Texas Company	10.5
4	Stanolind Oil & Gas Co.	9.9
5	Magnolia Petroleum Co.	7.5
6	Standard Oil Co. of California	4.5 (D)
7	Gulf Oil Corp.†	4.0
8	Pure Oil Co.	3.7
9	Skelly Oil Co.	2.3
10	Atlantic Refining Co.	2.2
11	Continental Oil Co.	2.2
12	Ohio Oil Co.	2.1
13	Delhi Oil Corp.	1.9 (D)
14	Tide Water Associated Oil Co.	1.8
15	Shamrock Oil & Gas Corp.‡	1.7
16	Sinclair Oil & Gas Co.	1.7

[1] *Hearings before Committee on Interstate and Foreign Commerce on H. R. 4560.* 84 Cong., 1 sess. (1955), 22; *Hearings before Committee on Interstate and Foreign Commerce on S. 1853,* 84 Cong., 1 sess. (1955), 1527, 1542.

Reserve-Ownership Rank	PRODUCER	Reserves TCF
17	Union Oil Co. of California§	1.6 (D)
18	Columbian Fuel Corp.	1.6 (D)
19	Sunray Oil Corp.	1.5
20	Western Natural Gas Co.	1.4
21	Southern Production Co.	1.3 (D)
22	Taylor Oil & Gas Co.	1.1 (D)
23	Three States Natural Gas Co.	1.0 (D)
24	Kerr-McGee Oil Industries	1.0 (D)
25	Sohio Petroleum Co.	0.7
26	Johnson Oil & Gas Co.	0.6 (D)
27	Hugoton Plains Gas & Oil Co.	0.5 (D)
28	Union Sulphur & Oil Corp.	0.5 (D)
29	Lion Oil Co.	0.4 (D)
30	Pubco Development Co.	0.3 (D)
	Others (26) reporting gas reserve ownership	1.7 (D)
	Subtotal	100.4
	Reserves owned by interstate pipe-line companies and affiliates‖	28.1
	Reserves for which ownership data are available	128.5
	Reserves for which ownership data are not available	83.0
	American Gas Association estimate of gas reserves in the U. S.—1953[#]	211.5

[*] The reserve data shown (excepting Gulf Oil Corp.) were compiled and presented by the Federal Power Commission, *Hearings before Committee on Interstate and Foreign Commerce on H. R. 4560,* 84 Cong., 1 sess. (1955), 22–23, unless indicated by a (D), in which case it has been obtained from Senator Douglas' presentation in *Hearings before Committee on Interstate and Foreign Commerce on S. 1853,* 84 Cong., 1 sess. (1955), 1527–28. Although most reserve estimates were as of December 31, 1953, in some cases the 1953 date is only an approximation.

[†] *Wall Street Journal,* December 21, 1955, 16.

[‡] FPC study assigns to this company a reserve estimate of 1.7 TCF as of November 30, 1954. Moody's *Industrial Manual–1955* records a reserve estimate of 2.8 TCF as of December 31, 1951. The Douglas compilation used the larger figure.

[§] FPC study gives a gross reserve estimate of 2.1 TCF, with net reserves of 1.6 TCF.

[‖] See Table 4 below.

[#] *American Gas Journal,* Vol. CLXXX (March, 1954), 19.

reserve holdings for the thirty largest sellers of natural gas to interstate pipe lines during 1953. It was able to obtain information for seventeen of these companies from an examination "of registration statements filed with the Securities and Exchange Commission, of annual reports to stockholders, Moody's Manual, and stock reports of Standard and Poor's Corp."[2] In addition to the FPC material, reserve ownership data were obtained from a presentation by Senator Paul Howard Douglas of Illinois before the Senate Committee on Interstate and Foreign Commerce, as well as from financial publications.

A compilation of reserve ownership data from the different sources is given in Table 1. An examination of this table indicates the existence of gas reserve data for thirty independent producers, whose total holdings amount to 98.7 trillion cubic feet.[3] If twenty-six unidentified concerns reporting very small reserves are included, a subtotal of 100.4 trillion cubic feet is obtained. The inclusion of holdings reported by interstate pipe lines brings the total reserves for which ownership is known to 128.5 TCF. On the other hand, ownership information is not available for 83.0 TCF of gas reserves. However, it has been possible to account for approximately 60 per cent of the 211.5 TCF of total U. S. gas reserves recorded on December 31, 1953.

Some indication of the gaps in reserve data is given in Table 2. Here, available reserve information is correlated with large sales to interstate pipe lines, the presumption being that such sales imply important reserve holdings. In this tabulation, independent producers are ranked by size of sales to interstate pipe lines in 1953, and all producers selling 25 million MCF or more per annum are included. In addition to the thirty-seven companies meeting this standard, six others for which reserve data are available have been included in the table.

Table 2 reveals that, of the thirty-seven producers making large interstate sales, reserve information is available for twenty-four companies, or approximately 65 per cent of this group. Of

[2] *Hearings—H. R. 4560*, 22.

[3] The following abbreviations are used in this book in reference to cubic feet: MCF=thousand cubic feet; MMCF=million cubic feet; M³CF=billion cubic feet; TCF=trillion cubic feet.

9

The Natural Gas Industry

Table 2

NATURAL GAS RESERVES OWNED BY INDEPENDENT PRODUCERS
SELLING TO INTERSTATE PIPE-LINE COMPANIES, 1953*

Sales Rank	Producer	Sales M³CF	Reserves TCF
1	Phillips Petroleum Co.	457.4	13.2
2	Stanolind Oil & Gas Co.	202.6	9.9
3	Humble Oil & Refining Co.	196.6	16.0
4	Magnolia Petroleum Co.	157.5	7.5
5	Shell Oil Co.	156.3	†
6	Chicago Corp.	155.6	†
7	Gulf Oil Corp. & Gulf Refining Co.	138.4	4.0
8	Atlantic Refining Co.	95.2	2.2
9	Shamrock Oil & Gas Corp.	81.4	1.7
10	Skelly Oil Co.	74.6	2.3
11	Sun Oil Co.	69.0	†
12	The Texas Company	67.4	10.5
13	Carthage Corp. plant	66.6	†
14	Republic Natural Gas Co.	63.2	†
15	Superior Oil Co.	62.5	†
16	Sunray Oil Corp.	53.7	1.5
17	Union Oil Co. of California	53.0	1.6
18	Continental Oil Co.	52.9	2.2
19	Southwest Gas Producing Co., Inc.	50.8	†
20	Panoma Corp.	48.6	†
21	La Gloria Corp.	48.0	†
22	Pure Oil Co.	48.0	3.7
23	Ohio Oil Co.	47.8	2.1
24	Abercrombie, J. S., Co.	46.9	†
25	Tide Water Associated Oil Co.	45.4	1.8
26	Sinclair Oil & Gas Co.	43.4	1.7
27	American Gas Produc. Co.	43.3	†
28	Southern Production Co.	42.1	1.3
29	Western Natural Gas Co.	39.2	1.4
30	Taylor Oil & Gas Co.	32.9	1.1
31	Union Sulphur & Oil Corp.	28.2	0.5
32	United Carbon Co.	28.1	†
33	California Co. (Standard Oil of California subsidiary)‡	26.4	4.5
34	Columbian Fuel Corp. (Columbian Carbon Co. subsidiary)	26.3	1.6

10

Sales Rank	PRODUCER	Sales M³CF	Reserves TCF
35	Sohio Petroleum Co.	25.8	0.7
36	Cullen, H. R.	25.6	†
37	Hugoton Plains Gas & Oil Co.	25.5	0.5
	Subtotal		93.5
	Other producers with interstate sales of less than 25 million MCF		6.9
	Total		100.4

* Sales data were compiled by the Federal Power Commission. Tabulation includes all producers selling 25 million MCF or more to interstate pipe lines during 1953, exclusive of producer sales to associated pipe-line companies. See *Hearings before Committee on Interstate and Foreign Commerce on S. 1853*, 84 Cong. 1 sess. (1955), 1639. Reserve data from Table 1 above.

† Not available.

‡ Sales are for the subsidiary only, while reserve data are for all of Standard of California's holdings in the United States.

interest is the fact that the known reserve data are almost entirely accounted for within this group of thirty-seven producers selling to interstate pipe lines. Furthermore, reserve information is known for the four largest sellers of gas and for eight of the ten largest gas producers. In the matter of unreported gas reserve holdings, it is unlikely that any one company's holdings, with the possible exception of the Shell Oil Company, would exceed 5.0 TCF. They are more apt to fall within a range of 1.0 to 4.0 TCF, which is characteristic of most of the reported holdings.

In Table 3, the ratio of gas reserves to sales is shown for twenty-three producers for whom reserve data are available. This tabulation makes evident the considerable variation in reserve-sales relationships, with a range extending from a low of 17.7 to a high of 155.8 and a median value of 33.4. The majority of these producers, however, fall within a reserve-sales ratio range of 20.0 to 40.0.

This variation in reserve-sales ratios is partially due to the use of sales data limited to interstate pipe-line transactions, while reserve data are not similarly restricted. For example, a firm selling a large fraction of its gas in intrastate markets would show a higher reserve-sales ratio than a firm with the same reserves and total sales but selling predominantly to interstate pipe lines. Relative differences in the intrastate sales made by different producers would, therefore, tend to accentuate variability in the reserve-sales data presented in Table 3.

In addition, two other factors would account for any significant differences in reserve-sales ratios among the producers.

Table 3

RESERVE-SALES RATIOS FOR TWENTY-THREE
INDEPENDENT PRODUCERS, 1953[*]

PRODUCER	Reserve-Sales Ratio[†]
The Texas Company	155.8
Humble Oil & Refining Co.	81.4
Pure Oil Co.	77.1
Columbian Fuel Corp.	60.8
Stanolind Oil & Gas Co.	48.9
Magnolia Petroleum Co.	47.6
Ohio Oil Co.	43.9
Continental Oil Co.	41.6
Tide Water Associated Oil Co.	39.6
Sinclair Oil & Gas Co.	39.2
Western Natural Gas Co.	35.7
Taylor Oil & Gas Co.	33.4
Southern Production Co.	30.9
Skelly Oil Co.	30.8
Union Oil Co.	30.2
Phillips Petroleum Co.	28.9
Gulf Oil Corp. & Gulf Refining Co.	28.9
Sunray Oil Corp.	27.9
Sohio Petroleum Co.	27.1
Atlantic Refining Co.	23.1
Shamrock Oil & Gas Corp.	20.9
Hugoton Plains Gas & Oil Co.	19.6
Union Sulphur & Oil Corp.	17.7

[*] Based on data of Table 2. Excludes the California Co., the sales and reserve data for which are not fully comparable.

[†] Ratio of gas reserves to gas sales.

One would be the amount of uncommitted reserves held; the other would be the period of time reserves are contractually committed to sustain current sales. The former is more likely to be responsible for variations than the latter, in view of the common practice of supporting interstate pipe-line sales with twenty-year reserves.

Subject to limitations noted above, the reserve-sales ratio data of Table 3 can be used to identify those producers who were likely holders of large uncommitted gas reserves in 1953. Certainly the very high reserve-sales ratios shown for the Texas Company and the Humble Oil and Refining Company imply such a situation. As a generalization, it could be asserted that producers recording reserve-sales ratios in excess of 40.0 were probably holders of large uncommitted gas reserves.

The possibility of deducing the degree of reserve concentration from the more complete data available for measuring sales concentration can also be examined in light of Table 3. Essential to such a projection of reserve concentration from sales data is the existence of a reasonable similarity in the reserve-sales ratios for different gas producers. The considerable variation in such ratios for the single test year, however, does not lead to a confident conclusion that sales concentration is apt to be an accurate gauge of concentration in reserve holdings. Whether the lack of uniformity is great enough to invalidate entirely the use of sales concentration for this purpose is difficult to determine. In view of this uncertainty, only the most limited and qualified statements about reserve concentration can be legitimately derived from sales concentration data.

Of further interest in studying the pattern of reserve ownership is the extent to which interstate pipe-line companies are the owners of natural gas resources. This bears upon the question of monopolistic market control in the gas field insofar as reserve ownership strengthens the bargaining position of the pipe-line buyer and thus offsets the effects of seller concentration. Table 4 gives a picture of the reserve holdings of certain interstate pipe-line companies, while Table 5 summarizes such data in conjunction with other reserve information.

Table 4

OWNERSHIP OF NATURAL GAS RESERVES BY CERTAIN
INTERSTATE PIPE-LINE COMPANIES AND
AFFILIATES, 1953[*]

Name of Company	Reserves TCF
El Paso Natural Gas Co.	4.461
United Gas Pipe Line Co.	4.000
Panhandle Eastern Pipe Line Co.	3.536
Colorado Interstate Gas Co.	3.225
Cities Service Gas Co.	2.036
Natural Gas Pipeline Co. of America	1.532
Northern Natural Gas Co.	1.500
Columbia Gas System	1.111
Arkansas–Louisiana Gas Co.	0.951
Lone Star Gas Co.	0.700
Kentucky–West Virginia Gas Co.	0.652
Mountain Fuel Supply Co.	0.607
Southern Natural Gas Co.	0.473
Other companies	3.363
Total	28.147

[*] Federal Power Commission data, *Hearings before Committee on Interstate and Foreign Commerce on S. 1853,* 84 Cong., 1 sess. (1955), 1528.

From Table 4, it is evident that pipe-line companies are major factors in the ownership of natural gas reserves. The two pipe-line companies with the largest reserves rank seventh and eighth in size of reserves held when compared with the non-pipe-line owners. However, ownership of large gas reserves does not characterize all natural gas pipe lines, since—with the exception of the El Paso Natural Gas Company—none of the postwar pipe lines are included in this list. The pipe-line systems originating in the period before 1941 predominate as large reserve owners. The explanation is found in the fact that pipe lines constructed in that prewar period usually acquired their basic gas supplies by direct purchase rather than through the system of long-term contracts. In addition, their promoters usually included the original owners of the gas reserves, who exchanged their holdings for pipe-line stock.

The relative importance of reserve ownership by pipe lines is given in Table 5, from which it is seen that the 28.1 TCF owned by interstate pipe lines, or controlled through affiliates, represents only 22.5 per cent of their total gas reserves and 13.3 per cent of total reserves in the United States. Approximately 78 per cent, or 96.7 TCF of pipe-line gas reserves, are held under contract from nonaffiliates. Noteworthy, too, is the fact that 59 per cent of the total gas reserves in the United States in 1953 was dedicated to an interstate pipe-line market, with approximately 40 per cent either uncommitted or dedicated to intrastate markets.

From the foregoing, it is possible to conclude that the available reserve information, while not complete, is sufficient to support useful generalizations. At the very least, an accurate picture of the minimum level of concentration in reserve ownership and

Table 5

NATURAL GAS RESERVES OWNED OR CONTROLLED BY AND UNDER
CONTRACT TO INTERSTATE PIPE-LINE COMPANIES, 1953[*]

	NATURAL GAS RESERVES		
ITEM	*TCF*	*Total Pipe-Line Reserves %*	*Total U. S. Reserves %*
Owned by interstate pipe lines	19.889	15.9	9.4
Owned by pipe-line affiliates	8.250	6.6	3.9
	28.139	22.5	13.3
Under contract to interstate pipe lines, excluding affiliates (104.977 TCF total under contract, including affiliates, less 8.250 TCF held by affiliates)	96.727	77.5	45.7
Total	124.866	100.0	59.0
American Gas Association estimate of gas reserves—12/31/53[†]	211.500		100.0

* Based on Federal Power Commission data reported in *Hearings before Committee on Interstate and Foreign Commerce on S. 1853,* 84 Cong., 1 sess. (1955) 1527.

† *American Gas Journal,* Vol. CLXXX (March, 1954), 19.

plausible approximations of the actual concentration level can be obtained from the data.

Utilizing available reserve data, the various concentration ratios can be derived with total gas reserves in the United States as a measurement base. (Table 6). The validity of such a concentration base, which includes the reserves held by the interstate pipe-line companies and their affiliates might be questioned. It could be argued that the degree of concentration is more accurately measured by relating the gas holdings of the largest independent producers to reserves in the United States, exclusive of pipe-line holdings. However, since the total supply of gas which influences long-term field prices necessarily includes pipe-line holdings, the market power of independent producers is limited by the existence of such alternative supplies, and the use of the broader concentration base is to be preferred.[4]

Consequently, the reserve holdings of independent producers for whom information has been disclosed are related to the total gas reserves in the United States. The resulting concentration ratios, also given in Table 6, column 2, are as follows:

5 largest holdings	27.0%
10 largest holdings	34.9%
15 largest holdings	39.5%
25 largest holdings	45.6%

These ratios, based entirely on the known data, may be said to describe the minimum level of concentration in reserve ownership. Thus, if all the 83.0 TCF of unreported gas reserves were, in fact, widely distributed in many small holdings—smaller in size than any already included in the list of reported ownerships—there would be no shift either upward or downward in the con-

---

[4] If the smaller concentration base were used, namely, 183.4 TCF (total U. S. reserves, 211.5, less pipe-line reserves, 28.1 TCF), minimum concentration ratios would become:

5 largest holdings	31.1%
10 largest holdings	40.2%
15 largest holdings	45.5%
25 largest holdings	52.5%

centration level by the inclusion of those data, since the rankings upon which the measurement of concentration depends would be unchanged. And the concentration base of 211.5 TCF, which already includes the undisclosed individual reserve holdings, would be unaffected.

But the gas reserves for which ownership data are not known may be expected to include some large holdings. The inclusion of these in the rankings can only have the effect of increasing the concentration ratios. The downward displacement in rank of some of the currently known holdings would increase the amount of gas reserves contained in the five, ten, or fifteen largest holdings. Since the base value of 211.5 TCF again is not affected by such inclusions, the concentration ratios must become larger.

With respect to maximum or upper limit concentration ratios, estimates are possible by making appropriate assumptions regarding the distribution of the unassigned gas reserves. For example, the entire 83.0 TCF of unreported gas reserve holdings might be assumed to be held in five large ownerships of approximately 16.6 TCF each. Certainly this would be a maximum possibility, for the largest single reported holding of 16.0 TCF is not likely to be greatly exceeded. On this assumption, a maximum level of concentration may be approximated, as shown in column 3 of Table 6.

It would be a decided gain if a closer approximation of the probable level of concentration could be obtained than that afforded by either minimum limits or an undoubtedly exaggerated maximum limit. One simple possibility is an average of the two limits, as shown in column 4. Another is to assume that the unreported reserve holdings are distributed in the same pattern as known ownerships. If quantitative values are assigned to undisclosed reserve holdings in the manner defined in footnote 4 of Table 6, concentration ratios may be calculated, with results as shown in column 5 of that tabulation.

Referring to the estimated concentration ratios of column 5, the 31.3 per cent for the five largest reserve holdings probably overstates the true situation. Reserve data are known for the four largest sellers of gas to interstate pipe lines, and it is most unlikely that many holdings of that size are to be found among sellers for whom data are not available. An offsetting factor is that the over-statement is not large in view of the minimum concentration ratio of 27 per cent. The same problem exists to a lesser extent for the ten largest reserve holdings. In general, the estimated concentration ratios shown in column 5 become more reliable as the size groupings of reserve holdings become larger.

The final estimates shown in column 6 of Table 6 are based on the assumption that reserves are related to current sales made to interstate pipe lines. Estimates of unreported reserves are obtained by multiplying producer sales by a reserve-sales ratio of 43.1. This factor, an average for the producers reporting reserves, was derived from the data of Table 3.

The concentration ratios obtained by this procedure are given in column 6; they are substantially less than the estimates of columns 4 and 5. The main limitation of the procedure followed in this case is that large reserve holdings are assumed to be found only in association with large interstate sales. The method thus allocates only 34.9 TCF of the 83.0 TCF of unreported reserves among the twenty-five largest reserve holdings, which probably understates somewhat the true situation.

Taking all these estimates into account, a usable approximation of the degree of concentration in the ownership of natural gas reserves may be attempted. The following summary estimate of concentration is offered:

ESTIMATED CONCENTRATION: INDEPENDENT PRODUCER GAS
RESERVE HOLDINGS, 1953

	Total Gas Reserves
5 largest holdings	30%
10 largest holdings	45%
25 largest holdings	60%

B. Concentration in Natural Gas Field Sales

As already noted, reserve concentration deals with a market power which can be sustained over a long period of time and

Table 6

CONCENTRATION IN THE OWNERSHIP OF NATURAL GAS RESERVES, 1953

ITEM	1 Natural Gas Reserves* TCF	2 Minimum Concentration Ratios† %	3 Estimated Maximum Concentration Ratios‡ %	4 Average of Min. and Max. Ratios %	5 Estimated Concentration Ratios§ %	6 Estimated Concentration Ratios‖ %
American Gas Association estimate of gas reserves in the U.S.—12/31/53	211.5	100.0	100.0	100.0	100.0	100.0
5 largest gas reserve holdings owned by independent producers reporting reserve-ownership data.	57.1	27.0	39.2	33.1	31.3	27.0
10 largest gas reserve holdings	73.8	34.9	66.2	50.5	51.3	39.1
15 largest gas reserve holdings	83.5	39.5	74.1	56.8	60.9	45.5
25 largest gas reserve holdings	96.4	45.6	82.4	64.0	71.4	55.2

* Data of Table 1.

† Based on known reserve-ownership data and assumes unaccounted-for gas reserves to be widely distributed in small holdings which do not affect rankings of the twenty-five largest producers.

‡ Based on the assumption that 83.0 TCF of unaccounted-for gas reserves are held by five owners, each holding 16.6 TCF. Since the largest known holding is 16.0 TCF, these five hypothetical ownerships become the five largest gas reserve holdings. The known holdings are then displaced downward.

§ Based on the assumption that ownership of unaccounted-for reserves is distributed in the same general pattern as known data. The unaccounted-for reserves are interleaved among the known data, at magnitudes which are obtained by averaging the two known and adjoining reserve magnitudes. For example, the first five known ownerships are 16.0, 13.2, 10.5, 9.9, and 7.5; interleaved among these are four hypothetical reserve-ownerships of 14.6, 11.8, 10.2, and 8.7. After the entire 83.0 TCF of unaccounted-for reserves are distributed in this manner, concentration ratios are calculated. Using this method, approximately 71.0 TCF of the 83.0 TCF of unaccounted-for reserves are allocated within the new group of twenty-five largest producers. In addition, 80.0 TCF of the known holdings are included in this unit.

‖ Based on the assumption that unaccounted-for reserves are distributed in proportion to interstate pipe-line sales. Reserve estimates for those producers for whom reserve data are not known were obtained by multiplying sales by a factor of 43.1. This factor is the average reserve-sales ratio of twenty-three producers for whom reserve data are available (see Table 3).

which results in the greatest control over price and output. Its determination is, therefore, basic to a study of the monopolistic potential in natural gas production. However, the possibility of short-run market power remains, and, to explore this possibility, the degree of concentration in current field sales of gas must be ascertained.

Concentration in field sales, as in reserve ownership, is to be measured by a set of concentration ratios—the percentage relationship between the sales made by different-sized groups of independent gas producers and a relevant base amount of sales. The latter, the so-called concentration base, should be related to a market unit that includes only the effective options available to buyers if the market strength of sellers is to be accurately determined.

Setting the limits of the market unit, therefore, becomes a matter of some importance. For it may be argued that the market for gas should be viewed functionally, that is, in terms of gas as a residential space-heating fuel and as an industrial heat energy source. A proper concentration base would then include the substitutes for natural gas such as coal, fuel oil, manufactured or synthetic gas, electric power, etc. Essential to this position is the proposition that the really important economic unit for the issue of monopolistic control over price is the final consumer market, since the availability of options at this final stage sets a limit to market power in the gas field.

An objection to this view is that the cost differential between natural gas and substitute fuels is so large, in many cases, that a monopolistic position in natural gas field markets may allow gas producers to secure returns well in excess of those likely to prevail under competitive conditions. Since the possibility of securing such noncompetitive returns is under consideration, the exclusion of substitute fuels would be warranted. On this ground, the choice of a concentration base is to be confined to actual sales of natural gas.

But other questions still remain regarding the selection of a natural gas sales concentration base. These concern geographical limits, as well as the matter of pipe-line-controlled gas produc-

tion as an effective buyer supply option. The alternatives are
shown below, with some indication of their size in 1953:[5]

Market Unit	Size (TCF)
1. Total marketed gas production in the U. S.	8.4
2. All gas supplied to interstate pipe lines in the U. S.	5.4
3. All gas supplied to interstate pipe lines from a 7-state area of the southwestern U. S.	5.0
4. Independent producer gas supplied to interstate pipe lines in the U. S.	4.2
5. Independent producer gas supplied to interstate pipe lines from a 7-state area of the southwestern U. S.	4.0

Among the above, the most widely defined market is that
represented by total marketed production in the United States.
It includes sales to both interstate and intrastate pipe lines, as
well as the field use and sale of gas for industrial purposes. It is
equivalent to an industry-wide output and would provide the
broadest concentration base for measuring the competitive structure of gas production. In this respect, the base is comparable in
scope to that used in ascertaining the degree of concentration in
reserve ownership.

If total marketed production is to be used as the concentration base, data which include the gas sales of individual producers to both interstate pipe lines and other purchasers would
have to be assembled. One such study was prepared by Dr.
John W. Boatwright, economist for the Standard Oil Company
of Indiana. It was presented in the hearings held on the Harris and
Fulbright bills.[6]

In the Boatwright study, which sought to determine gas
producer sales in the United States without recourse to Federal
Power Commission records, approximately 8,100 producers were
identified. These were defined as units making reports to state

[5] Total marketed gas production is obtained from U.S. Bureau of Mines,
Minerals Yearbook. For data relating to the other market units, see Table 7 below.
[6] *Hearings–H. R. 4560*, 321–46; *Hearings–S. 1853*, 159–215.

regulatory or taxing agencies. The natural gas output of each was obtained for 1953, and the production of the largest producers was related to an industry-wide output, although the amount of gas production which was used as the base for calculating concentration ratios was not given. Reference in the hearings was made to the fact that the producer group analyzed "supplies both interstate and intrastate requirements." It was also asserted that concentration was measured "on a national market," and reference was made to a combined interstate and intrastate use of gas which equaled the total 1953 marketed production of 8.4 TCF in the United States. The assumption is therefore made that total marketed production was used as the concentration base. The concentration ratios calculated in the Boatwright study are given below:

CONCENTRATION IN NATURAL GAS PRODUCTION
BOATWRIGHT STUDY

4 largest producers	17%
8 largest producers	28%
20 largest producers	46%
50 largest producers	66%
100 largest producers	78%

Aside from a certain identity of results in the matter of concentration ratios, which will be discussed later, the Boatwright study has a limited use for present purposes. A main objective, here, is to ascertain the monopolistic power of sellers in the markets where interstate pipe lines acquire their gas supplies. Consequently, a concentration base of total marketed production presents the difficulty that an unknown but probably large proportion of the gas included within it is not available to interstate pipe lines. For example, gas devoted to field use and carbon black manufacture has not been generally available in the pipe-line market, and, in 1953, 1.8 TCF out of a total marketed production of 8.4 TCF were devoted to these two uses.

The alternative to total marketed production as a concentration base is the quantity of gas supplied to the interstate pipe-line market. The latter has two important variants: the first consists of all gas available to interstate pipe lines, from their own or affiliated production and from nonaffiliated independent producers; the second would include only the gas supplied to interstate pipe lines by independent producers. A further refinement is possible by narrowing each of these variants to gas supplied to interstate pipe lines from a seven-state area of the southwestern United States. The relative size of the market units defined has already been given in summary form. A more detailed presentation appears in Table 7.

The main factor governing the addition to or omission from the concentration base of gas production controlled by interstate pipe-line purchasers is whether or not a unit constitutes an effective alternative for such buyers in dealing with independent

Table 7

GAS SUPPLY OF INTERSTATE PIPE-LINE COMPANIES, 1947 AND 1953

| ITEM | UNITED STATES | | | | SOUTHWEST* | | | |
| | *1947* | | *1953* | | *1947* | | *1953* | |
	TCF	%	TCF	%	TCF	%	TCF	%
Produced by pipe-line companies and affiliates	0.953	42.1	1.168	21.5	0.627	38.2	0.954	19.0
Purchased from independent producers	1.313	57.9	4.255	78.5	1.012	61.8	4.056	81.0
Total	2.266	100.0	5.423†	100.0	1.639	100.0	5.010	100.0

Source: Federal Power Commission data—1947: *Hearings before Subcommittee of the Committee on Interstate and Foreign Commerce on S. 1498*, 81 Cong., 1 sess. (1949), Tables 7 and 8, p. 16; 1953: *Hearings before Committee on Interstate and Foreign Commerce on S. 1853*, 84 Cong., 1 sess. (1955), Table 9, p. 1636.

* Includes interstate pipe lines operating in the seven-state area of Ark., La., Miss., Kansas, N. Mex., Okla., and Texas.
† Does not include the Pacific Coast.

23

producers. In this connection, there has been a considerable decline in the relative importance of pipe-line production as a source of gas supply. Referring to Table 7, in 1947 interstate pipe lines met approximately 40 per cent of their gas requirements by their own production. This percentage decreased rapidly and by 1953 had fallen to about 20 per cent.

Moreover, this pipe-line production was found mainly among the older pipe-line projects. With the exception of the El Paso Natural Gas Company, none of the newer, postwar projects have had significant gas reserve holdings or gas production of their own. Even the pipe lines with large reserve holdings have found it expedient, in the course of postwar expansion, to purchase gas required to meet that growth. In Table 8 gas supply data for the years 1947 and 1953 are recorded for each of the

Table 8

NATURAL GAS PRODUCTION AND PURCHASES OF
TEN INTERSTATE PIPE LINES, 1947 AND 1953

PIPE-LINE COMPANY	1947		1953	
	Produced M^3CF	Purchased M^3CF	Produced M^3CF	Purchased M^3CF
Arkansas–Louisiana Gas Co.	46.4	74.9	46.8	150.7
Cities Service Gas Co.	75.6	97.3	22.6	283.4
Colorado Interstate Gas Co.	74.3*	—	140.8	33.6
Interstate Natural Gas Co.	51.4	46.6	38.0	115.8
Mississippi River Fuel Corp.	—	55.7	—	157.2
Natural Gas Pipeline Co.	72.4†	32.7	83.0	137.8
Northern Natural Gas Co.	23.8	83.5	—	250.1‡
Panhandle Eastern Pipe Line Co.	45.3	104.5	73.3	267.7
Southern Natural Gas Co.	0.4	79.9‡	16.3	215.4‡
United Gas Pipe Line Co.	—	394.6‡	—	1,050.0‡

Source: Federal Power Commission, *Statistics of Natural Gas Companies— 1947 and 1953.*

* Includes production of producing affiliate, Canadian River Gas Co., merged 1951.

† Includes production of producing affiliate, Texoma Natural Gas Co., merged 1950.

‡ Includes output of producing affiliate, for which separate data are not available.

24

ten major prewar interstate pipe lines utilizing the gas supply sources of the Southwest.

In some instances, postwar pipe-line production actually declined, and, in almost all cases, such production fell relative to total needs. Since the postwar pipe-line projects were almost exclusively dependent on purchased gas, there is little doubt that independent producers became the predominant supply source for pipe-line gas. Therefore, a concentration base consisting only of gas purchased from independent producers could well be claimed the most relevant for current measurements of market power in the gas field.

Still, pipe-line production constitutes an alternative available to some pipe-line purchasers which, while diminished in effectiveness by 1953, was nonetheless a factor in the immediate postwar period. Moreover, the concentration ratios which would be obtained differ markedly, depending upon the concentration base chosen. In order to secure the broadest view of structural characteristics in gas field markets, the results of using both concentration bases should be given.

Selecting a proper geographical dimension for the concentration base, whether the United States or the seven-state southwestern area, presents a less difficult problem, since concentration levels for the two geographical market units were not significantly different in 1953. This situation is due to the increasing dominance of the Southwest as the source of interstate gas supplies, to the extent that its structural characteristics have been impressed on the national market unit.

In 1953, twenty-four of the twenty-five largest independent producers selling gas to interstate pipe lines in the United States were the same twenty-four largest producers making similar sales in a seven-state area of the Southwest. While the rankings and sales of individual producers in these two groups were also virtually identical, a substantial difference in concentration levels for the two market units could occur only if their concentration bases were markedly different. But reference to Table 7 indicates that interstate gas supplies obtained in 1953 from the Southwest constituted approximately 92 per cent of the total supplies secured in the United States. For all practical purposes, the concentration bases were the same in size.

This was not the case, however, for the earlier 1947 period tested, since in that year the Southwest supplied only 72 per cent of the United States total. Even if the Pacific Coast were excluded from this total to make the data fully comparable with that of 1953, no more than 80 per cent would have been supplied by the Southwest. The resulting difference in the size of concentration bases would affect concentration measurements substantially. If changes in concentration between 1947 and 1953, as well as the effect of the increased importance of southwestern supply sources, are to be presented accurately, concentration levels for both geographical market units should be determined.

Concentration ratio sets for the four market units discussed above are presented in Tables 9 and 10. The supporting data are given in detail in Tables 11 and 12, which show the sales volume and ranking of the twenty-five independent producers making the largest sales to interstate pipe lines. In Table 9, the geographical unit is the United States, and concentration levels on the two bases of total interstate pipe-line gas supplies and of independent producer gas supplies are shown. Similar concentration ratios for the market unit of the Southwest are given in Table 10. In order to summarize this information, the two sets of concentration ratios, which are perhaps most significant and which also define the upper and lower limits for sales concentration in 1953, are given in brief form below:

CONCENTRATION IN INDEPENDENT PRODUCER SALES TO
INTERSTATE PIPE LINES, 1953

	Independent Producer Gas—Southwest (per cent)	Total Interstate Pipe-line Gas—U.S. (per cent)
5 largest producers	28.5	21.6
10 largest producers	42.0	31.6
15 largest producers	50.0	37.7
25 largest producers	62.0	46.8

Field Market Concentration

Table 9

CONCENTRATION IN THE SALES OF NATURAL GAS TO INTERSTATE
PIPE LINES IN THE UNITED STATES, 1947 AND 1953

ITEM	1947			1953		
	Gas Supply TCF	Independent Producer Gas %	Total Interstate Pipe-Line Gas %	Gas Supply TCF	Independent Producer Gas %	Total Interstate Pipe-Line Gas %
Total gas supplies obtained by interstate pipe lines in the U. S., including own and affiliated production*	2.060	—	100.0	5.423	—	100.0
Gas supply purchased by interstate pipe lines in the U. S. from independent producers*	1.168	100.0	56.7	4.255	100.0	78.5
Gas supplied by 5 largest independent producers selling to interstate pipe lines in the U. S.†	0.329	28.2	16.0	1.170	27.5	21.6
Gas supplied by 10 largest independent producers†	0.472	40.4	22.9	1.715	40.3	31.6
Gas supplied by 15 largest independent producers†	0.563	48.2	27.3	2.044	48.0	37.7
Gas supplied by 25 largest independent producers†	0.667	57.1	32.4	2.539	59.7	46.8

* Data of Table 7. To make 1947 data fully comparable with 1953, the former has been adjusted to exclude Pacific Coast gas supplies.
† Based on data of Tables 11 and 12.

Table 10

CONCENTRATION IN THE SALES OF NATURAL GAS TO INTERSTATE
PIPE LINES IN SEVEN-STATE AREA* OF SOUTHWEST,
1947 AND 1953

	1947			1953		
ITEM	Gas Supply TCF	Independent Producer Gas %	Total Interstate Pipe-Line Gas %	Gas Supply TCF	Independent Producer Gas %	Total Interstate Pipe-Line Gas %
Total gas supplies obtained by inter-state pipe lines in Southwest, including own and affiliated production†	1.639	—	100.0	5.010	—	100.0
Gas supply purchased by interstate pipe lines in Southwest from independent producers†	1.012	100.0	61.8	4.056	100.0	80.9
Gas supplied by 5 largest independent producers selling to interstate pipe lines in Southwest‡	0.324	32.0	19.8	1.158	28.5	23.1
Gas supplied by 10 largest independent producers‡	0.458	45.2	27.9	1.703	42.0	34.0
Gas supplied by 15 largest independent producers‡	0.542	53.6	33.1	2.028	50.0	40.5
Gas supplied by 25 largest independent producers‡	0.641	63.3	39.1	2.517	62.0	50.2

* Ark., La., Miss., Kansas, N. Mex., Okla., and Texas.
† Data of Table 7.
‡ Based on data of Tables 11 and 12.

Field Market Concentration

A comparison of the results of the Boatwright study, mentioned earlier, with the concentration levels determined here can yield important conclusions. Boatwright based his work upon a broader market unit than even total interstate pipe-line gas, namely, total marketed gas production—in effect, a combined interstate pipe-line, intrastate, and field-use concentration base. Furthermore, the producer sales information utilized in the Boatwright analysis was neither limited to interstate pipe-line sales nor based on Federal Power Commission sales records. If the FPC data used in the present study are analyzed in terms of the concentration-size classes used in the Boatwright study, the following is obtained:

Natural Gas Sales—1953	Present Study (FPC data) (per cent)	Boatwright Study (per cent)
Total marketed production	—	100.0
Interstate pipe-line gas supply	100.0	—
4 largest producers	18.7	17.0
8 largest producers	28.7	28.0
20 largest producers	42.5	46.0

In view of their derivation from independent collections of basic sales data, as well as the different concentration bases used, the close results in the above table are highly significant. They provide considerable support for a conclusion that the level of concentration characterizing the interstate pipe-line market for gas was substantially the same as for a broader industry-wide market unit. By inference, too, a similar concentration level would have prevailed in the intrastate portion of the over-all field market for gas. Since the pattern of similarity occurs in each of the various concentration-size classes, it is also probable that the same producers were dominant in both interstate and intrastate markets for gas.

This concurrence in the concentration levels derived for an interstate pipe-line unit and for the larger industry-wide market has value in two respects: First, the concentration levels for an interstate pipe-line market would truly constitute a minimum in the sense that no larger market unit would show a lesser degree of concentration. Second, sales concentration in an interstate pipe-line market could be safely used as an indication of the structural characteristics of natural gas field markets in general. The gain here is the more complete information available with respect to producer sales to interstate pipe lines.

Relying upon data already given, it is possible to analyze the nature and extent of changes in sales concentration between 1947 and 1953. The period is especially significant, since the major part of the postwar expansion of long-distance interstate pipe lines occurred within these dates. The relevant concentration ratios are summarized below:

SALES CONCENTRATION, 1947 AND 1953

	Percentage of Independent Producer Gas— Southwest		Percentage of Total Interstate Pipe-line Gas—U.S.	
	1947	*1953*	*1947*	*1953*
5 largest producers	32.0	28.5	16.0	21.6
10 largest producers	45.2	42.0	22.0	31.6
15 largest producers	53.6	50.0	27.3	37.7
25 largest producers	63.3	62.0	32.4	46.8

Conflicting trends are evident in this comparison of concentration ratios, depending upon the concentration base selected. If the base of total interstate pipe-line gas in the United States is used, then a substantial increase in concentration levels is recorded. On the other hand, if gas supplied by independent producers in the Southwest is taken as the market unit, then a decrease in concentration is shown. In this latter case, the level of sales concentration for the five largest independent producers declined from 32.0 per cent in 1947 to 28.5 per cent in 1953. Comparable decreases in concentration for the other size classes also occurred.

The key to these contradictory changes in the level of sales concentration is to be found in the nature of the increase in total gas supplies available to interstate pipe lines. These increased from

2.060 TCF in 1947 to 5.423 TCF in 1953, almost all of the growth being accounted for by independent producers. In effect, the generally higher level of concentration characterizing the independent producer market unit in 1947 was transferred to the interstate pipe-line market unit as independent producers became a relatively more important source of supply.

The increase in sales concentration recorded for the total interstate pipe-line market is not, by itself, inconsistent with a stability or even a decrease in the degree of concentration among independent producers. But the increase in concentration for the larger market unit would merely have been greater had there also been an increase in independent producer concentration. Actually, for the market unit encompassing only gas supplied by independent producers, concentration ratios declined between 1947 and 1953. While the decrease was too small to permit inference of a downward trend, it does give firm support to the conclusion that there was no increase in concentration among independent producers during this period.

Although concentration among independent producers as a group actually did not increase, the higher level of sales concentration in the total interstate pipe-line market implied a growth in the market power of independent producers. Even if the concentration level which characterizes one particular group of sellers—independent producers—does not increase, a growing reliance upon that source of supply, relative to others, augments and strengthens its market position.

The change between 1947 and 1953 may be viewed from another direction by considering the shift in ranking of the twenty-five producers making the largest sales to interstate pipe lines in these two years. This information is contained in Tables 11 and 12. Thus, while the general level of concentration among independent producers remained constant between 1947 and 1953, the same is not the case with respect to rankings. Marked changes in sales position occurred; ten producers not among the first twenty-five in 1947 were found in that class in 1953. Other producers shifted their position within the class, both upward and downward; five in the bottom half of the list during 1947 moved

Table 11

(excludes sales to associated pipe-line companies)

PRODUCER	UNITED STATES		SOUTHWEST*	
	Sales M³CF	Rank	Sales M³CF	Rank
Phillips Petroleum Co.	457.4	1	457.4	1
Stanolind Oil & Gas Co.	202.6	2	190.5	3
Humble Oil & Refining Co.	196.6†	3	196.6†	2
Magnolia Petroleum Co.	157.5	4	157.5	4
Shell Oil Co.	156.3	5	156.3	5
Chicago Corp.	155.6	6	155.6	6
Gulf Oil Corp. and Gulf Refining Co.	138.4	7	138.4	7
Atlantic Refining Co.	95.2	8	94.3	8
Shamrock Oil & Gas Corp.	81.4	9	81.4	9
Skelly Oil Co.	74.6	10	74.6	10
Sun Oil Co.	69.0	11	69.0	11
The Texas Company	67.4	12	64.5	13
Carthage Corp.	66.6	13	66.6	12
Republic Natural Gas Co.	63.2	14	63.2	14
Superior Oil Co.	62.5	15	62.5	15
Sunray Oil Corp.	53.7	16	53.7	16
Union Oil Co. of California	53.0	17	53.0	17
Continental Oil Co.	52.9	18	51.6	18
Southwest Gas Producing Co., Inc.	50.8	19	50.8	19
Panoma Corp.‡	48.6	20	48.6	20
La Gloria Corp.	48.0	21	48.0	21
Pure Oil Co.	48.0	22	—§	—
Ohio Oil Co.	47.8	23	47.6	22
Abercrombie, J. S., Co.	46.9	24	46.9	23
Tide Water Associated Oil Co.	45.4	25	45.4	24
American Gas Produc. Co.	—§	—	43.3	25

Source: Federal Power Commission data—United States: *Hearings before Committee on Interstate and Foreign Commerce on S. 1853*, 84 Cong., 1 sess. (1955), 1639; Southwest: obtained by deducting from U. S. totals those sales made outside of a seven-state area of the Southwest, as given in *Hearings—S. 1853*, Table 5, p. 1246.

* Ark., La., Miss., Kansas, N. Mex., Okla., and Texas.

† Includes sales of 20.5 million MCF to an affiliate, Interstate Natural Gas Co.

‡ Formerly Hagy, Harrington, & Marsh.

§ Not included among twenty-five largest producers.

Table 12

TWENTY-FIVE INDEPENDENT PRODUCERS MAKING LARGEST SALES
OF NATURAL GAS TO INTERSTATE PIPE LINES IN THE U. S.
AND IN THE SOUTHWEST, 1947

(excludes sales to associated pipe-line companies)

PRODUCER	UNITED STATES		SOUTHWEST*	
	Sales M^3CF	*Rank*	*Sales* M^3CF	*Rank*
Phillips Petroleum Co.	116.2	1	116.2†	1
Chicago Corp.	66.6	2	66.6	2
Republic Natural Gas Co.	56.4	3	56.4	3
Humble Oil & Refining Co.	49.3	4	49.3	4
Stanolind Oil & Gas Co.	41.0	5	34.8	5
United Carbon Co.	33.9	6	20.3	12
Skelly Oil Co.	28.2	7	28.2	6
Continental Oil Co.	27.7	8	27.7†	7
Gulf Oil Corp. and Gulf Refining Co.	26.5	9	26.5	8
Hagy, Harrington, & Marsh	26.4	10	26.4	9
Hunt, H. L. & Hassie Hunt Trust	26.0	11	26.0	10
Southern Carbon Co.	22.7	12	22.7	11
Sun Oil Co.	14.5	13	13.5	14
Southwest Gas Producing Co., Inc.	14.3	14	14.3	13
Texas Gulf Prod. Co.	12.9	15	12.9	15
Magnolia Petroleum Co.	12.0	16	12.0	16
Shell Oil Co.	11.3	17	11.3	17
The Texas Company	11.1	18	8.7	22
Columbian Fuel Corp.	10.8	19	—‡	—
Shamrock Oil & Gas Corp.	10.8	20	10.8	18
Fin-Ker Oil & Gas Prod. Co.	10.4	21	10.4	19
Glassell & Glassell	10.2	22	10.2	20
Ray Stephens, Inc.	9.9	23	9.9	21
United Producing Co.	9.5	24	—‡	—
Barber Oil Co.	8.7	25	8.7	23
Barnsdall Oil Co.	—‡	—	8.5	24
Warren Petroleum Corp.	—‡	—	8.4	25

Source: Federal Power Commission data—United States: *96 Cong. Rec. 4209* (1950); Southwest: *Hearings before Subcommittee of the Committee on Interstate and Foreign Commerce on S. 1498,* 81 Cong., 1 sess. (1949), 365.

* Ark., La., Miss., Kansas, N. Mex., Okla., and Texas.

† The underlying data for the Southwest show separately sales of 23.5 million MCF made jointly by Phillips Petroleum Co. and Continental Oil Co. However, these sales are not recorded in the data for the U. S. No explanation for the omission is apparent. They have therefore been excluded from this tabulation to make the two series comparable.

‡ Not included among twenty-five largest producers.

to the upper half by 1953. In fact, only one producer, the Phillips Petroleum Company, maintained its position in the rankings for the two years.

This high degree of variation in the sales rank of particular producers, which characterized the period, is a condition suggestive of competition in natural gas field markets. Certainly it supports the proposition that expansion of pipe-line markets for natural gas after 1947 brought into existence as large-sized supply sources many producers who were not previously important.

In concluding this analysis of field market structure, a judgment concerning the level of sales concentration might well be offered. Two basic sets of concentration ratios were presented: one was derived from the broader concentration base of total interstate pipe-line gas supplies in the United States; the other set was founded on a concentration base or market unit limited to gas supplied to interstate pipe lines by independent producers in the Southwest. Both have their uses, although, as the analysis indicated, the latter and somewhat narrower concentration base is more suitable under present circumstances. If a market unit limited to independent producers in the Southwest is used, the five largest sellers were responsible for approximately 28 per cent of total sales in 1953, which was significantly higher than the 21.6 per cent determined on the broader concentration base. Similar divergences prevailed for the other size classes. Fortunately, the difference between the two sets of concentration ratios was not excessive to the point of rendering them incompatible.

Consequently, if a single series of sales concentration ratios is desired, a creditable estimate founded on the two sets of calculations can be made. Perhaps the following would not be too far from the mark:

ESTIMATED CONCENTRATION IN INDEPENDENT PRODUCER
SALES TO INTERSTATE PIPE LINES, 1953

5 largest producers	25%
10 largest producers	33%
25 largest producers	50%

C. Concentration in Gas Supply Submarkets

The preceding analysis has examined the question of concentration in national or large regional gas supply markets, but, in many cases, a narrower geographical area defines the effective supply options open to pipe lines without a major extension of facilities. A knowledge of concentration levels in such smaller geographical units—gas supply submarkets—can contribute greatly to an understanding of monopolistic potentials in natural gas production.

Sales information as complete in coverage as the FPC data used previously is not, however, available for submarkets. Instead, a different and less complete data source must be used, namely, the purchase contracts negotiated by producers and interstate pipe lines during the period 1944–53. These data can be analyzed to secure sales information for relatively small geographical gas supply areas which, when appropriately grouped, constitute natural gas submarkets within an over-all southwestern supply region.

Use of the purchase contract data for ascertaining submarket concentration has limitations, for the most part because of the incompleteness of available sales information: First, the purchase contract data sources did not show volume for all contracts. Second, the annual gas volume contractually agreed upon was not necessarily the amount actually delivered. Last, it was not known in all cases whether or not contracts negotiated in 1948 were still effective in 1953. With these deficiencies in mind, the submarket concentration results are best viewed as approximations, not assignable to any given year but, nevertheless, representative of conditions prevailing at the end of the period covered. These limitations in the data do not impair certain broad and important conclusions deducible from the submarket analysis.

The scope and coverage of the purchase contract data to be used in this analysis of submarket concentration, as well as certain general structural features of the nine gas supply areas identified, are summarized in Table 13. With one exception, 50 or more contracts were recorded for each of the various supply areas. For six of the nine supply areas, 80 or more contracts were

35

available. Of the total purchase contracts recorded, 425, or almost 60 per cent, reported gas volumes and were thus available for a submarket concentration analysis. In all but one of the individual supply areas, one-half or more of the contracts assigned to them contained gas volume information.

Of further interest is the distribution of large sellers among the various supply areas. Two classifications of sellers, in terms of size, are shown in Table 13: first, those whose total contracts over the period examined resulted in sales of 5.0 million MCF or more each year; second, those whose total contractual sales equaled 2.0 million MCF or more per annum. Excluding the San Juan–New Mexico and the East Texas–North Louisiana units, which are not comparable in size to the other supply areas, the number of sellers in the 5.0 million MCF or more category ranges between 10 and 19. For the sales category of 2.0 million MCF or more, the range is between 14 and 24 sellers.

Not represented in Table 13 is a characteristic structural feature of gas supply areas which is of some importance in the analysis of submarket concentration. It relates to what may be called large-seller diversity. An examination of the purchase contract data disclosed that, to a considerable degree, the same producers were not the largest sellers in each of the supply areas. For example, after identifying the five largest sellers in each of eight supply areas (excluding the minor San Juan–New Mexico unit), it was discovered that twenty-eight of forty possible separate sellers, or about two-thirds of the group, were independent of one another. Using the same procedure for the ten largest sellers, fifty of eighty possible separate producers, or almost two-thirds, were identifiable as separate sellers.

Some purchase contracts were large-volume agreements, although not containing volume information. Such contracts were found mainly in the Panhandle-Hugoton, the Southwest Louisiana, and the Southeast Louisiana–Mississippi gas supply areas. Consequently, use of the concentration ratios for the three areas must provide for a substantial margin of error. For other supply areas, the distortion attributable to this factor would not be troublesome. As gas supply areas are aggregated into larger submar-

Table 13

SUMMARY OF 723 NATURAL GAS PURCHASE CONTRACTS NEGOTIATED BY
INTERSTATE PIPE LINES IN VARIOUS GAS SUPPLY AREAS, 1944–53

Gas Supply Area	Annual Gas Volumes Reported M³CF	Number of Contracts	Contracts Reporting Gas Volumes	Number of Sellers	Sellers Reporting Gas Volumes	Sellers having Sales of 5.0 M³CF or More	Sellers having Sales of 2.0 M³CF or More	Number of Buyers	
								P*	D†
Panhandle–Hugoton	741.6	86	45	43	22	16	17	10	—
West Texas–Permian Basin	546.5	85	51	46	30	19	24	2	—
San Juan–New Mexico	70.5	18	9	15	7	5	6	1	—
East Texas–North Louisiana	624.9	155	86	96	56	29	40	10	1
Texas Gulf Coast–Dist. No. 2	173.2	86	42	62	36	12	19	5	—
Texas Gulf Coast–Dist. No. 4	328.6	81	45	50	35	15	21	4	2
Texas Gulf Coast–Dist. No. 3	342.3	73	46	50	32	17	21	7	1
Southwest Louisiana	463.5	83	69	47	43	16	22	7	2
Southeast Louisiana–Mississippi	167.1	56	32	33	17	10	14	3	1
Total	3458.2	723	425						

* P denotes pipe-line buyers.
† D denotes non pipe-line, distribution company buyers.

ket units, the disturbing effect of incomplete data for particular supply areas is diminished.

In other respects, the purchase contract data are more than adequate for the analysis of submarket concentration. Their coverage of field market transactions, in general, is relatively complete. This may be seen by comparing annual contract gas volumes recorded for all gas supply areas with gas sales made by independent producers to interstate pipe lines in 1953 as reported by the FPC. The FPC information constitutes a second data source which may be considered complete in coverage. Moreover, since independent producer sales in 1953 were based largely on purchase contracts negotiated between 1944 and 1953, the two data sources may be meaningfully compared. Such a comparison indicates that the total annual contract volume of approximately 3.5 TCF reported in the purchase contracts is over 80 per cent of the almost 4.1 TCF sold in 1953 by independent producers in the Southwest to interstate pipe lines.

Concentration ratios calculated from annual contract volumes reported in the purchase contract data for all gas supply areas combined may be compared with sales concentration measurements developed previously from FPC sales data for a similar market unit. The comparison is given below:

	1953 Sales; Independent Producers Southwestern U.S. (per cent) (see Table 10)	Annual Contract Volume; All Gas Supply Areas Combined (per cent) (see Table 14)
5 largest sellers	28.5	32.2
10 largest sellers	42.0	46.4
15 largest sellers	50.0	55.2
25 largest sellers	62.0	68.1

It is evident that there is no large difference in concentration levels derived from the two data sources. The results are, in fact, unusually close, and, coupled with the relatively complete coverage provided by the purchase contract data, they support the use of these data for an investigation of submarket concentration.

Table 14

SALES CONCENTRATION IN GAS SUPPLY SUBMARKETS

Gas Supply Submarket	Concentration Ratio*				Annual Contract Gas Volume M³CF
	5 Largest Sellers %	10 Largest Sellers %	15 Largest Sellers %	25 Largest Sellers %	
Texas Gulf Coast— Districts 2, 3, and 4	37.8	56.5	69.1	—	844.1
La. Gulf Coast—Southwest La. and Southeast La.	38.6	62.6	80.5	—	630.6
East Texas–North La.	39.4	60.5	72.8	—	624.9
All Gulf Coast plus East Texas–North La.	23.6	39.3	51.0	—	2,099.6
Panhandle–Hugoton— West Texas–New Mexico	59.4	74.7	82.9	—	1,358.6
All gas supply areas combined	32.2	46.4	55.2	68.1	3,458.2

*Concentration base consists of total contract gas volumes reported in each group of supply areas designated a submarket.

Having established the general suitability of the available data for the purpose at hand, concentration levels may be determined for the various gas supply areas, as well as for appropriate sub-market units. The former are examined first, and since errors resulting from incomplete contract data are likely to be largest here, only approximations are given. Using total reported contract volumes in each supply area as the concentration base, the resulting concentration ratios are presented below:

CONCENTRATION RATIOS IN GAS SUPPLY AREAS

Gas Supply Area	Five Largest Sellers (per cent)	Ten Largest Sellers (per cent)
Panhandle-Hugoton	80.0	90.0
West Texas–Permian Basin	60.0	80.0
Texas Gulf Coast—District 2	50.0	70.0
Texas Gulf Coast—District 4	50.0	80.0
Texas Gulf Coast—District 3	60.0	80.0
Southwest Louisiana	50.0	80.0
Southeast Louisiana–Mississippi	60.0	90.0
East Texas–North Louisiana	40.0	60.0

The levels of concentration in the individual supply areas are high, an expected consequence of the smaller size of the market unit, and a concentration ratio of 50–60 per cent for the five largest sellers is common. The highest level of concentration is found in the Panhandle-Hugoton supply area, reflecting the dominant position of a single seller. Least concentration is shown in the East Texas–North Louisiana supply source.

Concentration in gas supply submarkets is shown in Table 14. The submarkets are aggregations of the smaller supply areas, representing geographically homogeneous areas which are judged to encompass the immediate supply options available to pipe-line buyers. In many instances, therefore, the submarkets are more suitable market units than the supply areas for testing the competitive structure of gas field markets.

With an increase in the size of the market unit goes a decrease in concentration ratios which can represent an actual increase in the competitiveness of market structure. For example, even though conditions within Districts 2, 3, and 4 individually are not changed by aggregation into a Texas Gulf Coast submarket unit, nevertheless the competitive potential becomes greater if the number of alternatives open to buyers is enlarged. This effect is achieved if the supply areas aggregated contain different dominant sellers or are characterized by large-seller diversity.

This change in competitive characteristics attendant upon aggregation can be indicated by concentration ratios, if the supply areas brought together have approximately the same concentration level. If the same sellers were dominant in each supply area, there would be no increase in competitive structure by combining such areas, and the concentration ratio for the larger unit would not be different from the combined ratios of its components.

These effects of aggregation can be illustrated: Assume the existence of two market units having the same distribution of sales among sellers who are not the same in both market areas. These market units are then aggregated, with the result that the concentration ratio of the larger market area is less than the ratio of the two smaller units, as shown below:

Market Unit	Sales of Five Largest Sellers	Total Sales	Concentration Ratio
A	25, 20, 15, 10, 5	100	75%
B	25, 20, 15, 10, 5	100	75%
A+B	25, 25, 20, 20, 15	200	52%

However, if the dominant sellers were the same in both market units A and B, aggregation would not lead to a change in the concentration ratio, as demonstrated in the following:

A+B	50, 40, 30, 20, 10	200	75%

Based on the preceding analysis, the lower concentration levels recorded for natural gas submarkets in Table 14 indicate a lower monopolistic potential than for individual supply areas; and the extremely low concentration level for the All Gulf Coast plus East Texas–North Louisiana unit represents a further decrease.

An apparent exception to the rule is encountered when the All Gulf Coast plus East Texas–North Louisiana submarket is combined with its Panhandle-Hugoton–West Texas–New Mexico counterpart, for the previously experienced pattern of a diminishing concentration level with an enlarged market unit is reversed, despite considerable seller diversity. In this case, the higher concentration ratio resulting from aggregation is not to be interpreted as a diminution in structural competition.

Basically, the higher concentration ratio was due to an unusually wide divergence in concentration levels for the two submarket units which were combined. When such submarkets are aggregated, an averaging effect influences the concentration ratio obtained for the new larger market unit. Thus, the level characterizing the highly concentrated submarket is reduced by the increase in the concentration base, while the low level of the other submarket unit is raised by adding new dominant sellers.

Specifically, the competitive structure of the Gulf Coast–East Texas submarket was not diminished substantially by combining it with the Panhandle–West Texas supply source. Indeed, given large-seller diversity between the two areas, an increase in competitive potential is to be expected, since, whatever the effect on concentration ratios, the aggregation of submarkets increases the number of sellers providing supply alternatives for Gulf Coast buyers. Widening the supply unit also enlarges competitive options for pipe lines restricted to the Panhandle–West Texas submarket unit.

Thus the importance of exercising caution in the interpretation of changes in concentration levels resulting from an aggregation of submarket units is clearly shown. Evidently, choosing the market unit—gas supply area, submarket, or producing region—is the key to the question: Are the field markets for gas competitively structured? The basis for that choice is selection of a market unit which includes the important supply alternatives actually and readily available to pipe-line buyers. But the range of alternatives differs under varying circumstances, hence the need for a variety of market units and concentration measurements, such as those presented in this chapter.

CHAPTER 2

Field Market Price Levels and Demand Patterns

LIKE CONCENTRATION DATA, information concerning field price movements is vital in any analysis of seller market control. Market power must be brought to bear upon price if that power is to be advantageous. Depending upon the patterns of price changes, many useful inferences which aid in resolving the problem of monopolistic producer control in the gas field can be drawn from field price data. For the purposes of this inquiry, then, determination of field price levels and changes in various gas supply areas over the period of 1945–53 is essential.

The most widely used indicator of gas field price levels and trends is the average wellhead value series compiled by the U. S. Bureau of Mines. This statistical series is obtained by dividing the estimated total value of natural gas at the wellhead by the marketed production of gas for that period of time and the area under consideration.

While the average value series secured by this procedure is useful as an indicator of trends, it is not adequate as a measure of field prices in an interstate pipe-line market. The Bureau of Mines data do not discriminate between the different markets for field gas; for example, the high value uses of gas, as in the interstate pipe-line market, are not differentiated from the lower value uses of gas, as in carbon black manufacture. Furthermore, the Bureau of Mines series does not take into account the time lags introduced by long-term supply contracts, nor does it give appropriate weight to the volume of gas committed at a particular price.

Generally, the Bureau of Mines data seem to underestimate both the level and the rate of change in natural gas field prices for an interstate pipe-line market. This shortcoming limits the uses

43

to which the data can be put, although they still provide a broad view of trends.

The average wellhead value of gas in the United States for the period 1937–54 is given in Table 15. This tabulation discloses the large postwar increase in the unit value of field gas. The pattern of this change is noteworthy. From 1937 to 1945, field values were relatively uniform, but, coinciding with the postwar expansion of consumer markets, a new price level approximately 30 per cent higher than before was reached by 1948. This new level was maintained, within .2 cent, through 1950, after which time a second and more rapid increase occurred. According to these data, almost three-fourths of the doubling of field values between 1945 and 1954 took place after 1950.

A second indicator of field price levels is the average cost of natural gas purchased by interstate pipe lines. While this statistical series has the advantage of excluding the non-pipe-line uses of gas and of focusing upon the interstate sector of the market, it includes in the average those lower costs prevailing in earlier periods and perpetuated by long-term contracts. As a conse-

Table 15

AVERAGE WELLHEAD VALUE OF NATURAL GAS

IN THE UNITED STATES, 1937–54

Year	Cents per MCF	Index (1945 =100)	Year	Cents per MCF	Index (1945 =100)
1937	5.1	104.0	1946	5.3	108.2
1938	4.9	100.0	1947	6.0	122.4
1939	4.9	100.0	1948	6.5	132.7
1940	4.5	91.8	1949	6.3	128.6
			1950	6.5	132.7
1941	4.9	100.0			
1942	5.1	104.1	1951	7.3	149.0
1943	5.2	106.1	1952	7.8	159.2
1944	5.1	104.1	1953	9.2	187.8
1945	4.9	100.0	1954	10.0	204.1

Source: U. S. Bureau of Mines, *Minerals Yearbook*.

quence, the average purchase cost values will lag behind current field prices, and this series, therefore, cannot accurately reflect the current price level in a period of changing prices. Its main function is to demonstrate the cost impact of rising field prices upon interstate pipe lines.

A. NATURAL GAS FIELD PRICES—SOUTHWESTERN UNITED STATES

In both the average wellhead value series of the Bureau of Mines and data relating to the average cost of gas to interstate pipe lines, deficiencies exist which lead to an underestimate of field price levels in pipe-line markets. To arrive at a satisfactory approximation of field prices in the pipe-line market, specific gas purchase contracts negotiated between interstate pipe-line buyers and natural gas producers must be consulted. The price values shown in these contracts are basic evidence of the market price prevailing at a specific time for the gas field covered in the contract; an estimate of field price levels can be derived from these values.

Determination of price levels and price patterns is to be based upon a sample of 723 gas purchase contracts, which were negotiated between interstate pipe lines and independent gas producers in the southwestern gas producing region over a period which extends generally from 1944 through 1953. The geographical distribution and certain other features of these contracts have already been presented in Table 13. Although FPC records were the ultimate source for almost all contracts analyzed, compilations of purchase agreements were obtained from various other documents (see appendix).

Two broad groups of contracts may be identified: One is the Kerr-Douglas group, prepared by the FPC and placed in the Congressional Record by Senators Paul H. Douglas and Robert S. Kerr during the 1950 debate on the Kerr bill, seeking exemption from federal price regulation for independent gas producers. The second, which may be called the FPC group, consists of various compilations prepared by that agency after 1950. The

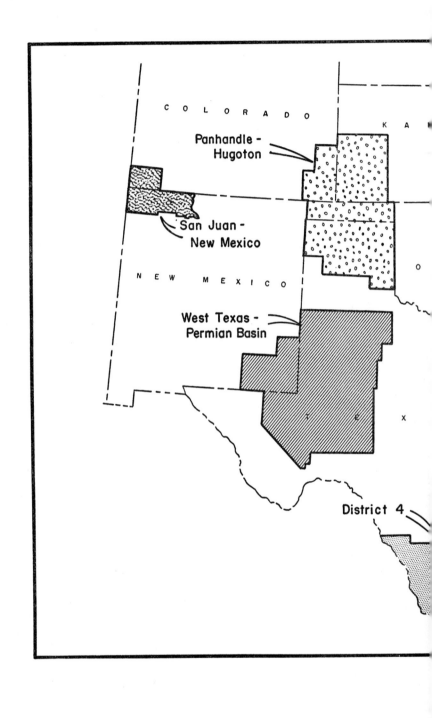

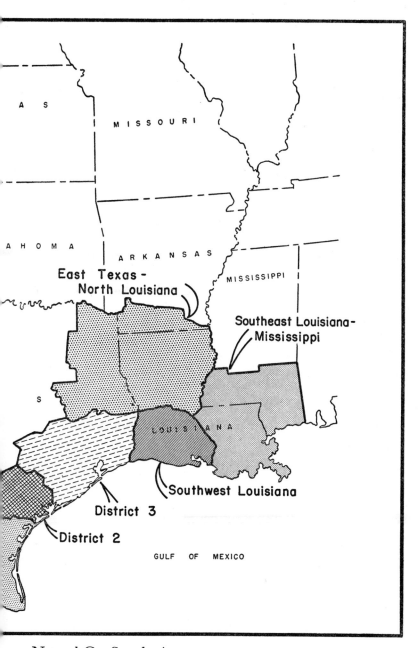

Natural Gas Supply Areas

Kerr-Douglas contract group is more complete than the FPC unit in coverage of gas volume information, as well as in other contract details.

To organize this purchase contract material, a geographical classification was undertaken, in which nine natural gas supply areas in the Southwest were identified: the Panhandle-Hugoton; the West Texas–Permian Basin; the San Juan–New Mexico; three Texas Gulf Coast gas supply areas, consisting of Texas Railroad Commission districts nos. 2, 3, and 4; the Southwest Louisiana; the Southeast Louisiana–Mississippi, and the East Texas–North Louisiana areas.

Geographical homogeneity was a primary consideration in distinguishing these supply areas, although other factors, such as the time pattern of their development, were taken into account. In general, these appear to be valid units for a field price analysis, but for some purposes the supply areas on the Texas Gulf Coast and in southern Louisiana might well be combined.

In addition to the geographical differentiation, the average price to be paid for natural gas over the effective term of each contract was determined. Such an average was used to represent the price element in all of the purchase agreements, with the exception of a few (approximately thirty-one contracts negotiated prior to 1949), for which only initial prices were known and used.

The necessity for calculating an average price arises from the practice of periodic fixed price escalation. In practically all long-term gas contracts, an initial price was stipulated and increased by given amounts at the end of designated time periods throughout the life of the contract. Illustrative of such arrangements might be the following price provision in a twenty-year contract:

	Cents per MCF
First 5 years	12.0
Second 5 years	14.0
Third 5 years	16.0
Fourth 5 years	18.0

In the above, the initial price is 12.0 cents per MCF, and the weighted average price over the term of the contract would be equal to 15.0 cents per MCF. Unless the weighted average price had been used, a creditable approximation of the price at which the transaction was completed could not have been made. Moreover, since the amount and rapidity of price escalation was an important pricing element which differed between contracts, determination of average prices was required to adjust such variations.

Another problem was presented by the need for a uniform pressure base. Since gas volumes vary inversely with pressure, prices per MCF would not be comparable unless the same pressure base were used for the measurement of an MCF unit. To illustrate, assume a given quantity of gas, measured on a 16.7 psi pressure base and priced at 15.0 cents per MCF, leading to a certain total expenditure by the purchaser. If the same quantity of gas were measured on a 14.65 psi pressure base, more MCF units would be obtained, and, at the 15.0 cent unit price, a larger total expenditure would be made by the purchaser. A reduction of pressure base, without an offsetting change in unit price, thus constitutes an effective price increase.

In view of the preceding discussion, a notable feature of the price charts is the statement that all prices are calculated on a 16.7 psi pressure base. The main reason for choosing this measurement base was its consistent use in the FPC contract data sources. Moreover, before 1950, most purchase contracts evidently used this pressure base; the widespread appearance of a 14.65 psi base after 1950, without a change in unit price values, was actually a price increase.

Additional procedures followed in determining volume and term of contract require explanation. Annual gas volumes are given in the charts wherever possible; but, in a few cases, amounts were not given in the sources for contracts which were renegotiated later. In these instances, to reflect more accurately the period in which the gas was actually committed, gas volumes given in the renegotiated versions were also attributed to the earliest date at which the contract was signed. As a consequence of this duplication, the annual gas volumes shown in the price charts may not be added together, without proper adjustment, if the total gas committed from a given supply area is to be obtained.

For the contracts after 1950, very little usable information about annual volume is given in the source material. The annual volume specified is frequently indefinite, being equal to ratable take—the proportion of field production allowed by state conservation authorities—or given as a certain quantity per well annually, without information about the number of gas wells involved. Wherever possible, though, estimates and approximations of gas volumes were made and used.

The terms of contracts shown in the charts do not represent the legal contract periods. Many times, the latter is given in the sources as "indefinite," "life of the field," or "life of commercial production." In other cases, the legal term of the contract is greater than the period for which a definite and known price is stipulated. For example, many of the twenty-year contracts do not specify a price after the tenth or fifteenth year, providing instead for a redetermination of price at that time. Frequently, prices are given for the full term of the contract, but they are declared to be minimum prices, subject to further negotiation, after the fifth or tenth year.

From the above, the difficulties encountered in selecting a proper contract period for the calculation of average prices are evident. If weighted average prices over the contract period were to be used in determining price values, a principle for selecting the relevant term of contract was essential. An effective contract term was thus defined as the period during which contract prices were firm maximum prices, except for the possible operation of two-party favored-nation provisos.[1] Consequently, in many cases the effective contract term is less than the legal contract term.

Equally important as a justification for this effective term of

[1] An explanation of this type of contract provision is given in Chapter 3. Such favored-nation clauses are, within their terms, operative at any time, and no contract containing these stipulations would, strictly speaking, have a firm price. However, two-party favored-nation clauses come into operation only as a result of buyer actions and are thus within the control of pipe-line purchasers.

contract concept is the great consequence of contract price flexibility in gas field bargaining transactions. The real significance of the contract term to pipe-line buyers is the price stability and cost certainty afforded by agreements of long duration. On the other hand, in periods of rising field prices, an opposite interest is found among sellers. Gas producers desire the pricing flexibility obtained by short-term agreements or by limiting the period during which prices are to be firm. It was therefore concluded that one of the purposes to be served by charting a term of contract series was to depict the changing pattern and trends with respect to contract price flexibility. This objective is achieved by the concept of an effective term of contract.

Field price information obtained by the procedures described is summarized in Figures 1 through 8, corresponding to eight of the nine gas supply areas distinguished in the southwestern United States. The paucity of contract data for the San Juan–New Mexico supply area through 1952 does not warrant presentation in chart form. Exact demarcations of these supply areas, as well as sources for the purchase contract data shown in Figures 1 through 8, have been included in the appendix to this volume.

B. Gas Supply Area Price Levels: 1945–53

The purchase contract data introduced in Figures 1 through 8 are the factual bases for an analysis of natural gas field prices. Their presentation in chart form, with observations given in chronological order, serves well as a means of depicting general price movements in individual supply areas. Nevertheless, the picture of field prices thus afforded is subjective and unsuitable for many purposes. For example, the important task of comparing the various supply areas is not possible without a commensurable quantitative measure of their respective price changes. Even within a single gas supply area, the variation in price between individual contracts in juxtaposition makes it difficult to ascertain over-all price levels and rates of change in recent years. Unless further summarization of the data is accomplished, many useful and necessary generalizations cannot be made.

51

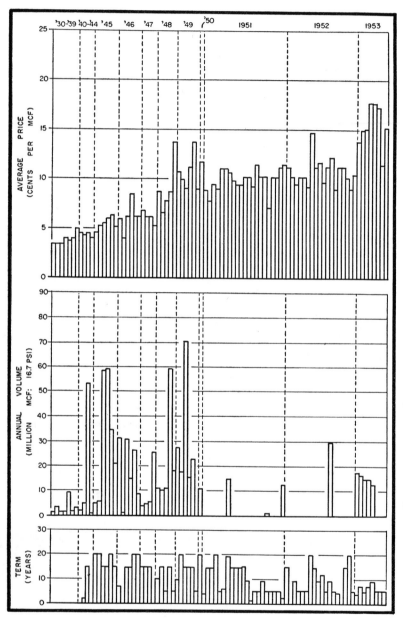

Fig. 1.—Natural Gas Purchase Contracts in the Panhandle–Hugoton Gas Supply Area

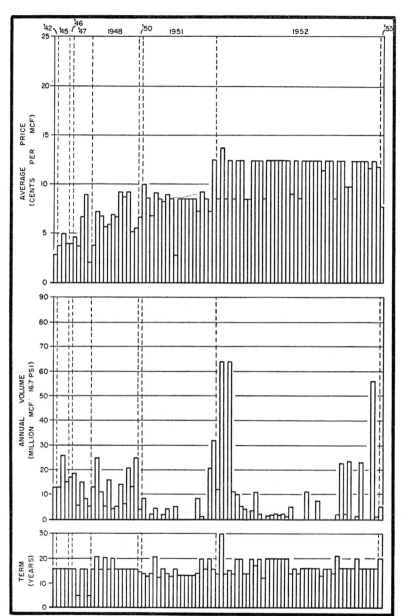

FIG. 2.—Natural Gas Purchase Contracts in the West Texas–
Permian Basin Gas Supply Area

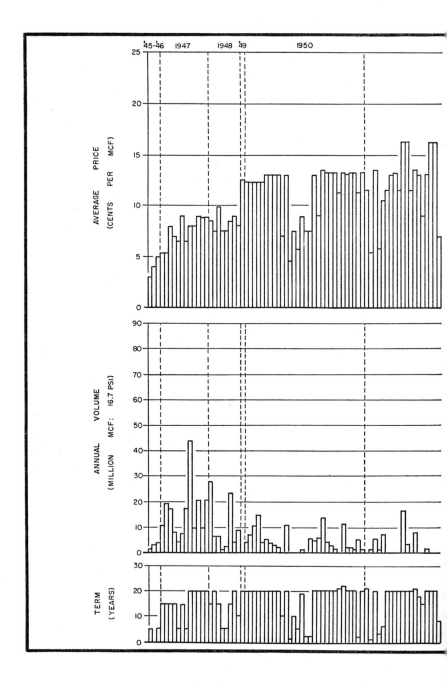

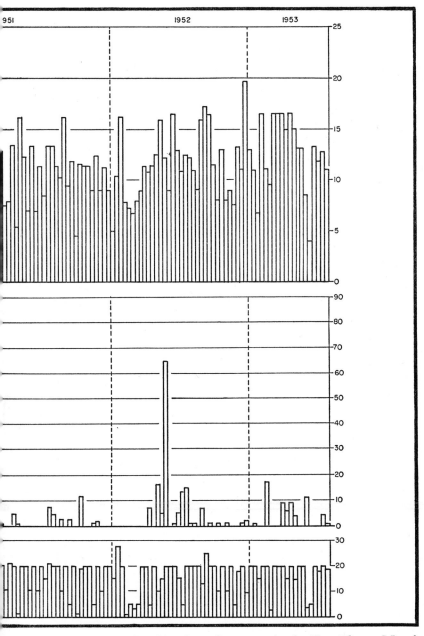

Fig. 3.—Natural Gas Purchase Contracts in the East Texas–North
Louisiana Gas Supply Area

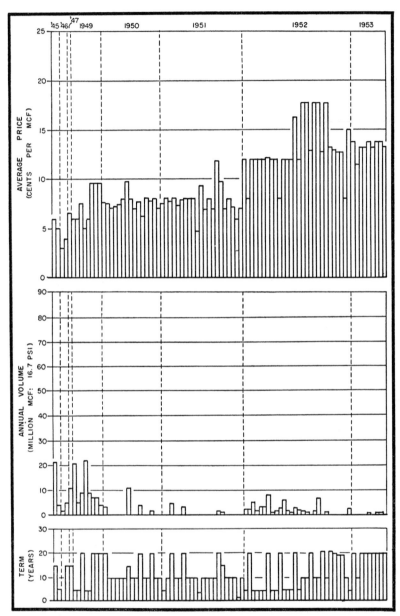

Fig. 4.—Natural Gas Purchase Contracts in the Texas Gulf Coast
Gas Supply Area—Texas R. R. Comm. Dist. No. 2

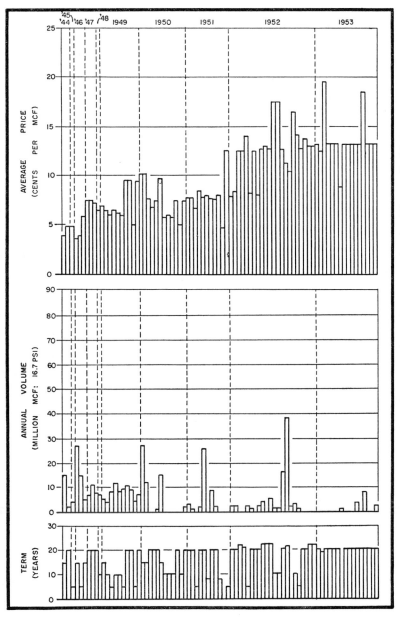

Fig. 5.—Natural Gas Purchase Contracts in the Texas Gulf Coast Gas Supply Area—Texas R. R. Comm. Dist. No. 4

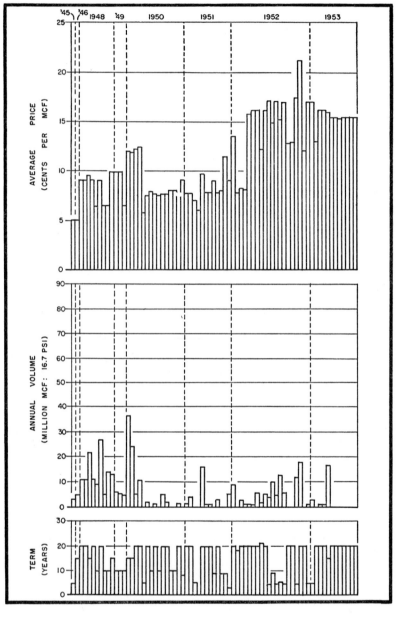

Fig. 6.—Natural Gas Purchase Contracts in the Texas Gulf Coast Gas Supply Area—Texas R. R. Comm. Dist. No. 3

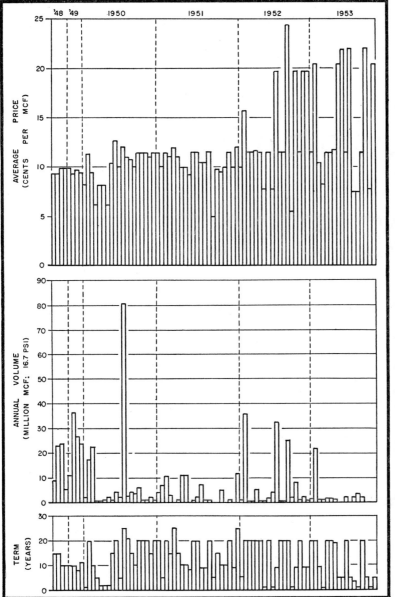

Fig. 7—Natural Gas Purchase Contracts in the Southwest Louisiana Gas Supply Area

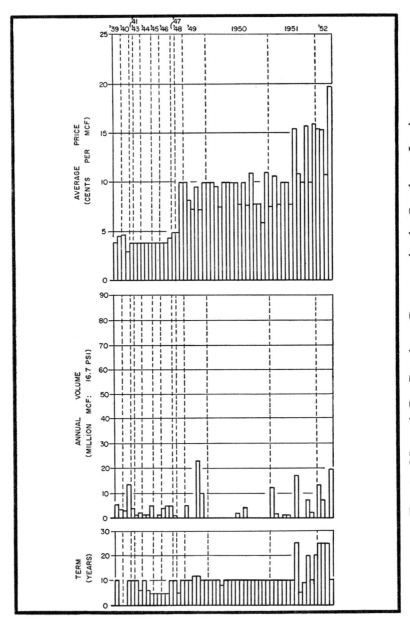

Fig. 8.—Natural Gas Purchase Contracts in the Southeast Louisiana–Mississippi Gas Supply Area

One means of achieving such condensation is a statistical approximation of representative field prices; an average might be taken of the price observations for a given year in a supply area. The success of this procedure depends heavily upon a careful weighting of the price observations, for it soon becomes evident in any investigation of gas supply markets that the price "bargain" in a natural gas purchase contract is exceedingly complex. The total consideration given and received in these agreements is much more than the stipulated unit price—necessarily including volume and effective contract term, as well as other contract provisions. If an average price is representative, it must be properly adjusted to account for these factors.

Higher prices are generally found in contracts specifying a large gas volume, the relationship being important enough to require a distinction between large-volume and small-volume markets for field gas. For the data at hand, however, any attempt to apply weights for this factor is severely limited by the lack of complete gas volume information.

A second factor which disturbs the comparability of the price observations is variations in the effective terms of contract. A price of 10.0 cents in a contract stipulating a five-year effective term may really be higher than one of 15.0 cents which is firm over a twenty-year period. The price values going into an average field price must therefore be adjusted in some manner to equalize the effective terms of contracts. Unfortunately, there are no simple and obvious means whereby a quantitative weight for this factor can be developed. As an alternative, only agreements with the same effective contract periods might be included in the average, but this solution would result in an insufficient number of observations.

Thus, inability to obtain or to devise suitable quantitative weights makes it difficult to secure an accurate and reliable statistical average of field prices. An unweighted average of price values might be taken, in the hope of obtaining a rough but usable statistic; however, price levels and price movements derived in this manner were atypical, if not misleading.

Since a weighted average field price is not feasible, and an

61

unweighted average is likely to hide more than it reveals, a summarization of contract price data is not readily obtained through techniques of statistical approximation. It may, however, be satisfactorily achieved by a judgment approximation of representative field prices in the various gas supply areas. But this method is replete with its own hazards, two of which are a tendency toward arbitrariness and the necessity of meeting the problem of adjusting price values to assure comparability.

Reliable results from this method depend upon an extended review of the purchase contracts in each supply area in order to take into account non-price factors and to provide the factual base for a secure judgment. Since such a contract review is necessarily lengthy and serves other purposes besides substantiating field price estimates, it has been segregated and appears as Part II of this study. Accordingly, only the final estimates of representative field prices for the various supply areas are presented here. A summary tabulation of these prices appears in Table 16, and the graphic representation of the data is plotted in Figure 9.

These field price approximations are indicative of average contract prices over a twenty-year purchase contract term. However, after 1950, firm contracts of that duration were uncommon, although many did specify minimum prices for a twenty-year term. Under these circumstances, basing an average contract price upon such minima understates the price which would have been paid for a firm twenty-year contract. Also, the field price estimates shown have reference to a large-volume pipe-line market. Price differentials were found in the contract data which could be explained rationally only by relating them to gas volume. These differentials were sufficiently large and consistent to necessitate a distinction between large-volume and small-volume gas markets to assure accuracy in depicting field price levels.

In arriving at the field price approximations shown in Table 16, underlying contract values were adjusted wherever possible to assure comparability. Volume factors were removed, as noted above, by separating contracts into large-volume and small-volume markets. The problem of price disparities stemming from different contract periods was met by adjusting prices to an

Table 16

REPRESENTATIVE NATURAL GAS FIELD PRICES, LARGE-VOLUME INTERSTATE PIPE-LINE MARKET, VARIOUS GAS SUPPLY AREAS, 1945–53

(cents per MCF: 16.7 psi)

Gas Supply Area	Prior to 1945	1945	1946	1947	1948	1949	1950	1951	1952	1953
Panhandle–Hugoton	4	6	6	7	9	10–11	—	11–12	12–13	18
West Texas–Permian Basin	3	4–5	—	6	(6–7)/(9)	—	—	9	13	—
East Texas–North Louisiana	—	3–4	5	(7–8)/(9)	9	(7.5)/(9.5)	12–13	16	16	16
Texas Gulf Coast—Dists. 2 and 4	—	5	6	7	—	10	10	10	18	18–19
Texas Gulf Coast—Dist. 3	—	—	5	—	9	11	12	12	18	18–20
Southwest Louisiana	—	—	—	—	11	12	12	12	23–25	25–27
Southeast Louisiana–Mississippi	4	5	5	5	6	11	11	(11)/(16)	20–22	—

Note: Prices represent average contract price over 20-year contract term. Where two sets of prices are given, in parentheses, the upper set applies to the first half of the year, the lower set applies to the second half year. Where prices are not shown, this is to be read as an absence of contract data.

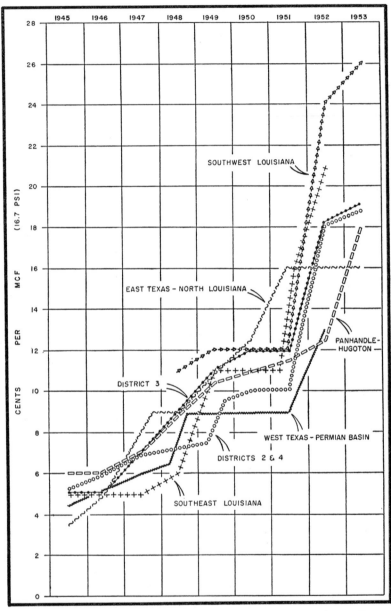

FIG. 9.—Natural Gas Field Price Levels—Large-Volume Inter-state Pipe-Line Market—Various Gas Supply Areas, 1945–53

assumed twenty-year term. Last, field prices were adjusted to include gas gathering taxes, whenever payment of such taxes was entirely a buyer obligation.

Turning to an analysis of these data, attention is directed to the price interrelationships prevailing among the supply areas. The price pattern clearly shows that effects of postwar expansion were first felt in the Panhandle-Hugoton supply area. Prices increased here to a level substantially higher than elsewhere, reflecting the presence of established pipe-line buyers whose available transportation capacity enabled an immediate response to postwar consumer demand. By 1945, prices in the Panhandle-Hugoton area attained a level of 6.0 cents per MCF, which was maintained through 1946.

However, after 1945, buying activity generally shifted to the East Texas and the Texas Gulf Coast supply areas. Prices in these areas rose, by the end of 1946, to levels approximating that of the older supply source. Moreover, the promotion of new pipe-line projects in 1947 brought additional buyers into the Gulf Coast–West Texas markets. The strongest pressure was exerted on prices in the East Texas–North Louisiana supply area; by the end of 1947, price levels here reached 9.0 cents per MCF, almost 30 per cent higher than the Panhandle-Hugoton level. Some price pressure was also felt in Districts 2 and 4 of the Texas Gulf Coast during 1947. At the same time, no purchase activity was recorded for District 3.

The high field price levels in East Texas led to a shift in buyer interest during 1948. District 3 became active, and prices soon rose to the 9.0 cents per MCF level of East Texas. Likewise, the Southwest Louisiana area, for which no contracts were recorded earlier, became a major supply source in 1948, establishing a price level of 11.0 cents per MCF or about 20 per cent higher than levels prevailing elsewhere. On the other hand, Districts 2 and 4, previously experiencing considerable purchase activity, were now apparently by-passed; no purchase contracts were recorded for these two supply areas during 1948, presupposing the absence of large-volume pipe-line buying.

A tendency toward price level equalization was also noted

during 1948. For example, the Panhandle-Hugoton region, in which prices up to that time had risen slightly above their 1945 level, experienced an increase to the more common 9.0 cent level. In a similar manner, the West Texas–Permian Basin supply area, which had consistently lagged behind most of the other sources, experienced a sharp rise from 6.0 to 9.0 cents per MCF between 1947 and the last half of 1948. An exception to this pattern of equalization was the Southeast Louisiana–Mississippi gas supply area, in which the 6.0 cents per MCF price level is presumably attributable to the presence of a single pipe-line buyer. However, the same condition in West Texas did not prevent an upward price adjustment there.

By 1949, the postwar pipe-line expansion was reaching its height. Evidently a response to its low field prices, buying activity was especially pronounced in Districts 2 and 4. As a result, prices soon rose to levels approximating those which prevailed elsewhere. Generally speaking, field prices in all of the active supply areas increased to an 11.0 cents per MCF level. Even the low prices in the Southeast Louisiana area were raised, notwithstanding the continued presence of only one pipe-line buyer.

A temporary peak in field prices for large-volume gas supplies was reached at the beginning of 1950 at a level of approximately 12.0 cents per MCF. From the middle of 1950 through 1951, relatively stable field prices characterized all supply areas except East Texas–North Louisiana, where prices rose from 13.0 to 16.0 cents, and Southeast Louisiana–Mississippi, where a price level rise from 11.0 to 16.0 cents occurred in the last half of 1951. There is little question that the beginning of Korean hostilities, and the consequent shortage of materials, impeded pipe-line expansion and diminished the immediate demand for field gas. Whether or not the rate of increase in field prices would have continued in the absence of these circumstances is problematical.

The East Texas price rise may not be entirely representative of activity in that area, since the price pattern after 1948 was highly erratic. By far the majority of contracts were small-volume purchases at prices of 13.0 cents or less, but a 16.0 cent price prevailed in a few gas fields which apparently contained reasonably large uncommitted gas reserves. It was on the basis of those fields that a large-volume price of 16.0 cents was selected; this price should be considered unique.

The period of stability in field prices ended in 1952. That year and the next saw a marked rise in the price of large-volume large-reserve gas supplies. Curiously enough, the increase began in previously laggard Southeast Louisiana in the latter half of 1951; by 1952, the increase in price was well established in the Gulf Coast supply areas. On the other hand, the Panhandle-Hugoton area was slow to change and experienced a comparatively small increase to about a 13.0 cent price level. The West Texas supply area also reached a 13.0 cent price, but, having started from a lower level, its increase was proportionately larger.

Although field price levels in general rose to new highs in 1952, a pattern of differentiation between the Louisiana Gulf Coast and the other Gulf Coast supply areas became evident. Field prices were above a 20.0 cent level in the Louisiana Gulf Coast, while in the Texas Gulf Coast and East Texas–North Louisiana supply areas they remained within the range of 16.0 to 18.0 cents per MCF.

In 1953, there was further upward pressure which, after confirming the price level established in 1952, raised it still higher. For the Texas Gulf Coast supply areas, prices increased to between 18.0 and 20.0 cents per MCF. In the case of the Louisiana Gulf Coast, the large-volume contracts negotiated were judged to involve purchase costs of 25.0 to 27.0 cents per MCF. Only in the East Texas–North Louisiana supply area did the price level remain unchanged at 16.0 cents. In the Panhandle-Hugoton area, field prices rose sharply to an estimated 18.0 cents per MCF, approximating Texas Gulf Coast levels. For the West Texas–Permian Basin supply area, no contract data were available for 1953; it would be expected, however, to follow the price movements of the companion Panhandle-Hugoton area.

Also of importance is the fact that the field price estimates shown for 1952 and 1953 must be viewed largely as minimum prices. Beginning in 1952, if not earlier, the contract prices in most large-volume large-reserve purchase agreements were firm only for short periods. Even when the legal term of contract was set at twenty years, these agreements usually provided for price redetermination at the end of an initial five-year period. At that time, prices could be renegotiated or adjusted to prevailing levels, such as an average of the three highest prices in the field. Furthermore, in many agreements the price escalation at the end of each five-year period was expressly stipulated as a minimum increase. Under these circumstances, the considerable upward flexibility of such purchase contracts clearly warrants viewing field price estimates based upon these contracts as only minima.

The preceding analysis of inter-supply area price levels discloses a number of interesting patterns. Of particular note is the step-like fashion in which the price level shifted from one supply area to another during the early postwar years. The main force behind this pattern was, of course, the shifting interest of buyers. As demand pressures in older supply areas raised prices to a high level or created the prospect of higher price levels, pipe-line buyers sought new producing areas. Both established operations and projects in a promotional stage responded in this fashion.

Accompanying buyer entry into a new supply area were substantial price jumps which tended first to become consolidated in the initiating supply area and then to diffuse. Thus, the first appearance of top field prices occurred in different supply areas, as buying activity shifted, but was soon transmitted to other supply sources as part of a tendency toward price equalization. Even those supply areas containing only one or two pipe-line buyers experienced this effect.

These price relationships among the supply areas were most evident during the period up to 1950 and were indicative of a market structure containing important buyer supply options. While entry into a new supply area might increase buyer utilization costs, expenditures would not be excessive for adjoining areas. In the interplay of bargaining, the possibility of such a buyer shift must have exerted considerable competitive pressure upon gas producers.

After 1950, inter-supply area patterns were not as obvious. By that time, a great quantity of gas reserves had already been

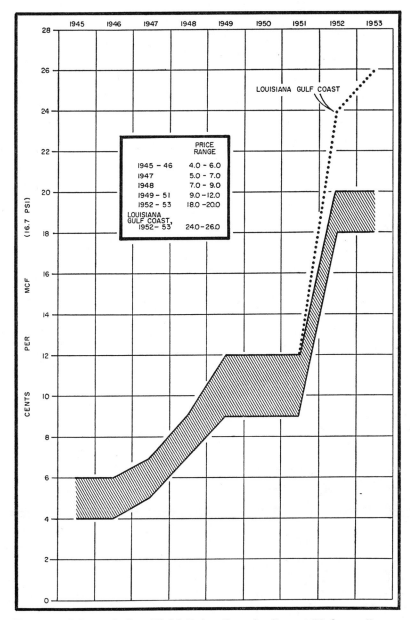

FIG. 10.—Natural Gas Field Price Levels—Large-Volume Interstate Pipe-Line Market—Southwestern U. S., 1945–53

committed, the number of new projects diminished, and the frequency of large-volume contracts reduced. Moreover, large, uncommitted gas reserves tended to become localized in the Louisiana Gulf Coast, a fact which may explain the diminution of pressures causing price equalization between supply areas.

Besides the ascertainment of price levels within individual gas supply areas, determination of changes in field price level for the entire southwestern gas producing region is desirable. Price ranges representing the over-all level of field prices for each year can be estimated from the data of Table 16. This information is given in Figure 10, which presents the broadest possible view of natural gas field prices during the period 1945–53.

Figure 10 shows that price levels rose steadily from a starting position of 4.0–6.0 cents per MCF before 1947 to a peak of 9.0–12.0 cents per MCF by 1949 and remained stable at that level until 1951. A new and sharp rise in field prices began in the latter part of 1951, and prices reached an 18.0–20.0 cent level in 1952–53. This upward movement was even stronger in the Louisiana Gulf Coast, where prices moved sharply to a level of 24.0–26.0 cents per MCF.

The data of Figure 10 indicate an approximate 300 per cent increase in field price levels between 1945 and 1953 for the large-volume large-reserve pipe-line market, about two-thirds of which took place after 1951.

C. INTERSTATE PIPE-LINE DEMANDS FOR FIELD GAS

There is little doubt that the large postwar expansion of interstate pipe-line facilities was a fundamental factor conditioning the rapid rise in field prices between 1945 and 1953. The growth in demand consequent to that expansion converted the gas field market from one of flush supplies and buyer supremacy to one of relative scarcity of supplies and seller ascendancy. To this larger demand must be assigned much of the responsibility for the demonstrated increase in field price levels.

Reasonably adequate quantitative indications of the growth in pipe-line demands for field gas are the purchases of interstate pipe lines from independent producers in the Southwest, as given in Table 7. These purchases increased from about 1.0 TCF in 1947 to approximately 4.0 TCF in 1953, or about 300 per cent within the six-year period during which most of the postwar field price increase occurred.

While interstate pipe lines did not represent the only demand force acting upon gas field prices, they did constitute by far the most important. This is shown in the following tabulation based on U. S. Bureau of Mines data:

	1946 TCF	Per cent	1954 TCF	Per cent	Change 1946–54 TCF
Marketed production	4.0	100.0	8.7	100.0	4.7
Interstate shipments	1.1	27.5	4.5	51.7	3.4
Intrastate use	2.9	72.5	4.2	48.3	1.3
Field use	0.9	22.5	1.5	17.2	0.6
Net intrastate use	2.0	50.0	2.7	31.1	0.7

According to these figures, 3.4 TCF of the 4.7 TCF increase in marketed production between 1946 and 1954, or approximately 72 per cent, occurred in the interstate market which is almost exclusively a pipe-line market. The remainder of the increase, including field use, has been assigned to an intrastate classification. But field use, which pertains mostly to the drilling and producing operations of gas and oil wells, should be attributed in part to the interstate market, since increased interstate shipments have been responsible for some of the growth in that area. To make the interstate and intrastate markets more comparable, field use should be omitted from both intrastate use and the marketed production base. If this is done, only a small part, approximately 17 per cent, of the increase in adjusted marketed production between 1946 and 1954 was accounted for by intrastate markets, while 83 per cent was attributable to interstate marketings.

These calculations give simple but cogent evidence of the magnitude of the postwar demand increase in the gas field. However, the effect of this increase in bringing about changes in the structural characteristics of natural gas supply is not fully demonstrated. This can be better accomplished by a descriptive presentation of pipe-line gas supply sources and the postwar development of natural gas pipe lines.

Two features characterized pipe-line gas supply in the period before 1945: First, the interstate pipe lines originating in the Southwest met a substantial if not a major part of their gas requirements from their own production or through purchases from closely tied affiliates. Second, most of these pipe lines secured their supplies from two geographically defined sources. The most important of these sources was the Panhandle-Hugoton gas supply area, consisting of the Panhandle field in northwestern Texas and the Hugoton field in Oklahoma and southwestern Kansas. The other source was the East Texas–North Louisiana gas supply area, especially the large dry-gas supplies of the Monroe field in northern Louisiana and, to a lesser extent, the Carthage field in northeastern Texas.

The reasons for this early geographical pattern are not difficult to find: Large quantities of gas were available to meet demands; the dry-gas supply was best suited to pipe-line operation; production and processing costs were low; and, perhaps most important, the fields had clear-cut advantages of location for the markets to be served.

In addition to the geographical pattern, the predominance, before 1945, of pipe-line-owned production relative to purchased gas is a noteworthy feature. The statistical evidence for this situation has been presented in Table 8. Again, a number of factors appear to have been responsible. One of the most important was that promoters of pipe-line projects frequently included individuals owning or controlling large gas reserves which were subsequently transferred to the newly formed companies. Since federal rate regulation, valuing pipe-line-owned gas reserves at original cost, was nonexistent, increments in the value of the reserves transferred to the newly formed pipe lines were expected to be obtained through an enhanced market value of pipe-line securities. Consequently, among the promoters of early pipe lines were many large petroleum companies. For example, the Standard Oil Company of New Jersey had considerable interests in the Colorado Interstate Gas Company, a pipe-line company serving Denver, Colorado, in the Mississippi River Fuel Corporation serving St. Louis, Missouri, and in the Interstate Natural Gas Company project serving New Orleans, Louisiana.[2]

In spite of owning large reserves, the prewar pipe lines did negotiate a certain number of purchase contracts with nonaffiliated producers. These were generally small-volume contracts, and the bargaining position of the sellers was not strong. To illustrate, a posted price system appeared to be operative in the Panhandle-Hugoton supply area, in which the buyer stipulated the prices at which gas would be purchased. Thus, from 1933 to 1944, the Northern Natural Gas Company apparently purchased gas in this supply area at only two prices—4.0 cents and 5.0 cents per MCF—while the Panhandle Eastern Pipe Line Company negotiated most of its gas purchase contracts at certain uniform prices —such as 3.56 cents, 4.07 cents, and 4.58 cents per MCF.[3]

The above factors indicate the absence of a large pipe-line demand for purchased gas supplies before 1945. Generally, there was much less demand for all gas, in comparison with the supply which was readily available. In particular, the gas reserves of the Texas and Louisiana Gulf Coast areas were without markets, and the low value of these supplies is well illustrated by the following statement:

> At present, in the south Texas fields when the Texas Corporation sinks a well and brings in a 'gaser,' it is delivered over to United Gas for cost, plus. If it is an oil well Texas Corporation retains it.[4]

This situation was sharply reversed during the postwar period by the great increase in consumer demands for natural gas. The most important causal factor was a change in the price rela-

---

[2] An early study which is especially informative regarding the promotion of various interstate pipe-line projects in the 1920's is J. C. Youngberg, *Natural Gas, America's Fastest Growing Industry.*

[3] See tabulation of natural gas purchase contracts for these pipe lines, *96 Cong. Rec. 4023-4024* (1950).

[4] Youngberg, *op. cit.,* 44.

73

tionship between gas and its competitive fuels—coal and oil. The more rapid postwar rise in coal and oil prices made economical the movement of southwestern gas to eastern and north-central consuming areas, and increased consumer demand in the mid-western markets already served.

Even prior to the war, expansion of ultimate consumer markets and pipe lines to serve them was under way. As early as 1940, at least five long-distance pipe lines, including one to New York City, were being projected.[5] But the greatest pipe-line growth was brought about by the large postwar disparity between costs of natural gas for domestic space-heating or for industrial uses and costs of alternative fuels.

Other factors were acting to enlarge field market demands within the southwestern gas supply areas: the depletion of the Appalachian gas fields made it necessary for the highly developed natural gas economy of the north central states to turn to the Southwest for replacement supplies; a similar depletion of local supplies, together with a rapidly expanding population, compelled California distributors to reach out for West Texas gas; the industrialization of the Southwest created new demands for gas within and among the producing states; and, last, the increasing costs of manufactured gas for mixed gas service resulted in a shift to straight natural gas service. Coalescing as they did, these factors added their strength to create an unusually large demand pressure in the field market for gas.

Nevertheless, the principal factor was still the growth in consumer markets, the scale and rapidity of which were well evidenced by the expansion of established pipe-line facilities and the promotion of new pipe-line projects. The economic feasibility of this activity seemed assured by the large and ready market for gas at resale prices equal to regulated transportation costs plus prevailing field prices. Furthermore, the promotional profits from new pipe-line projects were also dependent upon a ready consumer market, through which heavy bond financing was made possible, in some cases equaling 75 per cent to 80 per cent of total pipe-line capitalization. Large capital gains to promoters and

[5] 20 FPC Ann. Rep. (1940), 77.

74

equity holders resulted from such leverage; these were more than sufficient to provide the requisite entrepreneurial incentives. In fact, such capital gains may well have been an excessive stimulus for some projects, in the light of long-run field prices for gas. Finally, an attempt by the Federal Power Commission, in 1952, to adopt a rate-of-return policy which would have appropriated most of these leverage gains for consumers proved abortive.[6]

Expansion of the postwar market for natural gas affected the various gas supply areas differently. Expanded demands of Midwestern markets were among the first to stimulate a supply response. These needs were met by an enlargement of existing pipeline systems tapping the Panhandle-Hugoton gas supply area. For example, the Panhandle Eastern Pipe Line Company contracted in 1943 with the Phillips Petroleum Company for an annual volume of 53.5 million MCF, while the Northern Natural Gas Company and the Cities Service Gas Company secured comparable quantities from other producers in 1945 and 1946. An entirely new pipe-line system, the Michigan-Wisconsin Pipe Line Company, designed to serve the Detroit, Michigan, and the Milwaukee, Wisconsin, markets, was completed in 1949. It acquired a basic gas supply amounting to an annual volume of about 60 million MCF in 1945, again under purchase contract from the Phillips Petroleum Company.

To meet the needs of the California market, which had hitherto been served from local gas sources, the El Paso Natural Gas Company extended its facilities and built a major pipe line to the California border immediately after the war. The gas, supplied first to the Los Angeles market and subsequently to the San Francisco market, was obtained from a virtually new supply source—the West Texas–Permian Basin producing area. Although this area had been used previously to supply small local markets, it was for the most part undeveloped. Not until the large California market became accessible was an adequate outlet for West Texas gas provided; prior to that time, the gas had been wasted by venting or flaring. To supplement the variable supply of oil-

[6] See Edward J. Neuner, "Some Aspects of Natural Gas Regulation," Western Economic Association *Proceedings* —*1953 at Berkeley, California.*

well gas from this source, however, the El Paso Company had to contract for a large volume of gas in the Panhandle-Hugoton area, again from the Phillips Petroleum Company.

The other postwar interstate pipe-line projects were based upon East Texas and Gulf Coast gas supply sources. Not only were geographic relationships between these gas producing areas and the markets to be served more suitable than other areas, but, also, the rising prices after 1944 in the Panhandle-Hugoton area made other sources more economical. The postwar pipe-line projects based on the Gulf Coast, with the approximate date of their initial operation, are given below: the Tennessee Gas Transmission Co., 1944; the Texas Eastern Transmission Corp., 1947; the Texas Gas Transmission Corp., 1948; the Transcontinental Gas Pipe Line Corp., 1951; the Trunkline Gas Co., 1951; and the Texas Illinois Natural Gas Pipeline Co., 1951.

Three additional pipe-line projects, promoted after 1950, acquired gas reserves from the Gulf Coast producing region. The first was the Gulf Interstate Pipe Line Company, the reserves for which were obtained in 1952 from the Southwest Louisiana gas supply area. This pipe line functioned as common carrier, transporting gas to the Columbia Gas System in the Appalachian area. The second was the American Louisiana Pipe Line Company project, which was conditionally certificated in 1954 to serve the Detroit, Michigan, market and which contracted for a gas supply in the Southwest Louisiana gas supply area during 1953. The third was the Pacific Northwest Pipeline Company, certificated in 1954 to serve the states of Washington and Oregon with gas obtained from the San Juan–New Mexico gas supply area and from Canadian sources.

Thus, a total of eight completely or virtually new long-distance, large-capacity pipe-line projects were brought into existence between 1944 and 1951, and three others were initiated between 1950 and 1953. The first six projects tapping the Gulf Coast gas supply area contracted for their basic gas supplies over a much shorter time period—from about 1947 to 1950. The economic effects of numerous new projects seeking large gas supplies, combined with the expansion of established pipe-line systems, seem obvious. Even with a large supply of uncommitted gas, the resulting demands for field gas would have exerted extraordinary upward pressures upon field prices.

The impact of this large pipe-line demand can be explored still further. The postwar expansion of the Appalachian and the Eastern Seaboard markets for gas was at first met largely from the East Texas–North Louisiana supply area, particularly from the Carthage field, which underwent rapid development. The principal pipe-line purchasers in the East Texas supply area were the Texas Eastern Transmission Corporation and the Texas Gas Transmission Corporation, both of which contracted for large gas supplies in 1947 and 1948. Both companies served the Appalachian area, with the former finding an important market in the Philadelphia, Pennsylvania, area.

The Tennessee Gas Transmission Company, also serving the Appalachian market, had its main interests in the Texas Gulf Coast supply areas. It had contracted for gas in this area as early as 1944, and its purchases there were among the first to open up the Gulf Coast supply source. Although a major part of its gas reserves were obtained during 1945 and 1946, the company continued to contract for gas throughout the postwar period, purchases being largely concentrated within the three supply areas making up the Texas Gulf Coast.

In addition to these three purchasers, a fourth pipe-line project was actively contracting for gas during 1947 and 1948. This project, the Transcontinental Gas Pipeline Corporation, serving the New York City market, was principally interested in Districts 2 and 4 of the Texas Gulf Coast, although it did secure gas supplies from the Southwest Louisiana gas supply area.

In 1949 and early 1950, two other newly promoted pipe lines were seeking a gas supply in the Texas Gulf Coast area: The Trunkline Gas Company and the Texas Illinois Natural Gas Pipeline Company were or became affiliated with pipe-line systems for which the historical supply source was the Panhandle-Hugoton area. The first was affiliated with the Panhandle Eastern Pipe Line Company and provided additional gas for the expansion of the latter's markets. The second pipe-line project was affiliated with the Natural Gas Pipeline Company of America and was meant to meet the expanding requirements of the Chicago, Illinois, market. Both projects were apparently a response to the rise in Panhandle-Hugoton field prices.

By the middle of 1950, the promotion of new pipe-line projects came to a temporary halt. Established systems, however, continued to acquire gas supplies with increased interest in small volume purchases. While this interest reflects in part the more complete coverage of small volume transactions which characterized the contract data sources after 1950, it seemed to constitute a factual change in the field market demand pattern.

For example, gathering systems, such as the Wilcox Trend Gathering System, an affiliate of the Texas Eastern Company, were inaugurated to tap many small fields in the Texas Gulf Coast. Similarly, the Tennessee Gas Transmission Company contracted for much small-volume gas, and the Texas Gas Transmission Corporation organized gathering affiliates to cover the Southwest Louisiana gas supply area.

The period from 1950 through 1951 was also one of considerable price stability, which may have resulted in part from the curtailment of pipe-line expansion. However, during 1952 and 1953, a new upward price movement occurred in virtually all gas supply areas. This increase was not generally related to any market increase in demand, although established pipe-line systems continued to expand. Where the price rise was especially marked, however, in the Southwest Louisiana gas supply area, it was paralleled by the entry of two new pipe-line projects—the Gulf Interstate Pipe Line Company and the American Louisiana Pipe Line Company.

After 1952, the direct-distributor purchase developed. In this type of arrangement, gas is contracted for in the field by a distribution company or a concern affiliated with a distribution company, and long-distance pipe-line transportation is performed on a common carrier basis. The device was not unknown before 1952; when the Tennessee Gas Transmission Company was first organized, it had entered into such an arrangement with a subsidiary of the Columbia Gas System, Inc. During 1952, the Tennessee Gas Transmission Company also participated in similar agreements with the Iroquois Gas Corporation, the Niagara Gas Transmission Corporation, and the Equitable Gas Company.

Another significant feature of the period 1952–53 was the concentration of purchase activity for large-volume, new-project gas reserves in the Louisiana Gulf Coast supply areas. Although supporting data are not available, a considerable part of the remaining and uncommitted gas reserves in the United States seems to be located in that area. With future supplies likely to be found in the course of offshore tideland oil exploration, the Louisiana Gulf Coast supply area will undoubtedly retain its importance, in spite of growing pipe-line interest in Canadian gas supply sources.

CHAPTER III

Field Market Pricing Practices

A CHARACTERISTIC FEATURE of transactions in the field market for gas is the elaboration of contract provisions other than the direct price quotation. The total consideration in a natural gas purchase transaction is much more than that found in the contract price; it necessarily includes the "mix" of contract stipulations and the cost and value of these to buyer and seller. This feature has many consequences of considerable importance for a study of field markets and the problem of monopoly in the gas field.

First, modifications in the general pattern of contract provisions may lead to major changes in pricing conditions which are not fully represented by unit price levels. As noted in the analysis of field price levels, changes in the firmness of contract prices have altered the importance of long-term contracts. Current contract prices have become little more than minimum prices for the duration of the purchase agreements.

Second, variations in the cost burden of non-price provisions constitute price differences for buyers. Since these provisions, like price movements, are a product of market actions, an examination of their character and frequency may aid in establishing the degree of competition in field markets. Thus, price uniformity, under certain circumstances, is an indication of noncompetitive behavior, and excessive uniformity in contract practices and provisions might also imply monopolistic action on the part of sellers.

Even without complete uniformity of use, the prevalence of particular market practices may inhibit and restrain the operation of market forces enough to produce noncompetitive price results. For example, various contract provisions—such as favored-nation and spiral escalator clauses—are considered devices leading to

80

excessive field price increases. These provisions—by implication—have been viewed as monopolistic practices.[1]

The origins and purposes of these pricing practices have not been clearly established, nor have many of the suppositions about the subject been adequately grounded in fact. Consequently, more fully substantiated generalizations concerning the origin, character, and frequency of such pricing practices are essential to a correct evaluation of their noncompetitive significance.

Among the field pricing practices and purchase contract provisions to be examined are the following: fixed price escalation, tax-sharing, inflation adjustment and spiral escalator clauses, favored-nation and price redetermination provisions. Much attention has been devoted to these practices and clauses in various legislative proceedings, and general discussions of the purposes of these devices, as well as of the effect upon purchase costs of gas buyers, are available.[2] While these sources have been drawn upon where needed, the present analysis of field market practices rests largely upon information contained in basic purchase contract data.

A. FIXED PRICE ESCALATION, TAX-SHARING, AND SPIRAL ESCALATOR CLAUSES

Fixed price escalation involves periodic price increases which are known and stipulated at the time the gas purchase contract is first negotiated. To illustrate, a purchase agreement completed during 1952 in the Southwest Louisiana supply area provided for an initial price of 16.0 cents per MCF on a 14.65 psi pressure base, and this price was to be increased 0.4 cent each year for ten years.

---

[1] "We believe that if the producers are made to clean house of the malignant type of escalation clause which is the prime cause, in our opinion, of the present chaotic conditions, that the forces of competition can be freed to operate and that those forces of competition can be safely relied on in the public interest as a substitute for regulation." Testimony of Mr. Randall J. LeBoeuf, Jr., representing the Consolidated Edison Co. of New York, Inc., as well as other gas distributors in the northeastern United States, *Hearings—S. 1853*, 856.

[2] Representing gas producer interests, see testimony of David T. Searls, *Hearings—S. 1853*, 98–101; and testimony of John W. Boatwright, *ibid.*, 201–202. On the distributor side, see testimony of Randall J. LeBoeuf, Jr., *Hearings—H. R. 4560*, 704–709; and testimony of J. French Robinson, *Hearings—S. 1853*, 1267–74.

For the period covered by the purchase contract analysis, the practice of fixed price escalation is an almost universal feature of natural gas field pricing. Before 1944, the majority of contracts stipulated a uniform price per MCF, and there are examples of this practice even in recently negotiated contracts.

The purposes served by fixed price escalation are not obvious, since the same results, in terms of total producer revenues over the contract period, could be obtained with a uniform price per MCF. Generally, the explanation offered is that pipe lines are aided in their developmental stages by shifting some gas purchase costs to later years. If this is the case, the initial price in the contract with a fixed price escalation clause should be less than the price in an agreement without such a provision, since buyers would presumably insist that the average price in the first case be no greater than the single, uniform price in the second type of contract. However, such a pattern is not indicated in the contract sources, although the paucity of contracts without fixed price escalation necessarily limits the investigation.

It is more probable that the advent of this practice was the first reflection of a strengthening seller position in the field market. Granted that the initial price equaled prevailing prices, fixed price escalation increased the total revenue return of the seller and was therefore an effective price increase. For example, when initial prices are 5.0 cents per MCF, a 1.0 cent escalation each five years in a twenty-year contract results in a weighted average price of 6.5 cents per MCF. This is equal to a 30 per cent price increase when compared with a single, uniform price of 5.0 cents. But since the device of fixed price escalation postponed the price increase, it was probably much more acceptable to new pipe-line buyers. Of course, when fixed price escalation of a given magnitude has been used for some time, this price-increasing effect is removed, since the general level of field prices presumably adjusts to the practice.

The cost burden of fixed price escalation to the buyer is obviously dependent upon the amount of escalation and the frequency of occurrence. The most common pattern in the purchase contract data was a provision stipulating a 1.0 cent per

MCF increase in price at the end of each five-year period. As the bargaining advantage shifted to sellers, however, a tendency developed to decrease the length of the period; e.g., in some contracts escalation occurs each year. A second change was presented by increased amounts of escalation; e.g., in some relatively recent contracts, escalation was stipulated at 2.5 cents per MCF for each five-year period.

In spite of some contrary evidence, 1.0 cent escalation each five years still characterizes natural gas purchase contracts; the pattern has achieved an almost customary status. However, this consideration is not as important in present-day contracts as in an earlier period, since its relative price-increasing effect is greatly reduced when initial prices are at 15.0 to 20.0 cent levels. Furthermore, since most current purchase contracts have short effective terms of five years or less, the price escalation has little meaning in defining maximum purchase cost. Fixed price escalation serves only to establish the minimum increase in contract prices.

A second practice, almost as widespread as fixed price escalation, characterizing the field sale of gas is the tax-sharing clause. Its typical form is a requirement that the buyer pay a stipulated proportion of any future increase in "occupation, production, severance, gathering, or sales tax" levied upon the seller. An additional requirement, occurring rather frequently in the Louisiana gas supply areas, obligates the buyer to pay an existing 1.0 cent gathering tax levied by the state of Louisiana.

Tax-sharing provisions were common features of purchase contracts by 1948 and 1949. The purpose of these clauses, from the sellers' point of view, was to avoid the revenue loss which might result if tax levies were increased after a contract with firm prices had been negotiated. With rising field prices, state governments are more likely to appropriate, through severance taxation, some of the resulting scarcity returns or economic rents. Tax-sharing clauses have the added virtue of enlisting the interest of the pipe-line buyer in opposing such tax increases.

The burden of tax-sharing depends upon the division of responsibility for added taxes; any increase in the buyer's share constitutes an effective price increase. In earlier contracts, the

83

proportion borne by the buyer was small—typically one-third—while the seller bore two-thirds. With the increasing demand for gas, this proportion gradually changed in favor of the seller; the exact division of obligation was, in many instances, a bargaining item in the contract negotiations. In the most recent contracts, a tax-sharing proportion of three-fourths buyer and one-fourth seller became almost standard practice.

Tax-sharing proportions which differed from these relatively standard ratios were often the result of policies of particular pipe-line buyers. Thus, the United Gas Pipe Line Company evidently pursued, for as long as possible, a policy of not including tax-sharing clauses in its purchase contracts. Later, as a result of market pressures, it began accepting a one-half buyer and one-half seller division. Conversely, the Texas Eastern Transmission Corporation and the Texas Gas Transmission Corporation included seven-eighths buyer tax-sharing clauses in their purchase contracts. Since this fraction exceeded the normal proportion, it apparently functioned as a bargaining point to induce the completion of purchase agreements.

In spite of these exceptions, it is probably correct to conclude that tax-sharing, fixed at a proportion of three-fourths buyer and one-fourth seller, has also achieved a customary status. The importance of this clause as a factor determining field prices has not been great, although its effect would be significant if production and gathering taxes were substantially increased.

Another practice in the field pricing of gas is the inclusion in purchase contracts of price-index inflation clauses and an inflation adjustment proviso known as a spiral escalator clause—both of which can have a pronounced upward effect upon contract prices. However, these clauses do not seem to occur frequently in purchase contracts. The purpose which they serve is evident: to protect sellers under long-term contract from the value-eroding effects of inflation. These clauses may also be instruments for securing upward price adjustments when a seller's bargaining position is not strong enough to command larger and more flexible forms of upward price revision.

The price-index inflation clause brings about contract price increases proportional to defined changes in a general price level index, usually the Bureau of Labor Statistics Index of Wholesale Prices. An illustration is available in contracts negotiated by the Permian Basin Pipe Line Company during 1952.[3] In this instance, contract prices were not to be changed until the wholesale price index had increased above an adjustment level. The adjustment level was contractually defined as a given number of points above a stipulated base index value, the latter presumably measuring the position of the price index and therefore the general price level at the time the contract was negotiated. When the price index rose above the adjustment level, contract prices were to be modified in proportion to the increase of the price index above the stipulated base index value.

The effect of these requirements was to postpone any adjustment until a substantial price index increase occurred (in this case, approximately 18 per cent), but once that point was reached, price adjustments were to be made annually in proportion to price index changes. This inflation adjustment also functioned for price index decreases, but not below the prices originally stipulated in the agreement. If, subsequent to a rise, the price index fell below the level which brought the proviso into operation, then prices were restored to the amounts stated in the contract. In addition, an upper price limit was set, in the case of the Permian Basin contracts, by a stipulation that prices resulting from the inflation clause could not exceed the highest price paid by an interstate pipe line in District 3 for comparable quantities of gas.

A second form of inflation adjustment proviso is the spiral escalator clause. The requirements of this type of provision, however, permit increases in contract prices which are unrelated to price level changes. In the spiral escalator clause, a second condition must be fulfilled, in addition to the price level increase, before the proviso becomes operative. The contract price adjustment not only requires a defined increase in a price index, but it is also conditioned upon an increase in the resale rates of the pipe-

[3] *Hearings—H. R. 4560*, 690.

line buyer. When these requirements are met, contract prices are increased in proportion to the increase in the resale rates above a stipulated base level.

Since this clause was ostensibly an inflation adjustment device, it seems incongruous to make contract price adjustments dependent upon and limited to a percentage increase in buyer resale rates. The presumed explanation is that pipe-line buyers insisted upon protection for themselves against regulatory lags in the adjustment of their own revenues if purchased gas costs increased. The plausibility of the explanation is heightened by the fact that the most frequently cited instances of spiral escalator clauses occur in contracts dated prior to 1946, when the bargaining position of the pipe-line buyers involved was relatively strong.

Generally, in the event of an inflationary change in prices, the spiral escalator clause would be much less effective than a price-index inflation clause in assuring sellers of the desired protection. Whatever the degree of price level change, the producer would first have to wait for an increase in the pipe line's regulated resale rates before adjusting prices. The producer would then receive an adjustment which, under original-cost utility regulation, would almost certainly be less than the full price level change.

Apart from its inflation adjustment effects, the spiral escalator clause, once it becomes operative, assertedly leads to an indefinite upward movement of contract prices. Under this type of clause, rate increases obtained by the pipe-line buyer for any reason lead to an upward adjustment in purchase contract prices which, in turn, necessitates a second pipe-line rate increase, resulting in a new adjustment of purchase contract prices, and so on. The provision derives its distinctive name from this upward price spiraling effect.

The usual implication derived from this effect is that it may lead to unjustifiable price increases by gas producers, in the sense that they are unrelated to or exceed the inflation adjustment. But this implication may not always be correct, or at least the circumstances under which such increases would occur might be more limited than ordinarily supposed.

In a representative situation, where gas contract prices are in all other respects fixed, the total percentage increase in pipe-line gas costs attributable to spiral escalation cannot exceed the percentage increase in other pipe-line cost-of-service elements, which is initially responsible for raising resale rates.[4] Since the underlying assumption in spiral escalator clauses is that changes in costs other than purchased gas measure the degree of inflation, there would be no gain to the gas producer above and beyond an inflation adjustment. Actually, the regulatory delays in securing successive resale rate increases give the producer less advantage than he might obtain by other means, such as tying contract prices directly to a price index.

Under certain defined conditions, however, spiral escalation can result in gas price increases which are fortuitous and unrelated to an inflation adjustment. This occurs when prices in a contract containing such a provision are initially increased for some entirely different reason, such as fixed price escalation. Then an additional price increase is induced, the magnitude of which varies depending upon a number of factors. Under the circumstances likely to be encountered, the additional increase in purchased gas costs will not be particularly large—perhaps about 15 per cent.

To illustrate, if a 50 per cent increase in purchased gas costs were to occur as a result of fixed price escalation or similar causes, this initial increase in the cost of service would activate the spiral escalator. If purchased gas costs were 20 per cent of total costs, the ultimate outcome would be an additional 8.3 per cent increase

---

[4] With respect to the following illustration, assume a resale rate increase of 40 per cent in period 2 because of a 50 per cent increase in "other" costs between periods 1 and 2; then the cost of purchased gas affected by the spiral escalator is successively increased in periods 3, 4, etc., until an equilibrium is reached when the original position of purchased gas costs relative to the total cost of service is restored. In this case, the actual proportion of purchased gas costs to total cost of service is not significant; the change in purchased gas costs will be proportional to the change in "other" costs:

Cost	PERIOD					Change from Period 1
	1	2	3	4	Final	
			(dollars)			(per cent)
Purchased Gas Costs	20	20	28	29.6	30	50.0
Other Costs	80	120	120	120.0	120	50.0
Total Cost of Service	100	140	148	149.6	150	50.0

above that which would otherwise have been incurred.[5] The degree to which the spiral escalator would increase purchased gas costs depends upon the initial increase activating its operation and the proportionate significance of purchased gas costs in the total cost of service. Using probable combinations of these two factors, the increase caused by spiral escalation would range approximately between 5 per cent and 33 per cent.[6]

A third situation associated with the use of a spiral escalator clause may also be analyzed briefly. Such a practice assertedly operates to increase purchase contract prices with a rise in general field price levels. An increase in the price of one contract can "trigger" a price increase in others, if these agreements contain spiral escalator clauses. This result again derives from the impact of an increase in purchased gas costs upon total pipe-line cost of service which then leads to a resale rate increase. But the price increases obtained by the contracts with spiral escalator provisions, even after the full spiraling effect, will be considerably less than the increase obtained by the "trigger" contract.[7] If one of

[5] Relying upon the same illustration as before, but assuming a 50 per cent increase in purchased gas costs between periods 1 and 2 with no changes in "other" costs, the following results are obtained:

	Period					Change Due to Spiral
Cost	1	2	3	4	Final	Escalation
	(dollars)					(per cent)
Purchased Gas Costs	20	30	32	32.4	32.5	8.3
Other Costs	80	80	80	80.0	80.0	—
Total Cost of Service	100	110	112	112.4	112.5	2.3

The percentage change caused by spiral escalation is the percentage increase between period 2 and the final outcome, since the purchased gas costs of period 2 would have been incurred even in the absence of the spiral escalator.

[6] A tabulation of the additional percentage increase in purchased gas costs resulting from the operation of a spiral escalator, assuming likely combinations of the two factors, is presented below:

INITIAL INCREASE IN PURCHASED GAS COSTS ACTIVATING SPIRAL ESCALATION	RATIO OF PURCHASED GAS COST TO TOTAL COST OF SERVICE		
	20%	30%	40%
25%	5.0	8.5	13.3
50%	8.3	14.3	22.2
100%	12.5	21.3	33.3

the purposes of the spiral escalator clause is contract price flexibility, i.e., the adjustment of purchase contract prices to the higher field price levels which may prevail in the future, the device has very little to recommend it.

Little information is available regarding the extent to which spiral escalator clauses are a feature of gas field pricing. The purchase contract data analyzed were not always explicit in indicating the presence or absence of this type of provision, and thus a quantitative measure of its occurrence cannot be made. From a general examination of field pricing transactions, however, it does not appear that the spiral escalator clause was very common or that it is currently used with any frequency.

Although other instances are known, its notoriety seems to rest largely upon one case: the widely discussed spiral escalator provision included in the basic gas supply contract of the Michigan-Wisconsin Pipe Line Company.[8] This contract, covering initially the entire gas supply requirements of the pipe-line buyer, was negotiated in 1945 with the Phillips Petroleum Company. Other contracts entered into by the Phillips Petroleum Company with the Panhandle Eastern Pipe Line Company and the El Paso Natural Gas Company, both evidently negotiated before 1945, also were asserted to contain such provisions.[9] Spiral escalator clauses were present, too, in a few of the earliest contracts negotiated by the Tennessee Gas Transmission Company, particularly in the Carthage field of East Texas.[10]

---

[7] If a pipe line has two gas supply contracts outstanding, each of which results in purchased gas costs equaling 10 per cent of the total cost of service incurred, and if purchased gas costs under only one contract are raised 50 per cent, the effect is, other factors being equal, to increase the cost of service 5 per cent. The initial percentage received by the second contract containing a spiral escalator is thus measured. The ultimate increase when the spiral is completed is only 5.55 per cent. Various factors again determine the exact amount of increase, but, even under the most favorable conditions, the increase obtained by the contract with the spiral escalator would still be considerably less than that secured by the "trigger" contract.

[8] See *Hearings—S. 1853*, 1011, for the contract provision in question. See also Opinion No. 275, *Michigan-Wisconsin Pipe Line Company*, Federal Power Commission (July 28, 1954), for a description of the clause and its impact upon the pipe line's cost of service.

[9] *Hearings—S. 1853*, 99.

[10] *Ibid.*, 1286.

The early dates of these spiral escalator contracts, as well as the strong positions of some of the pipe-line buyers, bears out a previously expressed view that these clauses were not the consequence of large seller market power, imposing onerous—if not monopolistic—burdens upon purchasers. Rather, they were the first efforts by gas producers to avoid the kinds of risks entailed by long-term contracts. At the time, it was apparently the risks of inflation which were of greatest concern.

The spiral escalator provision is unquestionably an important factor influencing prices in the markets served by the Michigan-Wisconsin Pipe Line Company, and, because of this, the clause has received a large amount of attention and criticism. However, the resulting emphasis may have given the practice a weight which is not commensurate with its over-all significance.[11] As a factor conditioning gas field prices in general, spiral escalation is not very important. All available evidence indicates that it is not widely used. Its value to the seller as a means of securing an inflation adjustment is less than that obtainable by a price-index inflation clause. As a means of bringing about an upward adjustment of contract prices to prevailing field price levels, spiral escalation is far less efficient than price redetermination. These more effective alternatives more than likely explain the relatively infrequent use of spiral escalator clauses.

B. Favored-Nation Pricing Provisions

A widely followed practice in postwar gas field markets, warranting considerable attention, has been inclusion of favored-nation clauses in gas purchase contracts. The use of these clauses has produced considerable repercussions in field markets with attendant effects upon field price levels, since the result of their operation is to bring about an upward adjustment in purchase contract prices. Their objective, moreover, is much greater than securing an inflation adjustment. The general effect of such pric-

[11] See the presentation before Congressional committees of consumer and regulatory interests in those markets, especially the Wisconsin Public Service Commission, in *Hearings—S. 1853*, 471–73, 491–96.

ing provisions is to assure the seller of some adjustment in contract prices if future market prices rise because of changing demand and supply relationships. Efficiency of the clauses in this respect can vary over a wide range, depending upon form and terms of particular favored-nation stipulations.

Two forms of the favored-nation clause differ markedly in potential impact upon contract prices and in cost burdens to buyers: One is the two-party favored-nation proviso, sometimes designated a first-party favored-nation clause; the other is known as a third-party favored-nation clause. The two are distinguishable as follows:

Two-Party Favored-Nation Clause: the buyer is obligated to pay to the seller the equivalent of any higher price which the buyer may subsequently pay for a comparable quantity of gas from another seller within a defined geographical area.

Third-Party Favored-Nation Clause:[12] *the buyer is obligated to pay to the seller the equivalent of any higher price which a third-party purchaser may subsequently pay for a comparable quantity of gas within a defined geographical area.*

The basic difference between these two forms lies in the control retained by the pipe-line purchaser over the operation of the clause. Little or no buyer control accompanies the third-party type of provision, since the actions of others—beyond buyer control—can bring about an increase in the contract prices of existing purchase agreements. Furthermore, a single contract containing a third-party clause, in a supply area where otherwise the pipe-line buyer has only two-party favored-nation contracts, can "trigger" all of the agreements. The higher price paid to the contracting seller with a third-party clause must be paid to all other

[12] The third-party favored-nation clause is, strictly speaking, not a "favored-nation" stipulation. As a general rule, a "favored-nation" stipulation is intended to prevent discrimination; one party agrees to accord a second party as favorable treatment as is given anyone else under like circumstances. It does not require that the second party receive from the first party treatment as favorable as the former can obtain from anyone else.

sellers with contracts having two-party clauses if the same defined geographical area is involved.[13] In effect, a single third-party favored-nation contract converts all two-party arrangements in the same geographical area into third-party variants.

It is evident, then, that the third-party type of favored-nation clause can be quite burdensome to the pipe-line buyer. It increases uncertainty regarding future purchased gas costs and reduces the cost assurance upon which the economic and financial feasibility of a pipe-line project may depend.

Under the two-party favored-nation clause, however, considerable control is retained by the purchaser. Assuming no third-party favored-nation contracts in a given supply area (and no price redetermination clauses, which have the same effect to a lesser degree), the buyer can control supply costs by making no new purchases at higher prices in that supply area. This element of control prevents an increase in gas purchase costs to the extent that a pipe-line project would become unprofitable. A burden is imposed, however, since the buyer must meet expanding gas supply needs by entering new gas fields and supply areas, which necessitates additional gathering facilities and pipe-line extensions.

The circumstances under which a pipe-line buyer may actuate a two-party favored-nation clause can be illustrated. Part of the initial gas supplies for the Transcontinental Gas Pipe Line project was contracted for in Districts 2 and 4 during 1947 at an average price of 7.5 cents per MCF over a twenty-year term. By 1949, an expanding market for gas evidently justified an enlargement of pipe-line capacity, even before construction began, by increasing pipe-line diameter from 26 inches to 30 inches. To acquire the additional gas needed, an average price of 9.5 cents was paid in three new contracts within the same supply area. The effect was to raise prices in the older contracts which contained two-party favored-nation clauses by 2.0 cents per MCF. Presumably, the buyer balanced the higher cost of the additional gas —including the extra cost incurred for old supplies—against a

13 As a consequence of a price increase in a third-party favored-nation contract from 9.0 cents to 16.0 cents per MCF, the Transcontinental Gas Pipe Line Corp. activated all two-party favored-nation contracts in the same supply area of Southwest Louisiana. See *Hearings—S. 1853*, 1027.

smaller investment per unit of pipe-line capacity for the larger-sized facility and consequently a lowering of unit transportation costs for a given load factor.

It is interesting to note that, while the new 1949 contracts also contained two-party favored-nation clauses, they included a proviso not previously present. This clause gave the buyer the option of terminating the contract if its price were increased by the operation of the favored-nation clause. Such an option might serve as a bargaining weapon against the seller, since the full price increase permitted by a favored-nation clause would leave the buyer indifferent to the prospect of either continuing to take the old gas or substituting new gas supplies.

Two purposes appear to be served by the favored-nation clause: first, it equalizes the bargaining positions of different sellers at the time the contract is negotiated; second, it enables sellers to obtain in otherwise firm agreements, some upward adjustment of contract prices to reflect price levels which may prevail in the future. The first of these is efficiently served by the two-party favored-nation clause. Such a provision equalizes the seller bargaining position by removing the gain to the buyer from any ability to differentiate or to discriminate among sellers.

In the bargaining transactions within gas field markets, imperfect knowledge prevails; the prices acceptable to different sellers are really known only to the buyer. He could effectively discriminate by completing contracts in a sequence beginning with the seller offering the lowest-priced gas, who is presumably the weakest or the least knowing in the market. Since the contract would be valid for extended periods, price realignments would not occur readily, and there would be little or no tendency toward a uniform price. A two-party favored-nation clause, however, would assure the first seller negotiating a contract of receiving a price equal to that eventually needed to bring forth the buyer's supply requirements.

The above has assertedly been the purpose of the two-party clause; it may well have been the origin of the clause.[14] However,

[14] See testimony of E. O. Thompson, Texas Railroad Commission, *Hearings—H. R. 4560*, 116.

93

equalization of sellers' positions is no longer the sole or primary aim, since achievement of that purpose requires only a time-limited clause like that used in a few purchase contracts. Thus, the Texas Illinois Natural Gas Pipeline Company, negotiating a number of contracts at the beginning of 1950, included two-party favored-nation clauses which were operative only for the period prior to the delivery of gas. As this pipe line increased its purchase activity, market conditions apparently required negotiation of contracts without such limits on the favored-nation clause.

The time limitation upon the two-party favored-nation clause, such as that noted, was infrequently used; most clauses were operative over the full legal term of contract. The second function served by the provision more likely reflects the objective sought by sellers through the use of the device: to provide a mechanism for bringing about an upward adjustment in contract prices which parallels anticipated rises in future field price levels. The point is illustrated rather neatly in certain agreements negotiated by the Texas Gas Transmission Corporation, in the Southwest Louisiana gas supply area during 1950 and 1951. These contracts stipulated that the two-party favored-nation clause was not to come into operation until after gas deliveries had begun. Consequently, during the period that the pipe-line buyer was acquiring his gas supply, protection against discrimination was not secured by the gas seller, but future adjustments in contract prices were possible.

The interest of gas producers in contract price adjustments is not difficult to appreciate. However, although it may provide for some change, the two-party favored-nation clause does not assure the seller that his contract prices will rise parallel to a rising field price level. Under this type of favored-nation clause, the upward adjustment depends upon buyer initiative. Unless a pipe-line buyer finds it the more economical alternative, he presumably will not purchase gas in certain supply areas if the effect is to activate the two-party favored-nation clauses in his gas supply contracts. When existing field prices are substantially higher than those stipulated in older contracts making up the bulk of supply, the economy of such action diminishes; the full increase in the buyer's cost of additional gas is likely to be prohibitive. Thus, there are numerous two-party favored-nation contracts in force which were negotiated during 1948–50 at much lower prices than those now prevailing and which have not benefited from price adjustments.

It would appear, then, that two-party favored-nation provisions may not be particularly advantageous to gas producers. Alone, they may not be effective in securing price increases for committed gas supplies. Moreover, they may lead to lower field prices for uncommitted gas in old supply areas. Established pipeline buyers simply go to new supply areas to meet additional gas requirements.[15] There the heavy demand may force prices above levels which would otherwise prevail, while the smaller demand in older supply areas would have an opposite effect. Alternatively, the device of a direct-distributor purchase may come into use to avoid the "triggering" of old contracts.[16]

On the other hand, full and immediate contract price adjustment appears to be enjoyed by the gas producer with a contract containing a third-party favored-nation clause. Contract prices are raised to the level paid by any other buyer for comparable gas. Or, if sales of comparable quantities of gas are not available, a contract price adjustment may still be made if higher prices are paid for a non-comparable gas supply. In this case, contract prices are renegotiated, taking into account the differences, and, in the absence of agreement, are subject to arbitration.[17]

Even with a third-party clause, field prices must rise within the geographical area covered by the favored-nation provision before the provision becomes effective. The strength of the third-party provision also depends upon the option of the buyer to withdraw from the contract. Having the right to withdraw, the

[15] For example, the Transcontinental Gas Pipe Line Corp. has found it expedient to purchase additional gas in the Southeast Louisiana–Mississippi gas supply area, a source not previously tapped. See *Hearings–H. R. 4560*, 720.

[16] See *ibid.*, 1692, for the assertion that the direct-distributor purchase of the Iroquois Gas Corp. in District 3 during 1952 was motivated by the refusal of the Tennessee Gas Transmission Co. to supply additional gas, the purchase of which would have activated favored-nation clauses.

[17] See text of the third-party favored-nation clause in the Union Oil–Transcontinental Gas Pipe Line contract, *ibid.*, 688–89.

buyer can negotiate something less than a full increase to prevailing price levels. In spite of these considerations, however, there is little question that the third-party favored-nation provision gives the gas producer an exceptionally strong position in contract price adjustment. As far as the seller is concerned, it renders the price provisions of the long-term gas supply contract completely flexible.

The above discussion has indicated the pertinent aspects of two-party, as well as third-party, favored-nation clauses. Since important policy judgments depend upon the extent of their use in natural gas markets, information regarding their occurrence is essential. A determination of their frequency, based upon the purchase contract analysis, is presented in Table 17.

Two conclusions are to be drawn from this tabulation: First, and most important, where favored-nation provisions have been used, they have been almost exclusively of the two-party variety.[18] Only 13 contracts of approximately 400 reporting favored-nation clauses were identified as third-party agreements. Even allowing for possible inadequacies in the data, the two-party favored-nation clause seems clearly predominant. Moreover, some of the third-party favored-nation provisions were subsequently eliminated by renegotiation.[19]

The second conclusion is that the use of the two-party favored-nation clause has not been uniform among the various supply areas. In the Panhandle-Hugoton and the Southeast Louisiana–Mississippi supply areas, its use has been negligible. It was present to a high degree in West Texas, as well as in Districts 3 and 4, and in the supply areas of District 2 and Southwest Louisiana about 60 per cent of the contracts contained favored-nation

[18] Some uncertainty exists concerning whether or not favored-nation clauses in contracts after 1950 were two-party or third-party variants. There is evidence in the contract data sources which suggests that the third-party variants were identified. No uncertainty exists about the contracts between 1947 and 1950, since the sources for these included complete details regarding the type of provision.

[19] *Trunkline Gas Supply Co.,* 9 FPC (1950), 721. The third-party favored-nation contract of the Transcontinental Gas Pipe Line Corp. was reportedly modified, but not without an upward price adjustment. See Moody's *Public Utility Manual–1955,* 54; see also *Hearings–S. 1853,* 1027.

Table 17

ANALYSIS OF FAVORED-NATION CLAUSES IN NATURAL GAS PURCHASE CONTRACTS
NEGOTIATED IN VARIOUS GAS SUPPLY AREAS, 1944–53

Gas Supply Area	Total Contracts	No Favored-Nation Clause	2-Party Favored-Nation Clause	3-Party Favored-Nation Clause	Date of First 2-Party Favored-Nation	Date of First 3-Party Favored-Nation
Panhandle–Hugoton	86	74	12	0	*	—
West Texas–Permian Basin	85	16	69	0	3/47	—
San Juan–New Mexico	18	0	18	0	4/51	—
East Texas–North Louisiana	155	76	75	4	9/47	4/48
Texas Gulf Coast—Dist. No. 2	86	35	51	0	9/47	—
Texas Gulf Coast—Dist. No. 4	81	17	63	1	8/47	2/53
Texas Gulf Coast—Dist. No. 3	73	19	50	4	4/48	5/48
Southwest Louisiana	83	32	47	4	5/48	6/48
Southeast Louisiana–Mississippi	56	55	1	0	10/52	—
Total	723	324	386	13	—	—

*First contract which indicates the presence of a favored-nation clause is dated September, 1935. No detail regarding this purchase agreement is given. First postwar favored-nation contract is dated August, 1945.

provisions. For all the supply areas taken together, a little more than one-half of the contracts contained two-party favored-nation clauses.

The dates on which these provisions first appeared in the contract sources are also shown in Table 17. The practice evidently came into use in almost all Gulf Coast supply areas by the end of 1947 and the beginning of 1948. Its late arrival and almost complete absence in the Southeast Louisiana–Mississippi supply area was apparently due to the buying policy of the United Gas Pipe Line Company. Except for a few contracts, this pipe line was the sole purchaser in the supply area mentioned, and the company's contracts did not usually include favored-nation clauses.

Furthermore, since the United Gas Pipe Line Company was an active purchaser in almost all other Gulf Coast and East Texas supply areas, its policy in this matter accounts for many of the agreements without favored-nation provisions. Generally, the prewar pipe lines had a greater tendency to exclude such provisions from their gas purchase agreements. But a frequent offset was some form of price redetermination clause or a shorter-term contract; the United Gas Pipe Line Company, for example, made extensive use of ten-year contracts.

Not shown in the tabulation, but evident from the contract analysis, is another pattern relating to favored-nation clauses, namely, that relating to the geographical areas over which the provisions were operative. This factor was one of the most common elements of variation in favored-nation clauses.[20] Once the provision was accepted in principle, its geographical scope apparently became a matter of further bargaining. The buyer's interest was to narrow the geographical scope—to minimize restriction upon future purchase activity; the seller's was to widen the area —to increase the probability of upward price adjustments.

One of the more prevalent patterns relative to geographical scope was to have the favored-nation provision encompass an area conterminous with the various gas supply areas. To illustrate,

---

[20] A second element of possible variation could be the time periods over which the provisions were effective. Although a few exceptions were noted, this period was, in almost all cases, the same as the legal term of the contract.

in the Texas Gulf Coast the provisos usually covered the district in which the producer was located or some combination of adjoining districts. In the Louisiana Gulf Coast, the favored-nation area often included the parishes by which that supply area was defined for this study.

In the West Texas–Permian Basin supply area, and to some extent in others, the favored-nation area was frequently a territory within a given number of miles from the point of production or delivery. This did not always encompass the entire supply area. As a rule, the favored-nation area varied, depending upon the bargaining strength of buyer and seller. It could be limited to a single gas field, or a small area surrounding the producing wells, or, in unusual cases, it could be broadly and vaguely stated that the area included the Gulf Coast area of Texas. The most common situation, however, was to limit the geographical boundary to a supply area or some smaller portion of it. This would minimize the restraining effect upon buyers.

Some of the later developments in the use of favored-nation provisions may be noted. Among the large-volume purchase contracts negotiated during 1952–53 in the Gulf Coast supply areas, the pattern has been to use two-party provisos with limited favored-nation areas. The Iroquois Gas Corporation contract of 1952 contained a two-party provision based on District 3. The United Fuel contracts in Southwest Louisiana had two-party clauses based on that supply area. A similar arrangement characterized the American Louisiana Pipe Line Company contracts of 1953, except that, in this case, one agreement stipulated a favored-nation area which included offshore gas supplies.

An unusual agreement was the Niagara Gas Transmission contract of 1953 in Southwest Louisiana, which contained a third-party clause stipulating price adjustments "based on average of 3 highest prices paid by anyone." This agreement, however, had a twenty-year term, evidently without other provisions for price redetermination. Almost all the other contracts discussed had stipulations for price redetermination within a period of from four to five years.

An interesting combination was found in the West Texas

176356

supply area. Purchase contracts (1952) involving the Permian Basin Pipe Line Company, an affiliate of the Northern Natural Gas Company, provided that two-party favored-nation clauses were to be operative for the first fifteen years of the contracts and three-party provisos for the remainder of the twenty-year term.[21] Except for other provisos, such as inflation adjustment clauses, the effect of this combination was to make the contract price relatively firm for the first fifteen years, while making it more flexible thereafter.

C. PRICE REDETERMINATION PRACTICES AND CONTRACT PRICE FLEXIBILITY

Price redetermination provisions are related to favored-nation clauses insofar as the same general objective of contract price flexibility is sought. Both of these pricing practices are intended to loosen the restraints implicit in long-term purchase agreements; both are devices to assure sellers of upward price readjustments in relation to future field price levels. While the price redetermination provision, like the related favored-nation clause, has many variations, its general form may be described as follows:

Price Redetermination Clause: the seller may request a readjustment of contract prices at the end of a stipulated period or periods prior to the completion of the full legal term of contract, with new prices to be established by negotiation or in accordance with a defined procedure.

The main element of variation among price redetermination clauses was the length of the redetermination period. In the earlier purchase agreements, it was usually a ten- or fifteen-year period in contracts with twenty-year legal terms. More recent agreements have tended to become standardized at price redetermination periods of five years, with minimum contract prices established by fixed price escalation or by the contract prices of the previous period.

21 *Hearings—H. R. 4560,* 440.

A second element of variation in this type of contract provision concerns the procedure for redetermining prices. In many contracts, it was simply to be established by negotiation, but usually not below certain minima, since price redetermination was not intended to bring about a lowering of prices. In other cases, it was to be fixed at the average of the three highest prices for comparable amounts of gas in a defined area. Very commonly, it was to be decided by negotiation or some stipulated procedure, with resort to arbitration if agreement was not reached.

Generally speaking, as a means of securing contract price flexibility for sellers, price redetermination is more efficient than two-party favored-nation clauses, but less effective than third-party provisions. Although restricted in frequency of occurrence, contract price adjustments under price redetermination are not dependent upon buyer action, as in the two-party favored-nation clause. From a buyer's point of view, price redetermination provisions may be less objectionable than third-party favored-nation clauses. The latter can bring about contract price increases at any time, but price redetermination gives stable contract prices for five-year periods and possibly longer.

It would appear that, in the postwar evolution of field practices, short-term price redetermination replaced the relatively ineffective two-party favored-nation clause as the main instrument for securing contract price flexibility. At the same time, the price redetermination clause also apparently became a substitute for the third-party favored-nation clause. In the latter case, if contract prices were periodically redetermined to an average of the three highest prices in a given supply area, there would be little difference between the two contract devices, except for the time required to secure price adjustment. In a sense, a third-party favored-nation clause is the equivalent of one-year price redetermination, since this would probably be the minimum period needed to bring about a change in contract prices.

Furthermore, when five-year price redetermination is joined with a two-party favored-nation clause, as is frequently the case, upward price adjustments can be obtained even before the price redetermination period has elapsed. A price increase resulting from the operation of one price redetermination clause can lead to a similar price adjustment in all two-party favored-nation contracts. For example, if a pipe-line buyer has several purchase contracts in the same favored-nation area, all with five-year price redetermination and two-party clauses, the price redetermination of the earliest will raise the prices of the more recent contracts through the two-party favored-nation clauses. Granted the essential condition that all purchase contracts are in the same favored-nation area, contract prices—no matter when negotiated—will tend to move together, parallelling the current level of field prices. The result is an exceptionally high degree of contract price flexibility, virtually identical with that which is obtained if all the contracts stipulate third-party favored-nation clauses.

Illustrative of price redetermination practices are contract data available for the Tennessee Gas Transmission Company. One of the largest pipe-line buyers in the Gulf Coast area, this company made extensive use of a purchase contract in the Texas Gulf Coast area which included both five-year price redetermination and a two-party favored-nation clause. Under the price redetermination clauses, prices were to be adjusted to an average of the three highest prices paid by transporters of gas, including the Tennessee Gas Transmission Company, for comparable gas in the supply area or the district involved. In the event of disagreement, resort to arbitration was provided, with arbitrators bound to the use of a three-highest price formula. Included in some 1949 contracts, these price redetermination clauses came into operation during 1954. They resulted in an expected upward price adjustment, with comparable price changes in a number of two-party favored-nation contracts which would not have been adjusted otherwise.[22]

Of equal interest are somewhat different price redetermination practices found elsewhere. In the Panhandle-Hugoton supply area, favored-nation clauses of any sort were notably absent, while price redetermination provisions were widely used. In the early postwar contracts, price redetermination was operative only after a considerable part of the contract term had expired. The general

[22] *Hearings—S. 1853*, 1285–86.

stipulation was for price adjustment at the end of fifteen years, with new prices equal to the weighted average price of gas in a defined area but not less than a specified minimum.

By 1953, however, field market conditions appeared to require either short-term contracts or contracts with short price redetermination periods of five years or less. For example, one of the largest pipe-line purchasers in the supply area, the Northern Natural Gas Company, assertedly had five-year price redetermination clauses in virtually all of its Hugoton field purchase contracts.[23] The clauses in these contracts provided for establishment of new prices by negotiation, with a minimum fixed by the previous contract price. In the absence of agreement between the parties, the price was to be determined by arbitration. An additional proviso, of some interest, expressly stipulated the continued delivery of gas by the seller, pending the outcome of arbitration, with retroactivity for the redetermined price.[24] These agreements did not contain favored-nation provisions.

From the preceding discussion, it may be concluded that price redetermination gives sellers the assurance of upward price adjustments over reasonably short periods to levels reflecting current field prices. The gas supply covered by the agreement is, nevertheless, committed on a long-term basis to the pipe-line buyer who also receives some assurance of price stability from the five-year price redetermination period. Furthermore, retroactivity is protection to the buyer against the threat of supply withdrawal during price adjustment negotiations, and arbitration under a defined procedure for selecting arbitrators affords protection to both buyer and seller against the exploitation of any special bargaining strength which either may possess.

The obvious importance of price redetermination suggests a quantitative measurement of its prevalence. The major importance of price determination as a marketing device is its bearing upon the problem of the degree of upward price flexibility in natural gas purchase contracts. To deal with this problem properly, an analysis of the effective term of purchase contracts is

[23] *Hearings—H. R. 4560*, 438.
[24] See *ibid.*, 461, for the text of such a price redetermination provision.

required, since a flexibility almost equivalent to price redetermination may be achieved by reducing the legal term of a gas
supply agreement. Thus, the opportunity for price adjustment
in a five-year agreement is little different than that afforded by
a twenty-year contract with five-year price redetermination. The
need to consider effective contract terms and price redetermination jointly is further illustrated by the United Gas Pipe Line
Company's practice of negotiating many ten-year contracts without price redetermination, in which the shorter term evidently
offset redetermination. In any case, the ten-year contract is comparable to a longer-term agreement with ten-year price redetermination and should be viewed as such.

The most satisfactory means of ascertaining the degree of
contract price flexibility is a quantitative analysis of the effective
term of purchase contracts. This approach includes both price
redetermination contracts and agreements without such clauses
and differentiates according to the duration of firm contract
prices. Table 18 tabulates the effective contract terms with a
breakdown by gas supply areas.

Before examining this material, the possibility of a deficiency
which would affect conclusions drawn from it should be noted.
It is uncertain whether the data sources for contracts negotiated
during or after 1950 were complete or consistent in recording
price redetermination clauses. For example, purchase contracts
of the Tennessee Gas Transmission Company generally contained
five-year price retetermination provisions. However, the gas supply agreements of this pipe-line buyer after 1950 were usually
recorded as twenty-year contracts and have been treated accordingly in Table 18.

The result of this possible deficiency in the contract data is
overestimation of the number of contracts with effective terms
of twenty years or more and underestimation of those with five-
year effective terms. However, if this deficiency involves only or
mainly the Tennessee Gas Transmission Company's contracts—
a probable situation—conclusions from the data would not be
greatly affected. Also, only a limited supply area would be in-

Table 18

ANALYSIS OF THE EFFECTIVE CONTRACT TERMS OF NATURAL GAS PURCHASE CONTRACTS

NEGOTIATED IN VARIOUS GAS SUPPLY AREAS, 1944–53

Gas Supply Area	Total Contracts	Effective Contract Terms					
		20 Yrs. or More	15–19 Yrs.	10–14 Yrs.	5–9 Yrs.	Less than 5 Yrs.	Indefinite
Panhandle–Hugoton	86	10	24	9	23	7	13
West Texas–Permian Basin	85	20	39	24	2	—	—
San Juan–New Mexico	18	—	18	—	—	—	—
East Texas–North Louisiana	155	90	22	13	17	12	1
Texas Gulf Coast—Dist. No. 2	86	26	7	32	18	2	1
Texas Gulf Coast—Dist. No. 4	81	49	7	13	9	3	—
Texas Gulf Coast—Dist. No. 3	73	39	7	14	11	2	—
Southwest Louisiana	83	32	9	19	12	11	—
Southeast Louisiana–Mississippi	56	6	—	38	10	—	2
Total	723	272	133	162	102	37	17

volved, since these agreements are found—with the exception of three—in the Texas Gulf Coast supply area.[25]

From Table 18, it is seen that contracts having effective terms of twenty years or more constitute the largest group. This category and contracts having fifteen- to nineteen-year terms constitute a majority of the total contracts. Contracts with shorter terms—ten years or less—are also a sizable group.[26] They make up over 40 per cent of the total. Within individual supply areas, different patterns can be noted. In the Panhandle-Hugoton area, for example, there is a distinct gap between relatively long-term arrangements and the short-term agreements. This gap reflects a current tendency to short-term contracts in that supply area. In other gas supply areas, such as West Texas–Permian Basin and East Texas–North Louisiana, there is a heavy preponderance of long-term agreements. In the West Texas–Permian Basin area, this feature may reflect the predominance of a single buyer; for East Texas–North Louisiana, it may have been due to the earlier development of the supply area and the many small sellers. A marked general emphasis on contracts with terms of ten years or less in the Gulf Coast supply areas becomes evident if an adjustment for the Tennessee Gas Transmission contracts is made.

Assuming that the eighty-five Tennessee Gas Transmission contracts with twenty-year contract periods contain five-year redetermination clauses and therefore are more properly recorded as having short effective terms, the change in distribution of total contracts is shown below. More comprehensive classifications, which differentiate the effective contract periods between long-term, medium-term, and short-term, are used:

[25] The distribution of the affected Tennessee Gas contracts are given below:

District No. 2	18
District No. 4	40
District No. 3	24
Southwest Louisiana	3
Total	85

[26] The terms of natural gas purchase contracts are usually set at 5-year intervals, e.g., 5-10-15-20 years. Thus by far the largest number of contracts in the 10–14 year class, for example, are 10-year agreements.

DISTRIBUTION OF PURCHASE CONTRACTS BY
DURATION OF EFFECTIVE CONTRACT PERIOD

	UNADJUSTED		ADJUSTED FOR TENN. GAS CONTRACTS	
	Number	*Per cent*	*Number*	*Per cent*
Long-Term: 15 years or more	405	56.0	320	44.3
Medium-Term: 6 to 14 Years	175	24.2	175	24.2
Short-Term: 5 Years or Less	126	17.4	211	29.1
Indefinite	17	2.4	17	2.4
Total	723	100.0	723	100.0

The above tabulation presents a general, summarized view of the pattern of effective contract periods in the gas field. It is evident that a substantial shift in the proportion of short-term purchase contracts occurs with the Tennessee Gas adjustment. After the adjustment, agreements having effective terms of five years or less constitute approximately 30 per cent of the total purchase contracts examined. Since most of the contracts with five-year effective terms were classified as such because of redetermination clauses, it is also substantially correct to conclude that a factor of 30 per cent measures the incidence of short-term price redetermination. In spite of the large number of short-term agreements, long-term purchase contracts are still predominant, making up 44.3 per cent of the total. A sizable group of contracts, approximately 25 per cent of the total, falls within a medium-term classification.

While there is little question that effective contract terms are the dominant consideration, a complete picture of the degree of contract price flexibility requires the inclusion of favored-nation clauses. Both practices are aimed toward and determine the possibility of contract price adjustments in a natural gas purchase agreement. Presented together, they provide the most comprehensive view of contract price flexibility in gas supply markets. Moreover, an examination of this sort synthesizes and is a capstone to the entire discussion of pricing practices. As should be evident by now, the primary motive for the various practices examined is the gas producer's interest in securing an immediate market while retaining the possibility of a benefit from rising field prices.

An analysis of contract price flexibility is given in Table 19, in which purchase contracts in the supply areas are classified by effective contract period, with subclassifications according to the presence or absence of favored-nation clauses. Since virtually all favored-nation clauses recorded in the contract sources were two-party types, no distinction was drawn between these and a third-party type of provision. All third-party favored-nation clauses should be viewed as very short-term agreements regardless of the effective contract period.

Table 19 indicates that almost all purchase contracts contain some element of contract price flexibility. Only about 15 per cent of the purchase contracts were completely firm in price on a long-term basis. Most long-term agreements, about two-thirds of this classification, contained two-party favored-nation clauses. They were therefore subject to the possibility of some price adjustment. In the medium-term classification, the larger number of the agreements were without favored-nation provisos. To a considerable extent, however, this reflects the buying policy of a single pipe-line purchaser in Southeast Louisiana and District 2.

Among the classifications tabulated, short-term agreements with two-party favored-nation clauses represent a maximum contract price flexibility. A relatively large number of these agreements are recorded, making up approximately 17 per cent of the total included in the analysis. However, this classification is also heavily weighted by the contracts of a single pipe-line buyer. The inference that the short-term contract with a favored-nation clause is a representative combination of contract provisos would need careful qualification. Furthermore, a substantial number of short-term agreements do not contain favored-nation clauses. This fact, together with the heavy concentration of favored-nation clauses among long-term contracts, supports the conclusion that favored-nation clauses are and have been an offset for the burden of long-term supply agreements.

In general, the analysis of contract price flexibility establishes the absence of simple patterns or obvious uniformities. This mat-

Table 19

CONTRACT PRICE FLEXIBILITY—NATURAL GAS PURCHASE CONTRACTS

NEGOTIATED IN VARIOUS GAS SUPPLY AREAS, 1944–53

GAS SUPPLY AREA	EFFECTIVE CONTRACT TERM*						Total†
	Long-Term (15 Yrs. or More)		Medium-Term (6–14 Yrs.)		Short-Term (5 Yrs. or Less)		
	No Favored-Nation	Favored-Nation	No Favored-Nation	Favored-Nation	No Favored-Nation	Favored-Nation†	
Panhandle–Hugoton	27	7	11	2	25	1	86
West Texas–Permian Basin	15	44	—	24	1	1	85
San Juan–New Mexico	—	18	—	—	—	—	18
East Texas–North Louisiana	40	72	12	3	23	4	155
Texas Gulf Coast—District No. 2	3	12	27	5	4	34	86
Texas Gulf Coast—District No. 4	4	12	6	7	7	45	81
Texas Gulf Coast—District No. 3	4	18	9	6	6	30	73
Southwest Louisiana	8	30	9	12	15	9	83
Southeast Louisiana–Mississippi	6	—	41	1	6	—	56
Total	107	213	115	60	87	124	723

* Defined as period during which contract prices are firm.

† Adjusted to include eighty-five Tennessee Gas Transmission Co. contracts transferred from long-term, favored-nation classification.

† Includes seventeen contracts (2.4 per cent of total) with indefinite term. Two of these are favored-nation and fifteen are no favored-nation.

ter counts heavily with both the buyer and the seller, for in the bargaining arena of a field price market, contract price flexibility is second only to price as an objective. Sellers exert bargaining pressure to move from long-term contract combinations to short-term agreements with favored-nation clauses. Buyers seek to restrain the drift away from their objective of a firm-priced contract.

A tabulation of combinations encountered in the purchase contract data is relevant to the subject of buyer and seller interest. These range in order from the greatest to the least seller advantage:

1. 20 year contract; third-party favored-nation; multi-district favored-nation area.
2. 20 year contract; third-party favored-nation; single-district favored-nation area.
3. 20 year contract; two-party favored-nation; 5 year price redetermination at average of 3 highest prices.
4. 20 year contract; no favored-nation; 5 year price redetermination with arbitration.
5. 5 year contract; no favored-nation; no price redetermination.
6. 20 year contract; no favored-nation; 10 year price redetermination.
7. 10 year contract; no favored-nation; no price redetermination.
8. 20 year contract; two-party favored-nation; 15 year price redetermination; price-index inflation clause.
9. 20 year contract; two-party favored-nation; wide favored-nation area; no price redetermination.
10. 20 year contract; two-party favored-nation; narrow favored-nation area; no price redetermination.
11. 20 year contract; time-limited, two-party favored-nation; no price redetermination.
12. 20 year contract; no favored-nation; no price redetermination.

The primary conclusion of this chapter is that in the postwar history of natural gas field markets in the Southwest two major changes have taken place: one, the dramatic change from field price levels previously recorded; the other—less evident but equally important—the change in contract price flexibility. The second development has taken the form of a gradual ascendancy of those contract combinations most advantageous to gas producers. There were no sudden alterations or outstanding uniformities accompanying this change; it was simply a slow but persistent enlargement of seller advantage. Undoubtedly, the same forces which led to a substantial rise in field prices were at work. The competitive or noncompetitive character of these forces remains to be considered.

PART II

Market Behavior in the Gas Field

Essential to any study of conditions characterizing the field sale of natural gas is an examination of market transactions. Since only these data can provide the necessary factual base for generalizations concerning gas field markets, a detailed and systematic analysis of such transactions is fundamental. Without this type of analysis, hypotheses explaining market practices and market behavior cannot be adequately tested, and erroneous conclusions derived from a limited or special experience cannot be refuted. Therefore, one of the most desirable results of the contemplated investigation is an enlarged knowledge and understanding of natural gas field markets.

In addition to this broad value, more specific benefits may be expected. An analysis of market transactions provides the substantiation for estimating representative and comparable field prices in the various natural gas supply areas. It has already been established that such approximations are the only feasible approach to the problem of ascertaining price levels and price movements in the gas field.

Furthermore, a detailed review of market transactions is necessary if the forces and practices conditioning the formation of price are to be discovered. The general view of market behavior thus obtained also serves to disclose possible uniformities in seller actions. Since open and direct agreement is unlikely—if even necessary—these uniformities must be relied upon for inferential evidence of seller collusion.

The contemplated investigation is greatly aided by contractual arrangements characteristic of gas field markets which preserve and make available the detail of buyer and seller transactions. These purchase contracts constitute the core of this study and

113

must be examined in any treatment of market behavior in the gas field. However, isolated agreements reveal little or nothing concerning behavior. Each supply agreement must be related to the transactions which have preceded it and those which follow later. In short, a chronological analysis of the purchase contract data is the most effective means of revealing field-market behavior. Price charts, included earlier in the text, summarize the contract data for each gas supply area. Reference to these charts will assist the reader greatly in following the analysis given below.

CHAPTER 4

Panhandle, West Texas, and East Texas Supply Areas

THE SUPPLY SOURCES in this group include the Panhandle-Hugoton fields, the West Texas–Permian Basin gas-producing area—to which has been joined the related San Juan–New Mexico unit—and East Texas–North Louisiana. These supply areas constitute a meaningful unit for many reasons. Here was first experienced the impact of postwar expansion in natural gas markets, and, as a result, field price changes tended to be initiated in these regions until about 1948. Moreover, the purchase contracts negotiated in these areas from 1944 to 1953 committed a large fraction of the most economical gas reserves in the United States to interstate markets. An examination of market transactions in these supply sources therefore spotlights an important phase in the historical development of natural gas field markets. Also, the distinctive characteristics of each of the three gas-producing areas provide excellent illustrations of the widely different circumstances which condition and determine market behavior in the gas field.

A. PANHANDLE-HUGOTON

The Panhandle-Hugoton gas supply area encompasses the Texas and Oklahoma Panhandle region, as well as the southwestern portion of Kansas and a small part of southeastern Colorado. In the early development of the long-distance interstate pipe-line industry, this supply area was among the first to be tapped. It has been the main source of gas supply for the midwestern consumer markets of Chicago, Detroit, Minneapolis, Milwaukee, and Kansas City, as well as for Denver and—to a limited extent—Los Angeles and San Francisco.

The general structure of this supply area, in terms of the

number and size of sellers, is summarized in Table 20. Before dealing with this material, however, two limitations should be considered: First, the contract sources utilized do not record all transactions; therefore, the gas volumes shown for each seller are

Table 20

ANALYSIS OF NATURAL GAS PURCHASE CONTRACTS

IN THE PANHANDLE–HUGOTON GAS SUPPLY AREA, 1944–53

RANK OF SELLER BY ANNUAL GAS VOLUME	Annual Gas Volume M^3CF	Number of Contracts	Number of Buyers
1. Phillips Petroleum Co.	318.5	13	6
2. Shamrock Oil & Gas Corp.	103.3	6	3
3. Republic Natural Gas Co.	83.5	3	2
4. Panoma Corp. (formerly Hagy, Harrington, & Marsh)	54.6	2	2
5. Stanolind Oil & Gas Co.	31.7	1	1
6. Plains Natural Gas Co.	28.5	1	1
7. Hugoton Production Co.	18.4	1	1
8. Magnolia Petroleum Co.	15.8	1	1
9. Skelly Oil Co.	14.7	1	1
10. United Producing Co.	13.6	2	2
11. Combined Carbon Co.	12.3	1	1
12. Sinclair Oil & Gas Co.	10.2	1	1
13. Cities Service Oil Co.	10.1	2	2
14. White Eagle Oil Co.	6.0	1	1
15. Ray Stephens, Inc.	5.7	1	1
16. J. M. Huber	5.2	2	2
17. Saturn Oil & Gas Co.	3.0	1	1
5 sellers reporting less than 2.0 M^3CF of annual gas sales	6.5	5	
Subtotals	741.6	45	
21 sellers not included in above listing, having contracts with indefinite gas volumes	—	32	
Renegotiated and other indefinite gas volume contracts	—	9	
Totals	741.6	86	

not a measure of actual contract sales. Second, many of the contracts included in the tabulation do not contain complete gas volume information. Although many of these undoubtedly represent minor transactions, a significant number are known to involve large quantities of gas. Thus, at least the rankings of adjoining sellers are rendered uncertain, and possibly the market shares of the largest sellers would be reduced if complete volume information were available.

In spite of these limitations, the available contract data provide a generally useful outline of seller structure in this supply area. In Table 20, the contract data during the period covered indicate the presence of forty-three sellers, of which sixteen contracted to dispose of annual gas volumes in excess of 5.0 million MCF each. However, the dominant seller in this market was clearly the Phillips Petroleum Company; it was responsible for approximately 40 per cent of the gas volume recorded in these contracts. Although five other major sellers are to be noted, this dominance in sales by the Phillips Petroleum Company is undoubtedly the outstanding structural characteristic of the Panhandle-Hugoton supply area. A comparable situation is not found in any of the other supply areas.

On the demand side of this market, ten separate buyers were identified. The five largest purchasers, ranked by annual gas volumes acquired through these contracts, were the following: the Northern Natural Gas Company; the Cities Service Gas Company; the Michigan-Wisconsin Pipe Line Company; the Panhandle Eastern Pipe Line Company; and the El Paso Natural Gas Company. Four of these buyers met their needs from multiple sources of supply. The exception was the Michigan-Wisconsin Pipe Line Company, which obtained its entire supply from the Phillips Petroleum Company.

An additional structural feature of the Panhandle-Hugoton gas supply market is the ownership of large gas holdings by many of its pipe-line purchasers. Possessing substantial reserves, the pipe-line buyers in this field have bargaining advantages which undoubtedly affect the price pattern. A pipe-line buyer can offset seller demands by bringing into production its own undeveloped lands, or it may be able to increase the rate of withdrawal from existing reserves. However, the postwar development of state conservation regulations has seriously limited this pipe-line option. These state regulations fix maximum production allowables for individual gas wells; therefore, while a pipe line may bring undeveloped gas lands into use, the rate at which these and existing reserves can be exploited is curtailed. These controls operate even when the correlative rights of other gas producers in a field are not likely to be injured.

A factor which has been emphasized as a price-determining force in the Panhandle-Hugoton area is the condition of drainage. In gas fields consisting of common reservoirs, withdrawals at one point, by reducing pressure, bring a movement of gas to that point as a new equilibrium is sought. Thus, when lands overlying the common reservoir are in different ownerships, those producing first and most rapidly are apt to do so at the expense of other owners. Consequently, producers without markets are at a disadvantage, and a strong price-depressing effect is produced as the incentive to increase production adds to the market supply. Since both the Panhandle and the Hugoton fields are common reservoirs, drainage can and evidently did exist.[1] While this condition may have had some impact upon field prices in the past, its postwar role is probably minimal. The establishment of gas production allowables has generally prevented the most serious inequity inherent in the practice.[2]

[1] In *Peerless Oil and Gas Co.* v. *Cities Service Gas Co.*, Order No. 19515, December 9, 1946, the Corporation Commission of Oklahoma found the Cities Service Gas Co. to be draining gas from tracts owned by Peerless in the Hugoton field. See also *Natural Gas Investigation—Docket G-580*, Federal Power Commission (1948), 185–86, footnotes 31 and 32.

[2] Drainage may still be a problem, as is evident in the following testimony of Mr. E. O. Thompson of the Texas Railroad Commission, *Hearings—H. R. 4560*, 91:

> *Mr. Wolverton.* Who is asking for the [minimum field] price-fixing legislation in Texas?
> *Mr. Thompson.* Particularly a group of people in the northern part of the state that own land in the Hugoton field that overlaps from Texas into Oklahoma and Kansas, and the withdrawals are much heavier in Texas, where the price is 6 cents, than they are in Oklahoma and Kansas, where they are 8 and 9 cents. . . . Those people feel their gas is being taken out from under them and going in the line in competition with 8- and 9-cent gas.

Consideration of price and marketing patterns indicates that, until 1944, a price level of about 4.0 cents per MCF prevailed in this supply area. Most of the gas volumes included in the contracts of this period were insignificant, and the effective terms of the contracts were indefinite or unknown. One exception is a contract, dated April, 1943, between the Phillips Petroleum Company and the Panhandle Eastern Pipe Line Company, which provides for a large annual volume at a price of more than 4.0 cents per MCF.

From 1945 to 1947, the first phase of postwar pipe-line expansion was undertaken. Responding to the evident increases in both domestic and industrial demands, the existing pipe-line systems tapping this source acquired additional gas supplies. Also, the newly promoted Michigan-Wisconsin Pipe Line Company secured its basic gas supply at this time. A contract dated December 11, 1945 was the first commitment of natural gas to that project by the Phillips Petroleum Company. The annual volume specified was about 60.0 million MCF, and the average price over a fifteen-year effective term was approximately 6.0 cents per MCF. Shortly before this transaction, the El Paso Natural Gas Company had also contracted for a similar volume from the same seller at a comparable price.

During 1945–46, other producers negotiated contracts with the existing pipe lines. The volumes were relatively large, and the prices were approximately 6.0 cents per MCF. Additional contracts were completed during 1947. In this year, however, initial prices were already 6.0 cents per MCF, and, if consideration is given to the fixed price escalation provisions of these agreements, a 7.0 cent price level might well be approximated.

Thus, starting immediately at the close of the war, prices in the Panhandle-Hugoton supply area increased rapidly to a level of 6.0 to 7.0 cents per MCF, which was maintained through the end of 1947. This price change represented a considerable increase—50 to 75 per cent—over earlier levels. But there is little evidence in the purchase contract data to suggest that the price increase was due to monopolistic forces in the market and was not, in the main, a response to postwar demand expansion. A relatively large number of buyers and sellers were involved in the transactions, and the established pipe-line buyers were certainly not without their own bargaining advantages. Large gas volumes were also acquired in these transactions, and the bulk of Panhandle-Hugoton gas reserves were probably committed to a pipe-line market during this period. Most of these contracts were long-term arrangements; practically all have fifteen- to twenty-year effective terms. In short, the particular characteristics of this market, as well as the patterns emerging from the purchase contract data, do not suggest an undue seller market power during the period under consideration.

During 1948, a new price level of approximately 9.0 cents per MCF was established, being first recorded in a contract dated March of that year. Seemingly, this price change was a response to rising field price levels in other producing areas. For example, a 9.0 cent price had been established in the East Texas–North Louisiana supply unit by 1947.

Among the purchase agreements of 1948, two warrant attention. One was the first renegotiation of the 1945 Phillips–Michigan-Wisconsin transaction. Unable to fulfill certain terms of its original contract, the pipe-line buyer accepted renegotiation to prevent a cancellation of the purchase agreement. A new price was agreed upon, averaging 8.7 cents per MCF on a 16.7 psi base, for the fifteen-year effective term of the contract. This price was not incongruous with prevailing levels. In the month preceding this renegotiation, the Phillips Petroleum Company had completed a short-term agreement with the El Paso Natural Gas Company at a price which was identical to the initial price in the Michigan-Wisconsin contract.

An agreement between the Hugoton Production Company and the Kansas Power and Light Company was also unusual. In its stipulation of a 13.4 cents per MCF initial price, the contract recorded an exceptionally high price relative to prevailing levels and, in addition, included an uncommon five-year price redetermination provision. The Hugoton Production Company was organized by the Panhandle Eastern Pipe Line Company. Gas reserves owned by the pipe-line company were then sold to the newly formed affiliate in exchange for stock, which was distributed to Panhandle Eastern stockholders as a dividend. The Hugoton Production Company subsequently committed the acquired gas reserves to the Kansas Power and Light Company. Since the latter served markets close to the gas supply area, it may have been especially interested in securing a block of gas acreage in the Hugoton field. Thus, the unusually high price may have been due to advantages of location to the buyer.

Purchase contracts subsequent to the Hugoton Production transaction did not confirm its price. While prices during 1949 appeared to vary between 9.0 and 13.0 cents per MCF, this wide range reflects the peculiarities of the data. A field price level closer to 10.0 cents per MCF would be more accurate. In Figure 1 of the field price charts, three contracts negotiated in 1949 between Phillips Petroleum Company and Michigan-Wisconsin Pipe Line Company show widely different prices. However, these were all dated December 1, 1949, and should be treated as a single price observation. One of these contracts was a second renegotiation of the 1945 contract, committing an additional 11.0 million MCF at a new average price of 9.0 cents. The other two contracts, recording substantially higher prices, were negotiated at the same time for the same effective term, apparently as only part of the entire bargain. If these contracts are weighted by their respective gas volumes, averaging their prices results in a value of 10.2 cents per MCF. This amount may be more meaningful than the separate prices for approximating the level of field prices at that time.

From the above discussion, it may be concluded that field prices in this supply area continued their postwar rise, moving from a level of almost 9.0 cents in 1948 to approximately 10.0–11.0 cents per MCF in 1949, adjusted to a twenty-year effective contract term. Furthermore, between 1947 and the end of 1949, a change in marketing patterns was manifested. The annual gas volumes included in the contracts of this period were noticeably less than earlier. If account is taken of the fact that the two contracts with annual volumes in excess of 40 million MCF were renegotiations of agreements completed in 1945, then the small quantity of gas committed during the period is readily apparent.

None of the purchase agreements provided for gas volumes in excess of 30 million MCF, and most were for less than 20 million MCF. The effective contract periods also deviated from past patterns. Effective terms of less than fifteen years appeared much more frequently than before, and a number of short-term agreements of five years or less were negotiated. Of some note was the continued absence of favored-nation clauses; only two contracts negotiated during the period 1945–47 contained these provisions. This absence contrasts sharply with the pattern in other gas supply areas.

Virtually no purchase agreements were recorded for 1950 in the contract sources. However, from 1951 through 1952, a considerable number of contracts were completed, many of which were small-volume purchases. During 1951 and 1952, stability in field prices was indicated from the purchase contract data. This condition existed in other supply areas, also. In the Panhandle-Hugoton area, a price level of approximately 10.0–11.0 cents per MCF can be discerned during 1951. In view of the prevalence of short-term agreements, the level should be adjusted upward; on a twenty-year standard contract term, a correct price level would range between 11.0 and 12.0 cents per MCF. For 1952, a slight upward pressure was exerted, although not sufficient to invalidate a conclusion of continued price stability. A price level ranging between 12.0 and 13.0 cents per MCF—again adjusted to a twenty-year contract period—may be approximated. On August 1, 1952, the Oklahoma Corporation Commission increased minimum field prices in the Oklahoma portion of the gas supply area to 9.82 cents per MCF (14.65 psi), or approximately 11.2 cents per MCF on a 16.7 psi pressure base.

The price levels approximated above are applicable to large-volume contracts. Unlike the other gas supply areas, no clear-cut price differences, with relation to gas volumes, can be seen. Most of the contracts recorded for 1952 and 1953 contained indefinite gas volume information; the contract sources specified, in many instances, that the gas volume was to be taken "ratably." Such a volume stipulation in this supply area did not necessarily imply a small volume. Furthermore, interspersed throughout the contracts of this period were agreements in which volume information was expressed as committed gas-producing acreages, the sizes of which implied commitment of substantial annual gas volumes. In summary, many of the 1952–53 contracts were large-volume agreements, and their prices were not greatly different from contracts which were presumably small-volume purchases. Consequently, a small-volume gathering-system market with a distinctively lower price level could not be clearly distinguished.

By the beginning of 1953, price stability was broken, and a new upward movement was initiated. Among the contracts in which the new prices appeared were three purchase agreements, all dated January 1, 1953, between the Phillips Petroleum Company and the Northern Natural Gas Company. The average prices in these purchase agreements during their effective terms ranged between 14.0 and 16.0 cents per MCF, while initial prices were between 12.0 and 15.0 cents. Sizable gas volumes were involved in the transactions, and an outstanding feature was the very short legal term of contract. In one instance, it was only three years; in the others, the legal term was five and seven years.

The rising field price trend in 1953 was continued in a second group of contracts. In spite of variation in the effective term of contract—from five to ten years—each of these supply contracts provided for an average price of approximately 17.5 cents per MCF. The first of these contracts again involved the Phillips Petroleum Company as seller, with the Colorado Interstate Gas Company as purchaser. Other sellers were carbon-black manufacturers; the price level apparently attracted these owners of gas reserves into the market. All of the contracts in this group were relatively large-volume transactions.

Relying upon these data, a representative field price for large-volume gas supplies during 1953 may be approximated. For short-term contracts, having effective terms of seven years or less, the estimated field price level ranges between 15.0 and 17.0 cents. To secure comparability with earlier periods, this price level must be adjusted to a twenty-year standard contract period. If this is done, a long-term large-volume field price level of about 18.0 cents per MCF is calculated.

123

In addition to price, the marketing patterns associated with the contracts negotiated between 1950 and 1953 are important. First, a clearly marked change concerns the effective term of contract. The earlier pattern of fifteen-to twenty-year contracts no longer applies, and the contract with an effective term of five years or less has become very common. All of the 1953 purchase agreements mentioned above, for example, were under ten years, and most had effective contract periods of five years. The contracts negotiated by the Phillips Petroleum Company, in particular, had short legal terms coinciding with the effective contract periods. Other contracts committed gas reserves for indefinite periods, such as the "life of the field" or the "life of leases," but provision was made for the renegotiation of prices at the end of defined periods.

Concerning the use of favored-nation clauses, the pattern was clearly one of avoiding inclusion of such provisions. In comparison with other gas supply areas, this was an unusual pattern and was a continuation of an earlier feature of this supply area. Certainly, by the test of frequency, contracts without favored-nation clauses were far more usual than those containing such provisos. None of the large-volume contracts negotiated during 1953 included such clauses; however, the short effective terms in these supply agreements gave sellers considerable contract price flexibility.

The representative field prices derived from this analysis of purchase contracts recorded for the Panhandle-Hugoton gas supply area can be summarized. These values are judgment approximations based upon the detailed contract analysis. The prices, expressed as average contract prices adjusted to standard twenty-year contract terms and applicable to a large-volume market, are given below:

REPRESENTATIVE FIELD PRICES: PANHANDLE-
HUGOTON GAS SUPPLY AREA

Large Volume	Cents per MCF: (16.7 psi)
Prior to 1945	4.0
1945	6.0

1946	6.0
1947	7.0
1948	9.0
1949	10.0–11.0
1950	(no data)
1951	11.0–12.0
1952	12.0–13.0
1953 (short-term)	15.0–17.0
1953 (long-term)	18.0

B. West Texas–Permian Basin and San Juan–New Mexico

A second major gas supply area is represented by the West Texas–Permian Basin producing region. It not only encompasses the oil and gas fields of West Texas but also includes those of southeastern New Mexico. A closely related supply source is the San Juan area, located in the northwestern corner of New Mexico. The two are linked as supply sources for the pipe-line system serving the California market. Attention, however, is to be focused upon the more important West Texas area.

The West Texas–Permian Basin supply area has various distinctive features which are likely to affect price levels. First, the major market which it supplies is California. The region is a basic source of supply for the Los Angeles metropolitan area, as well as San Francisco and other communities in northern California. Second, the only major interstate pipe-line purchaser in this supply area until 1952 was the El Paso Natural Gas Company. Its long-distance large-diameter pipe-line facilities to the California-Arizona border were constructed in the postwar period. The El Paso Natural Gas Company was also the dominant buyer during the initial development of the San Juan–New Mexico gas supply area. By 1954, gas from the San Juan field was being purchased by the Pacific Northwest Pipeline Company, which, however, was subsequently affiliated with the El Paso Natural Gas Company.

A third feature affecting price levels in West Texas is the

fact that supplies in the area consist largely of casinghead gas. Such gas, defined generally as gas produced in association with oil, was—in the past at least—viewed as a by-product of the more lucrative oil operations. In the absence of a ready market, casinghead gas was either flared or offered at whatever price it would bring. In addition, the output of this gas, being dependent upon oil production, can vary substantially. A reduction in oil production allowables, for example, would reduce the availability of gas, with adverse effects on pipe-line operations. Taken together, the distinctive features noted undoubtedly operated to depress field prices during the early development of the West Texas gas supply area.

Table 21

ANALYSIS OF NATURAL GAS PURCHASE CONTRACTS

IN THE WEST TEXAS–PERMIAN BASIN

GAS SUPPLY AREA, 1944–53

RANK OF SELLER BY ANNUAL GAS VOLUME	Annual Gas Volume M³CF	Number of Contracts	Number of Buyers
1. Phillips Petroleum Co.	173.1	6	2
2. Magnolia Petroleum Co.	57.4	4	2
3. Humble Oil & Refining Co.	56.0	1	1
4. Shell Oil Co.	31.2	4	1
5. Sinclair Oil & Gas Co.	22.4	3	1
6. Plymouth Oil Co.	21.5	1	1
7. Warren Petroleum Co.	20.1	1	1
8. Gulf Oil Corp.	19.4	3	2
9. Skelly Oil Co.	19.2	4	2
10. Standard Oil Co. (Ohio)	19.2	1	1
11. Slaughter Field Producers Group	17.9	1	1
12. Slick-Urschel Oil Co.	14.3	1	1
13. Cities Service Oil Co.	11.2	2	2
14. Anchor Gasoline Corp., et al.	8.0	1	1
15. Harvey J. Wier, et al.	8.0	1	1
16. Stanolind Oil & Gas Co.	7.1	3	2
17. Slick Oil Co.	6.5	1	1
18. Columbian Carbon Co.	6.0	1	1
19. Texas & Pacific Coal & Oil Co.	6.0	1	1

RANK OF SELLER BY ANNUAL GAS VOLUME	Annual Gas Volume M³CF	Number of Contracts	Number of Buyers
20. Texas Gas Products Corp.	4.8	1	1
21. Amerada Petroleum Corp.	4.5	1	1
22. Wilshire Oil Co., Inc.	3.5	1	1
23. Pecos Petroleum Co.	3.2	1	1
24. Ohio Oil Co.	2.4	1	1
6 sellers reporting less than 2.0 M³CF of annual gas sales	3.6	6	
Subtotals	546.5	51	
16 sellers not included in above listing, having contracts with indefinite gas volumes	—	19	
Renegotiated and other indefinite gas volume contracts	—	15	
Totals	546.5	85	

The structure of the West Texas–Permian Basin gas supply area is presented in Table 21. Again, the predominance of the Phillips Petroleum Company is evident, its sales being almost one-third of the total volume of sales recorded for this supply area during the period under consideration. However, other large sellers were also active in this market. The existence of only two interstate pipe-line buyers is noteworthy. The El Paso Natural Gas Company was the sole interstate purchaser until 1952, when the Permian Basin Pipe Line Company, certificated in 1953, began contracting for large quantities of gas. This pipe-line company, an affiliate of the Northern Natural Gas Company, was organized to provide additional gas supplies to supplement Panhandle-Hugoton sources in serving Northern's markets in the Midwest.

Concerning price levels in the West Texas supply area, reference should be made to the field prices of Figure 2, Chapter 2. It is evident from the price chart that the contract data prior to 1948 do not show a well-defined price pattern. Only a limited number of contracts are available for this early period, but those do commit large volumes and involve important sellers. These purchase agreements may reasonably be assumed representative of prevailing prices. Consequently, a price level of about 3.0 cents per MCF is approximated for the period before 1945, and a level of about 4.0–5.0 cents is estimated for 1945 and 1946. In 1946, virtually no contract activity was recorded in the data sources, although it is quite probable that many small-volume agreements were completed.

During 1947, a highly erratic price pattern is evidenced, much of which is explained by the special features of individual contracts. By and large, the lower-priced agreements were the exceptional ones. Generally, a price level of about 6.0 cents per MCF may be approximated for 1947. One purchase contract, however, dated in October, 1947, reached a peak average price of 8.7 cents per MCF over a fifteen-year effective term.

In the first half of 1948, a price level of 6.0–7.0 cents per MCF was definitely established, and by the last half of that year, prices had moved to approximately 9.0 cents per MCF. An apparent break in the 9.0 cent price level toward the end of 1948 was not representative. The two contracts reflecting this price drop were renegotiations of earlier purchase agreements, and in this supply area, such renegotiated prices were generally below prevailing market levels.

The high frequency of contract renegotiation was actually a distinctive feature of the West Texas supply area. Even where the contract did not indicate the presence of favored-nation clauses, the buyer was apparently willing to renegotiate either to secure additional gas under the old contract or under a new purchase agreement covering a different field. For example, a contract between the Phillips Petroleum Company and the El Paso Company, first signed in 1942, was subjected to three renegotiations in a period extending through 1948. Two of the renegotiations were dated the same as new purchase agreements, suggesting that an adjustment of prices in the old contract was part of the bargain for additional gas supplies. Other similar renegotiation patterns can be found in the contract data.

Following the establishment of a 9.0 cent price level, a gap occurred in the contract data. No purchase information was available for 1949, and only one minor supply contract was dated in 1950. However, a substantial number of contract observations were recorded for 1951.[3] These were, to a large extent, renegotiations of contracts completed in 1949, implying the existence of contract activity for that year which was absent from the contract sources. It may also be assumed that these renegotiations were the result of favored-nation clauses. Furthermore, the purchase agreements completed by the El Paso Company during 1951 were negotiated at the 9.0 cent price level of 1948. The inference to be drawn is that a lower level of prices prevailed during 1949. Since the 1951 contracts tend toward smaller volumes, it is possible that both 1949 and 1951 prices characterize a small-volume market. Of interest is the great uniformity of price and terms among these agreements, a condition which becomes even more pronounced in the following year.

Beginning in 1952, a new price level was established, approximating 12.5 cents per MCF. About this time, the Permian Basin Pipe Line Company came into the supply area, and it is reasonable to assume that the entry of this second buyer was a primary factor in raising the price level. The contracts initiating the price rise, however, were arrangements in which the El Paso Company was buyer. Nevertheless, the close proximity in time and the similarity in pricing suggest a significant interaction between the El Paso and Permian Basin purchases.

Thus, the first contract to establish the new price level was dated in December, 1951, between the Magnolia Petroleum Company and the El Paso Natural Gas Company. It stipulated a large annual volume, approximately 32.0 million MCF, at an average price of 12.54 cents per MCF over a fifteen-year effective term. A second agreement, dated in February, 1952, with the Phillips Petroleum Company, was the renegotiation of a 1948 contract with a considerable increase in gas volume. The same initial price

[3] Not all of the renegotiated purchase contracts of 1951 were shown in the price chart, since they were completed at a uniform price and uniform terms. Thus, forty-two renegotiated contracts, extending over the period from June, 1951 to August, 1952, were not charted.

129

as the Magnolia agreement was stipulated, namely, 11.4 cents per MCF, which escalated 1.14 cents each five years. The contract, though, was recorded as having an effective term of thirty years, a factor of more advantage to the buyer than the seller, with a resulting average price of about 14.0 cents per MCF. Then, on the same date as the El Paso contract, the Permian Basin Pipe Line Company negotiated an agreement with the Phillips Petroleum Company for an identical annual gas volume, approximately 64.0 million MCF and providing for the same basic schedule of prices. The effective term in this case was only fifteen years, and therefore an average price of about 12.5 cents was established.

Evidence of interaction between the two pipe-line buyers is also to be found in other contract activity during 1952, mainly in the form of a virtual identity of average contract prices. Thus, of the twenty-eight purchase contracts in this period recording average prices of 12.5 cents per MCF, fifteen were El Paso contracts and thirteen were Permian Basin arrangements, all of which were distributed evenly over the year.

While the average contract prices in these purchase agreements were uniform when derived by the procedures established for this study, the actual price schedules and the auxiliary contract provisions were not identical. For example, the Permian Basin Pipe Line Company contracts typically contained the following price provisions:[4]

	Cents per MCF (16.7 psi)
First five years	10.83
Second five years	11.97
Third five years	13.11
Fourth five years	14.25

Furthermore, the contract provided for a legal term of twenty years and, in the absence of price redetermination, an effective term which was also twenty years. On this basis, the average contract price was calculated at 12.54 cents. The agreement, how-

[4] On the pressure base of 14.65 psi stipulated in the contract, prices would be 9.5, 10.5, 11.5, and 12.5 cents per MCF, respectively.

ever, contained a favored-nation provision which was a two-party stipulation for the first fifteen years and a third-party proviso thereafter. Strictly speaking, the contract was probably firm for only fifteen years.

On the other hand, the El Paso purchase contracts generally included the following price schedule:[5]

	Cents per MCF *(16.7 psi)*
First five years	11.40
Second five years	12.54
Third five years	13.68

Thereafter fair market price at the beginning of each five-year period, with minimum increase of 1.14 cents.

Since prices in this case are firm only over the first fifteen years—although legal contract terms were either twenty or twenty-five years—the average price over the effective contract period was again 12.54 cents per MCF. The El Paso contract also contained a two-party favored-nation clause. In addition, the agreements of both pipe-line buyers included a three-fourths buyer tax-sharing clause.

It is evident, then, that the purchase contracts of the two buyers were not identical in details. In this respect, the contracts demonstrate an important fact: the price bargain in natural gas field markets is a complex of provisions stipulating rights and obligations among which the actual price schedule is a primary but not necessarily exclusive element. Nevertheless, it may be reasonably claimed that the total consideration offered by each of the buyers was nicely balanced, a conclusion strengthened by the price-index inflation adjustment clause contained in the Permian Basin Company's contracts. This concession may well have offset the half-cent higher price offered by El Paso.

[5] Again, on the 14.65 psi pressure base actually stipulated, prices were 10.0, 11.0, and 12.0 cents per MCF for the first three 5-year periods, with a minimum increase of 1.0 cent in each succeeding period.

Consequently, despite differences in contract provisos, a basic price uniformity characterized the purchases of the two pipe-line buyers. Its implications for the issue of competitive market behavior remain to be explored. Actually, the reasons for the condition may not be too difficult to find; they appear to have resulted from forces on the buying side of the market. Both companies were contracting for additional reserves at the same time in the same general area. A basic identity in their purchase offers would be necessary if one company were not to be unsuccessful in its drive to secure new supplies. But this would hold true only for a given time, and it might be expected that active competition among buyers would lead to price variability around a particular level. It would seem, then, that the imperfection on the buying side of the market, inherent in the fact that there were only two purchasers, was largely responsible for the general uniformity of prices.

Market imperfection may also have accounted for the detailed differences in contract provisions. Although, when taken as a whole, they resulted in a nice balance between the two purchase offers, these contract stipulations were sufficiently different to have a varying attraction among sellers. In a very meaningful sense, the lack of standardization was an analogue of the product differentiation encountered among sellers in other market situations. Finally, with very many small-volume contracts to be handled, efficiency in purchasing would suggest the use of a posted price system, namely, to stand ready to contract for gas at a given schedule of prices under given terms. This factor would account for the uniformity found in the contracts concluded with different sellers by the same pipe-line buyer.

The possibility that the price uniformity was imposed from the selling side seems slight. First, a relatively large number of sellers were involved, and concerted action on their part would have required considerable organization. Second, the uniform price established was not incongruous with price levels in other supply areas at the time and was actually lower. Last, price uniformity is not necessarily in the interest of all sellers. Sellers with large volumes to sell would presumably insist upon higher prices.

Yet a feature of this period is the virtual absence of any correlation between volume and price. All transactions were made at the same price, thus strongly reinforcing the hypothesis of a posted price system.

Turning again from this consideration of market behavior to the approximation of price levels, an average contract price may be estimated for 1952, amounting to 13.0 cents per MCF on a twenty-year standard contract period. Moreover, this price level has been attributed to a large-volume market since, as noted, a feature of this supply area is the absence of any clear-cut price distinctions between a large-volume and a small-volume market. The price estimate for 1952 was stable, but whether or not it continued thus during 1953 is not known. The absence of contract data precludes the possibility of discovering whether a higher price level was reached in 1953, as occurred in the Panhandle-Hugoton supply area.

With regard to the non-price characteristics of purchase contracts in the West Texas–Permian supply area, the presence of only two buyers makes the task relatively simple. Two-party favored-nation clauses were almost universally found in the new purchase contracts after 1947. The Permian Basin Pipe Line Company, however, included a third party type of clause which came into operation after the fifteenth year of its contracts. Its operation would then have the same effect as a fifteen-year price redetermination proviso. The use of favored-nation clauses in this supply source was clearly in contrast to their absence in the Panhandle-Hugoton area. Similarly, the pattern of effective contract terms differed between the two supply areas. In the present case, they were largely held to a fifteen-year level, with no tendency to a shorter term evident.

The seller structure for the San Juan–New Mexico gas supply area can be ascertained from Table 22. Limitations of data preclude any extended analysis of this supply source. Only the purchases of the El Paso Natural Gas Company are recorded in the contract sources, and then only for the years 1951 and 1952. The general price trends just discussed also appear to be applicable in this market. Thus, a uniform price of 9.0 cents per MCF prevailed during 1951, while in the latter part of 1952 prices moved to a level of about 13 cents. Again, the uniformity of both price and contract terms seems to reflect the fact that El Paso was the only buyer. It is noteworthy that the price level in this supply area for the two years was slightly higher than in the West Texas area, possibly because of the more advantageous location of the field with respect to El Paso's California markets.

To conclude the contract analysis of the West Texas–Permian Basin gas supply area, a summary of field price approximations is given below. Since a distinctive small-volume market is not readily discernible, no attempt to ascertain a price level for it has been made.

Table 22

ANALYSIS OF NATURAL GAS PURCHASE CONTRACTS

IN THE SAN JUAN–NEW MEXICO GAS SUPPLY AREA, 1944–53

RANK OF SELLER BY ANNUAL GAS VOLUME	Annual Gas Volume M^3CF	Number of Contracts	Number of Buyers
1. Frontier Refining Co.	17.6	1	1
2. Benson & Martin	16.4	1	1
3. Stanolind Oil & Gas Co.	16.3	2	1
4. Blackwood & Nichols, *et al.*	9.8	1	1
5. Great Lakes Oil & Chemical Co.	6.5	1	1
6. Danube Oil Co.	3.6	2	1
1 seller reporting less than 2.0 M^3CF of annual gas sales	0.3	1	
Subtotals	70.5	9	
8 sellers not included in above listing, having contracts with indefinite gas volumes	—	8	
Renegotiated and other indefinite gas volume contracts	—	1	
Totals	70.5	18	

REPRESENTATIVE FIELD PRICES: WEST TEXAS–PERMIAN BASIN
GAS SUPPLY AREA

Large Volume	*Cents per MCF* *(16.7 psi)*
Prior to 1945	3.0
1945	4.0–5.0
1946	(no data)
1947	6.0
1948 (first half)	6.0–7.0
1948 (second half)	9.0
1949	(no data)
1950	(no data)
1951	9.0
1952	13.0
1953	(no data)

C. East Texas–North Louisiana

A third natural gas supply source of importance in the immediate postwar period is the East Texas–North Louisiana gas supply area. The geographical area encompassed by this supply area is evident from its descriptive title. In Texas it includes all of the Texas Railroad Commission District No. 6; in Louisiana it comprises the northern tier of parishes, particularly those in the northeastern gas-producing section of the state.

The most important source of gas in the area is the Carthage field in East Texas. It was among the first of the gas fields to be tapped in postwar expansion of the natural gas industry. Among the other important gas fields included in the supply area are Woodlawn, Waskom, North Lansing, Whelan, Bethany, and the Jefferson-Rodessa fields in Texas; the Sligo, Lisbon, Athens, East Haynesville, and Hico-Knowles fields in Louisiana.[6]

[6] The Monroe field in northern Louisiana is one of the larger fields located within the supply area. To a large extent, the field was fully developed in the prewar period and was evidently not available as a supply source for the new postwar pipe lines. No purchase agreements are recorded for this field in the contract sources.

135

The structure of this gas supply area is presented in Table 23 in a form comparable to previous analyses. A noteworthy feature is the many contracts recorded and the large number of sellers participating in this market. A total of 155 contracts is attributable to the supply area, which were negotiated by a total of 96 separate sellers. Concerning the size rankings of these producers, it is seen that 29 sellers have annual gas volumes in excess of 5.0 million MCF. Had a standard of 2.0 million MCF been applied for identifying individual sellers—as was done in other supply areas—the number of sellers listed would have been substantially larger.

The demand side of this market is likewise distinguished by a relatively large number of participants. A total of eleven pipe-line purchasers is recorded, including all of the pipe-line buyers operating in the Gulf Coast region in 1953, with the exception of the Texas Illinois Natural Gas Pipeline Company and the Transcontinental Gas Pipe Line Corporation. Although many pipe lines made purchases in the East Texas–North Louisiana gas

Table 23

ANALYSIS OF NATURAL GAS PURCHASE CONTRACTS

IN THE EAST TEXAS–NORTH LOUISIANA

GAS SUPPLY AREA, 1944–53

RANK OF SELLER BY ANNUAL GAS VOLUME	Annual Gas Volume M^3CF	Number of Contracts	Number of Buyers
1. S. E. Carthage Group	65.1	1	1
2. Southwest Gas Producing Co.	55.6	7	4
3. Skelly Oil Co.	47.1	4	3
4. H. L. Hunt	43.7	1	1
5. Stanolind Oil & Gas Co.	34.7	4	4
6. Atlantic Refining Co.	31.5	4	2
7. California Co.	30.2	2	1
8. R. Lacy, Inc., *et al.*	27.5	1	1
9. Continental Oil Co.	23.7	1	1
10. Glassell & Glassell	19.3	1	1
11. Hunt Oil Co., *et al.*	18.9	2	2

RANK OF SELLER BY ANNUAL GAS VOLUME	Annual Gas Volume M³CF	Number of Contracts	Number of Buyers
12. Whelan, D. E. & R. G.	16.2	1	1
13. Chicago Corp.	15.6	1	1
14. Phillips Petroleum Co., *et al.*	14.4	5	4
15. Natural Gas & Oil Corp.	11.4	1	1
16. Shell Oil Co.	11.4	2	2
17. M. A. Halsey, *et al.*	10.9	1	1
18. H. W. Klein, *et al.*	10.9	1	1
19. Hassie Hunt Trust	10.1	2	2
20. La Gloria Corp., *et al.*	10.1	1	1
21. Humble Oil & Refining Co.	8.5	2	2
22. John O. Harmon	8.2	1	1
23. Carter Oil Co.	7.9	2	2
24. Gulf Refining Co.	7.8	1	1
25. Southwest Natural Production Co.	7.7	2	2
26. Hope Producing Co.	7.1	1	1
27. Paul H. Pewitt	7.0	1	1
28. Sun Oil Co.	6.3	1	1
29. Lone Star Gas Co.	5.9	1	1
27 sellers reporting less than 5.0 M³CF of annual gas sales	50.2	31	
Subtotals	624.9	86	
40 sellers not included in above listing, having contracts with indefinite gas volumes	—	47	
Renegotiated and other indefinite gas volume contracts	—	22	
Totals	624.9	155	

supply area, not all were continually active buyers. Many negotiated only a few contracts, finding their main sources of supply elsewhere. Of the total, perhaps five purchasers may be considered important in the market. These include: United Gas Pipe Line Company; the Texas Eastern Transmission Corporation, the Texas Gas Transmission Corporation, the Mississippi River Fuel Corporation, and the Arkansas Louisiana Gas Company.

Price levels and price patterns for this area may be viewed

in summarized form in Figure 3, Chapter 2. The price chart points up a special characteristic of this supply area, namely, an unusual degree of price variability among the different contracts, which is not easily explained by variations in either annual gas volume or effective contract term. This characteristic, however, is evident only for the period beginning in 1950; prior to that year, more usual patterns prevailed.

A lack of correlation between annual volume, effective term, and price is, in general, verified by the contract data shown in the price chart. For example, effective contract terms are seen to be relatively stable at about twenty years and would not, therefore, account for the variability of prices. Furthermore, the correlation between price and volume is not impressively high. While some association between the highest field prices and large gas volumes does exist, the relationship is weak and obscure. Consequently, the existence of a large and almost random price variation between 1951 and 1953 is a feature of this supply area which requires explanation. Further attention will be given to it at a later point.

In the first phase of its development between 1945 and 1950, rather large gas volumes and gas reserves were committed from this supply source to the interstate pipe-line market. It was this area, and in particular the large dry gas reserves of the Carthage field, which provided the gas reserves for the Texas Eastern Transmission Corporation and the Texas Gas Transmission Corporation, two of the earliest postwar pipe-line projects. The advantageous location of the supply area relative to Appalachian and Eastern markets accounted for its rapid development.

Evidence of price levels before 1947 is meager, being recorded only in the first three contracts. These indicated a price level between 3.0 and 5.0 cents per MCF. In 1947, however, two large-volume contracts for gas from the Carthage field were negotiated by the Tennessee Gas Transmission Company. Although only initial prices of 5.5 cents are recorded in the contract sources, an average price over a twenty-year term may be estimated, based on the assumption of 1.0 cent escalation each five years. In this case, it would approximate 7.0 cents per MCF.

The validity of this estimate is confirmed in two large-volume agreements, negotiated during June, 1947, by the Texas Eastern Transmission Corporation and the Southern Natural Gas Company. In these contracts, gas was obtained from fields located in East Texas and in close proximity to the Carthage field. Prices in the two agreements were set at a straight 7.0 cents and 8.0 cents, respectively, over a fifteen-year effective term.

For the rest of 1947, the market in this supply area consisted entirely of the contract activity of the Texas Eastern Transmission Corporation. It negotiated seven contracts during a period from June, 1947, through September, 1947, acquiring gas from many different sellers under a variety of terms and conditions. It was evidently during this short period that the main gas reserves for its project were secured, since—by means of this group of agreements—the Texas Eastern Company was able to contract for an annual gas volume totaling 149.4 million MCF.

Pricing patterns in these Texas Eastern contracts were not uniform. Each agreement tended to contain its own "mix" of price, term of contract, and conditions. There were short-term agreements, having contract terms of five years and stipulating prices of 6.5 cents. Two agreements did not provide for price escalation and, instead, contained a straight 8.0 cents per MCF over a twenty-year effective term. The remainder of the contracts generally had twenty-year effective terms and initial prices of 7.5 cents, which escalated 1.0 to 1.5 cents each five years. Average prices on a twenty-year basis would then approximate 9.0 cents. The difference between the non-escalated price of 8.0 cents and the average price under escalation of 9.0 cents may reflect a discounting of the 9.0 cent price to adjust for the fact that the non-escalated average price would have to be paid immediately.

The non-price conditions of these contracts were somewhat more uniform. Thus, all contained a seven-eighths buyer tax clause. There was, furthermore, an absence of favored-nation clauses in all except the last three contracts, dated in September, 1947. The favored-nation provisions were two-party arrangements usually covering an area within a 100 mile radius.

From the above, it is concluded that a price level of 9.0 cents per MCF was established in the East Texas–North Louisiana gas supply area by the last half of 1947. No major change in this level occurred through 1948, despite the entry of the Texas Gas Transmission Corporation as an important new buyer. In addition, the Texas Eastern Transmission Corporation continued its purchase activity, as did certain other buyers. Finally, the reduction in the gas volumes committed in 1948 relative to the previous year is noteworthy.

The 1948 purchase contracts in this supply area are of further interest because of the appearance of the controversial third-party favored-nation clauses. Thus, the agreements completed by the new entrant into the market, the Texas Gas Transmission Corporation, established the price pattern during the last half of 1948. These contracts stipulated an initial price of 7.5 cents for the first five years, which escalated 1.0 cent in each subsequent five-year period. A two-party favored-nation clause was provided for the first fifteen years of the contract. For the last five-year period, however, a third-party favored-nation proviso was to become operative, in which the price could be increased to the "highest price then being paid in the Carthage field under any contract for minimum delivery of 25,000 M cubic feet per day."

The use of third-party favored-nation clauses was further exemplified in the three 1948 contracts negotiated by the Texas Eastern Transmission Corporation. In two of these, the buyer agreed to meet, after the first five years, the "top prevailing price within 100 mile radius of contract area." This provision was an effective third-party favored-nation clause. In the third Texas Eastern contract, negotiated with the Sun Oil Company, the favored-nation stipulation was an exceptionally broad third-party proviso. It provided that "buyer must meet higher price paid to other producers in Louisiana or Texas, giving due consideration to the deduction of 1.5 cents for handling costs." The scope of the favored-nation clause here, however, may have been balanced by the fact that the average contract price over twenty years was only 7.5 cents.

Following the establishment of the 9.0 cent price level in 1948, market activity in the East Texas–North Louisiana supply

140

area was apparently brought to a halt. At least, no purchase activity is recorded in the contract sources for this area during 1949. The one contract assignable to the year is dated December 30, 1949, and its inclusion in 1950 would be more meaningful. Undoubtedly, the absence of buying activity in 1949 reflects the shift of interest to the other supply areas along the Gulf Coast where lower prices prevailed.

When contract activity was renewed in this supply area, it was at a noticeably higher price level. Thus, in a group of six contracts negotiated by the Piedmont Natural Gas Company, Inc., a new pipe-line project which was unsuccessful in securing a FPC certificate, a price level of 12.25 cents per MCF on a twenty-year basis was established. These agreements were completed in the first two months of 1950 and covered gas to be obtained from various fields in northern Louisiana. The initial price in the contracts was 10.0 cents per MCF, with a rapid escalation at the rate of 0.5 cents each two years over a twenty-year effective term. A straightforward tax-sharing clause was also included, requiring the buyer to pay two-thirds of additional taxes. Moreover, the Piedmont contracts were firm price agreements over their contract term except for the inclusion of a two-party favored-nation clause which was based in most instances upon a 50 mile radius from the purchase area.

The new and higher price level reflected in the Piedmont contracts was confirmed in the group of contracts negotiated by the Mississippi River Fuel Corporation during the first half of 1950. In these, the buyer was seeking additional gas upon which to base an expansion of facilities. Between March, 1950, and June, 1950, it entered into a large number of contracts in the Dubach, Lisbon, Ruston, and other fields in northern Louisiana, in the course of which it secured a gas volume of approximately 75,000 MCF per day.[7]

Prices in the Mississippi River Fuel contracts were set at an initial level of 11.0 cents per MCF, escalating 0.5 cents each two years over a twenty-year term. The contracts contained a two-thirds buyer tax-sharing clause and what was evidently a two-

[7] *Mississippi River Fuel Corp.*, 9 FPC (1950), 198.

party favored-nation clause, based on a 50 mile radius from the point of delivery. These terms were identical in all of the Mississippi River Fuel contracts. Compared with the Piedmont contracts, which immediately preceded them, prices were 0.75 cents per MCF higher. On a twenty-year basis, the Mississippi River Fuel contracts averaged 12.95 cents as against the 12.25 cents of the other agreements.

After the Mississippi River Fuel contracts, price variability in this supply area became pronounced to an extent that detailed contract analysis is not likely to be informative about trends and patterns. Moreover, this variation in price was matched by an almost equal degree of variation in the non-price conditions of the purchase contracts, with the sole exception of effective contract periods which tended strongly to a twenty-year term. In the case of tax clauses, for example, variation in the proportion to be borne by the buyer among different purchasers was large. The same buyer would frequently make different tax-sharing concessions in agreements which were closely related in time. The same was true with regard to the burden of the 1.0 cent Louisiana gathering tax. Likewise, the inclusion of favored-nation clauses was highly variable and, when present, were generally of a two-party variety.

Despite the difficulties presented by the condition of price variability, some general approximations of price levels and price patterns are possible. Thus, field prices for the last part of 1950 were about 13.0 cents per MCF. The main purchaser at this time was still the Mississippi River Fuel Corporation, which continued its buying activity in northern Louisiana. The 13.0 cent price level was confirmed by three contracts negotiated by the Arkansas Louisiana Gas Company in Louisiana and Texas for substantial gas volumes at average prices up to 13.5 cents per MCF. It may be concluded that a price level of 12.0–13.0 cents prevailed in 1950, with a strong tendency toward the upper limit of that range.

In 1951, three price levels were identifiable. The bulk of the contracts were negotiated within an average price range of 11.5 to 13.5 cents per MCF on a twenty-year basis. Gas volumes acquired within this price range varied, but in a number of instances relatively large amounts of gas were obtained. A second price level is identifiable at about 7.0–8.0 cents and less. In general, the contracts at this level reflect the characteristic of relatively short contract terms; the lowest prices are spot purchases. In several cases, though, the agreements cannot be explained on this basis. In these cases special factors relating to the physical qualities of the gas and its accessibility to pipe-line facilities may have played a part. Last, none of the low-priced agreements involved any significant quantities of gas.

The third level of prices established during 1951 was one of approximately 16.0 cents per MCF. These prices were negotiated by only one buyer, the Mississippi River Fuel Corporation, and they were found only in contracts for gas from the Woodlawn field and the Waskom field in East Texas. With respect to its other purchases during 1951, Mississippi River Fuel Corporation maintained its earlier 13.2 cent price. In view of their concentration in two gas fields, the higher-priced contracts were clearly distinctive.

In the one contract of this high-priced group for which the annual gas volume is known, 16.0 million MCF was committed. This was the largest volume of any contract recorded during 1951 in this supply area. For the other 16.0 cent contracts, volume was given at some quantity such as 300,000 MCF per well per year. The annual volume then depended upon the number of wells; it is not unlikely that most of these contracts involved more than a single well. The other features of these Mississippi River Fuel contracts were not unusual, including a twenty-year effective term, a three-fourths buyer tax-sharing clause and a two-party favored-nation clause based on a 50 mile radius from the point of delivery. Finally, there is some basis for concluding that these purchase contracts represented the price level in 1951 for large-volume large-reserve gas supplies in this market area.

The general pattern of prices noted above was not changed significantly in 1952. At the most, the price level of 16.0 cents was confirmed by the appearance of contracts in other fields with average prices in this range. But the 11.5 to 13.5 cent range for twenty-year terms was still firmly fixed and was found in most of the contracts of the period. The gas volumes involved in such

purchases, however, were typically small. The larger volumes that
are associated with this price range were, in almost all instances,
renegotiated agreements. Thus, a contract, dated July 1, 1952,
and recording a volume of 65 million MCF at an average price of
12.2 cents, was evidently a renegotiation of certain contracts
completed in 1948 in the Carthage field by the Texas Gas Transmission Corporation. Whether or not new gas volumes were
added by the renegotiation is not known.

Renegotiations of four other earlier contracts involving the
Texas Eastern Transmission Corporation were also recorded in
1952 and in two of these, prices were renegotiated up to the 16.0
cent level. These renegotiated agreements, as well as some contracts for new gas, established that price level for 1952. The contracts for new gas supplies include one completed by the Mississippi River Fuel Corporation, again in the Woodlawn field. The
only other buyer of new gas at the 16.0 cent price level was the
Texas Eastern Transmission Corporation. This company obtained rather small gas volumes from three separate Texas and
Louisiana fields at average prices of 16.4 cents per MCF on a
twenty-year basis.

The highest price recorded in 1952 in East Texas–North
Louisiana was a 20.0 cent price negotiated by the United Fuel Gas
Company. While covering a gas field which falls within the East
Texas–North Louisiana gas supply area, this agreement is evidently connected with other purchases being made at the same
time by this pipe-line buyer in the Louisiana Gulf Coast area. Of
interest in this connection is that, despite its price, this contract
did not command a very large volume of gas. It cannot be considered representative of price levels in the supply area under
consideration.

For 1953, price levels and price patterns were again not basically different from the two previous years. There was some upward pressure; contracts in the 16.0 cent range were proportionately more common, but no break above this level occurred.
Moreover, all of the higher-priced agreements in 1953 were
negotiated by the Texas Eastern Company. Other pipe-line purchasers acquired gas in the 11.0 to 13.0 cent price range. The

number of low-priced spot purchase type of contracts declined noticeably from the previous year. Several renegotiated contracts appeared; many of the larger volume agreements were of this character, as had been the case in 1952. In general, price levels in the East Texas–North Louisiana gas supply area remained unchanged from the preceding year. Moreover, a general stability was maintained from 1951 through 1953–a distinctive pattern not characteristic of other supply areas.

With this general view of the price pattern and the price level in the East Texas–North Louisiana gas supply area completed, attention may be devoted to other features of this supply area. Of particular interest is the price variability noted earlier. This price variation was, first of all, not adequately explained by a parallel variation of either quantity or term of contract. Rather, it appears to have been due mainly to the existence of numerous gas fields in this supply area which, except for the Carthage field, are relatively small, particularly in Louisiana, and are held by many owners. Active bargaining between many small sellers and a rather large number of pipe-line buyers might easily result in substantially different prices in the same period. The fact that the five active pipe-line buyers were continually in this market, rather than being dominant in buying activity for successive time periods, would add to the variability of prices.

Another factor of some importance is also related to the existence of numerous small gas fields. The many gas fields contained within the gas supply area are likely to be quite different in their physical characteristics. Thus, differences in the quality of the gas, variations between fields in the pressures at which gas can be delivered to the buyer, and differences in the quantity of reserves to sustain an annual delivery could all lead to price variation. Support for this possibility is found in the fact that prices within individual fields show much less variation than prices over the entire supply area.

Moreover, the smaller volumes of gas available after 1950 would have emphasized the need to take into account, through price variation, the special physical characteristics of a particular field. Following the commitment of large gas volumes before

1950, the availability of gas supplies in the area was considerably reduced, as evidenced by the small volumes contained in even the higher-priced contracts. Small quantities of gas, however, were still attractive to buyers, in view of the advantages of location associated with this supply area. But the prices of very small gas volumes from diverse fields would have to reflect their unique physical characteristics if their purchase were to be rendered economical to the pipe-line buyer.

Although individual prices displayed considerable variability in the East Texas–North Louisiana gas supply area, which makes the determination of representative field prices more difficult, it is possible to identify the levels about which they tended to cluster. Of these, the most important (in terms of contract frequency) is the 11.0–13.0 cent price level which remained quite stable from 1950 through 1953, with some upward drift in the last year. A similar clustering around a 16.0 cent level and a 7.0–9.0 cent price level is identifiable. Among these three, the 16.0 cent price level would come closest to representing a large-volume market and certainly would be fairly reliable for this purpose during 1951 and 1952. For a small-volume market, an 11.0–13.0 cent range seems most relevant, although the 7.0–9.0 cent level warrants attention because of its frequency and should be considered as a second small-volume market.

These and other representative price levels which have prevailed at different times in the East Texas–North Louisiana gas supply area are estimated and summarized below:

REPRESENTATIVE FIELD PRICES: EAST TEXAS–NORTH LOUISIANA
GAS SUPPLY AREA

Large Volume	Cents per MCF (16.7 psi)
1945	3.0– 4.0
1946	5.0
1947 (first half)	7.0– 8.0
1947 (second half)	9.0
1948	9.0
1949	(no data)

Panhandle, West Texas, and East Texas Supply Areas

1950	12.0–13.0
1951	16.0
1952	16.0
1953	16.0

Small Volume

1951	11.5–13.5
	7.0– 8.0
1952	11.5–13.5
	7.0– 8.0
1953	12.5–13.5
	8.0– 9.0

CHAPTER 5

Texas Gulf Coast Supply Areas

THE MAJOR SUPPLY SOURCE for natural gas in the postwar period has been the gas and oil producing region extending along the entire Texas and Louisiana Gulf Coast. A study of natural gas field markets, however, would be greatly facilitated by a division of the region into smaller geographical supply units. Not only would a more accurate presentation of field prices be made possible for what appear to have been distinguishable markets, but a more precise analysis of market behavior would be achieved. As a consequence, the Texas portion of the Gulf Coast gas-producing region has been separated into three gas supply areas. These conform to the geographical districts established by the Texas Railroad Commission in the course of implementing its oil and gas conservation regulations.

A. TEXAS GULF COAST–DISTRICTS 2 AND 4

One of the above-mentioned gas supply areas includes District No. 2 and District No. 4, lying along the southernmost reaches of the Texas Gulf Coast. Since both districts were developed at about the same time by the same pipe-line purchasers, they should be considered together. A summary view of the price pattern in Districts 2 and 4 is to be found in Figures 4 and 5, respectively. The buyer and seller structure within these markets is shown in Tables 24 and 25.

With respect to the number and distribution of market participants, there were approximately twenty sellers reporting volumes of 2.0 million MCF or more in each of the two districts. If small producers—as well as those for whom volumes were not reported—were included, there would be fifty separately identi-

Texas Gulf Coast Supply Areas

Table 24

ANALYSIS OF NATURAL GAS PURCHASE CONTRACTS
IN THE TEXAS GULF COAST GAS SUPPLY AREA—
TEXAS R. R. COMM. DIST. NO. 2, 1944–53

RANK OF SELLER BY ANNUAL GAS VOLUME	Annual Gas Volume M³CF	Number of Contracts	Number of Buyers
1. Humble Oil & Refining Co.	21.9	1	1
2. Barnsdall Oil Co.	21.5	1	1
3. Stanolind Oil & Gas Co.	17.6	4	3
4. Atlantic Refining Co.	11.1	2	2
5. Western Natural Gas Co.	10.9	1	1
6. Blanco Oil Co.	9.1	1	1
7. Falcon-Seaboard Drill Co.	9.1	1	1
8. Alaska Steamship Co.	8.0	1	1
9. Continental Oil Co.	7.2	1	1
10. C. E. Starrett	6.4	1	1
11. Shell Oil Co.	6.4	1	1
12. Sinclair Oil & Gas Co.	5.4	2	2
13. Tide Water Associated Oil Co.	4.8	1	1
14. N. C. Ginter, et al.	3.6	1	1
15. Hewit & Dougherty, et al.	3.2	1	1
16. Seaboard Oil Co., et al.	3.2	1	1
17. Amerada Petroleum Corp.	3.2	1	1
18. Oil Drilling, Inc., et al.	2.5	2	2
19. Salt Dome Prod. & Skelly Oil Co.	2.4	1	1
17 sellers reporting less than 2.0 M³CF of annual gas sales	15.7	17	
Subtotals	173.2	42	
26 sellers not included in above listing, having contracts with indefinite gas volumes	—	29	
Renegotiated and other indefinite gas volume contracts	—	15	
Totals	173.2	86	

Table 25

ANALYSIS OF NATURAL GAS PURCHASE CONTRACTS

IN THE TEXAS GULF COAST GAS SUPPLY AREA—

TEXAS R. R. COMM. DIST. NO. 4, 1944–53

RANK OF SELLER BY ANNUAL GAS VOLUME	Annual Gas Volume M³CF	Number of Contracts	Number of Buyers
1. Chicago Corp.	51.5	3	1
2. Humble Oil & Refining Co.	46.6	4	2
3. Magnolia Petroleum Co., *et al.*	30.9	2	1
4. Argo Oil Corp.	28.4	2	1
5. D. M. Lockhart, *et al.*	25.6	1	1
6. La Gloria Corp.	22.5	2	2
7. Atlantic Refining Co., *et al.*	17.9	2	2
8. Western Natural Gas Co.	16.0	2	1
9. Ralph E. Fair, Inc.	9.1	1	1
10. Sun Oil Co.	8.4	1	1
11. Barnsdall Oil Co.	7.6	1	1
12. Rogers Lacy, *et al.*	7.3	1	1
13. L. M. Lockhart	7.3	1	1
14. D. H. Perry, *et al.*	7.3	1	1
15. C. V. Lyman	5.4	1	1
16. J. S. Abercrombie Co., *et al.*	4.8	1	1
17. Superior Oil Co.	3.8	1	1
18. Nueces Corp.	3.6	1	1
19. Stanolind Oil & Gas Co.	3.6	1	1
20. Clardy & Barnett	2.7	1	1
21. Clark Fuel Producing Co.	2.5	1	1
14 sellers reporting less than 2.0 M³CF of annual gas sales	15.8	14	
Subtotals	328.6	45	
15 sellers not included in above listing, having contracts with indefinite gas volumes	—	21	
Renegotiated and other indefinite gas volume contracts	—	15	
Totals	328.6	81	

fiable sellers in District 4 and sixty-two sellers in District 2. The variety and number of sellers is to be explained by the fact that the area consists of many separate oil and gas fields, most of which are relatively small. A few large dry gas fields are to be found, although none approach the Panhandle, Hugoton, or Carthage fields in size. Of further note is the extent to which the important gas producers and sellers included concerns other than the large oil companies. Although such large producers as Humble Oil and Refining Company, Magnolia Petroleum Company, and Stanolind Oil and Gas Company were listed as sellers, the supply area includes a substantial number of gas producers who are not important factors in the petroleum industry.

The contract data for the period under investigation disclosed the presence of four pipe-line purchasers in District 4, exclusive of the Texas Ohio Gas Company, a pipe-line project which was not successful in securing a Federal Power Commission certificate. These four included the Tennessee Gas Transmission Company, the Transcontinental Gas Pipe Line Corporation, the United Gas Pipe Line Company, and the Texas Illinois Natural Gas Pipeline Company. In addition, two non-pipe-line companies—the Equitable Gas Company and the Niagara Gas Transmission Company—purchased gas in this market, the transportation of which was undertaken on a common carrier basis by an existing interstate pipe line.

The four pipe lines mentioned above were also buyers in District 2, as was the unsuccessful Texas Ohio Gas Company. An additional buyer in this particular supply area was the Texas Eastern Transmission Corporation, which purchased directly in its own name, as well as through an affiliate—the Wilcox Trend Gathering System.

With reference to field prices prior to 1947, a level of about 5.0–6.0 cents per MCF prevailed in District 4. The only interstate pipe-line buyer at that time was the Tennessee Gas Transmission Company. A similar buyer and price situation existed in District 2, except that the United Gas Pipe Line Company was a second purchaser. In 1947, following the entry of the Transcontinental Gas Pipe Line Corporation into these two supply areas, the price level quickly rose to 7.5 cents per MCF. This substantial rise in prices illustrates a frequent occurrence in postwar gas field markets: sharp upward movements in field prices were associated with the entry of new pipe-line buyers into a gas supply area. Such new entrants not only brought about a general increase in demand but, in the relatively imperfect market for field gas, the advent of new buyers provided gas producers with an opportunity to stiffen their bargaining position. Moreover, in order to acquire needed reserves without undue delay, a new project was likely to offer a premium above the prices of existing and established buyers.

After Transcontinental's entry into the market in 1947, no other contracts are recorded in these two supply areas until 1949. During 1948, buyer interest apparently shifted to District 3 and Southwest Louisiana, where a substantial number of contracts were negotiated by the Tennessee Gas Transmission Company and the Transcontinental Gas Pipe Line Corporation at a price level of approximately 9.5 cents. This shift of buying activity over a relatively short-term period is further evidenced by the fact that in 1947 no purchases were recorded for District 3 and Southwest Louisiana, when buying activity was high in Districts 2 and 4. It serves to establish the existence of a significant competitive interaction between natural gas field markets in this period, whereby pipe-line buyers could and did gravitate to alternative supply areas, presumably in search of the most advantageous price and supplementary contract terms.

By 1949, the price level in both Districts 2 and 4 was under upward pressure. The Tennessee Gas Transmission Company, in the first half of 1949, was paying an average price of 7.5 cents per MCF when adjusted to a standard twenty-year term. Calculated on the shorter effective terms typical in the Tennessee Gas Transmission contracts, average prices were about 6.0 cents. In some instances, however, these 1949 contracts of Tennessee Gas Transmission were renegotiations of 1944–46 agreements, which may account for their price level. In 1949, too, favored-nation clauses came into wider use, although they had been included in the Transcontinental contracts of 1947. For example, the originals of these renegotiated contracts did not contain these provisions, but they were added in the later renegotiated versions.

While it would appear that Tennessee Gas Transmission's 1949 prices did no more than meet the Transcontinental contracts, they were effectively higher because of the greater advantage to sellers in the terms under which price modifications could be made. To illustrate this fact as well as pricing practices in general, a comparison of representative contract price schedules is given below:

TRANSCONTINENTAL GAS PIPE LINE CORP. DISTRICT 4— (AUG. 29, 1947)		TENNESSEE GAS TRANSMISSION CO.—DISTRICT 2 (APR. 22, 1949)	
First 2½ yrs.	5.0 cents	First 5 yrs.	6.0 cents
Next 4 yrs.	6.0 cents	Next 5 yrs.	7.0 cents
Next 4 yrs.	7.0 cents	Next 5 yrs.	8.0 cents
Next 3 yrs.	8.0 cents	Last 5 yrs.	9.0 cents
Next 3 years	9.0 cents		
Last 3½ years	10.0 cents		

If buyer pays higher price to any other seller in District 4, such higher price is payable under this contract. (Two-party favored-nation clause.)

Price to be redetermined at end of each five-year period—to be set at average of 3 highest prices paid by all transporters of gas in District 2. Also contains two-party favored-nation clause in District 2.

From a comparison of these contracts, it can be seen that the difference in initial price appears to be offset by the differences in fixed price escalation resulting in a virtually identical average price on a twenty-year term, namely 7.5 cents per MCF. This further demonstrates the importance of fixed price escalation as a pricing factor, as well as the necessity for using an average price, rather than an initial price in the measurement of field prices.

Despite the identity of average prices, however, the later Tennessee Gas Transmission contract was more advantageous to sellers because of the considerable degree of contract price flexibility which it contained. As a consequence of five-year price redetermination, the seller was able to avoid rigid price commitments in the face of a rising price trend. Relative to the redetermination provisions prevalent at that time, this substantial element of price flexibility must be viewed as a price increase. Its value to sellers can be inferred from the fact that the 7.5 cent price was probably below the true level of field prices obtainable in 1949. The pipe-line buyer presumably bargained off five-year price redetermination for prices below prevailing levels. Its ability to do so does reflect a continued—if diminished—buyer bargaining power, although in retrospect at least, the long-run advantage to the pipe line of its exercise seems dubious.

In the latter part of 1949, the Transcontinental Gas Pipe Line Corporation reentered these supply areas under circumstances which raised the level of prices to 9.5 cents. Six contracts were recorded for the Transcontinental Company, three of which represented price changes in the 1947 agreements caused by the activation of favored-nation clauses. These agreements, as well as the new contracts, contained the price schedule and terms of the 1947 supply arrangements but with a 2.0 cent per MCF increase in each of the price steps.

Although confirmed in subsequent contracts, this rise in field price levels was substantial. Some explanation for it is found in the special circumstances enhancing seller bargaining power relative to Transcontinental as buyer. Thus, the contracts were signed at a time when Transcontinental was attempting to add a sizable volume of gas to its reserves rather quickly to justify the enlargement of its certificated project from a 26-inch diameter pipe line to a 30-inch diameter line.[1]

In the first half of 1950, the price level established in the Transcontinental purchase agreements was maintained, if not increased, in transactions involving the Texas Illinois Natural Gas Pipeline Company, a new pipe-line project designed to serve the Chicago market. This company was affiliated with the Natural Gas Pipeline Company, which also served the Chicago market but obtained its gas supply from the Panhandle-Hugoton area.

[1] *Transcontinental Gas Pipe Line Corp.*, 9 FPC (1950), 32.

Two prices were paid by Texas Illinois in its gas supply contracts. In one group, an average price of 10.25 cents over a fifteen-year effective term was paid; in the others, a lower price prevailed —9.75 cents on a fifteen-year basis. This price difference reflected a variation in the strength of favored-nation clauses. In the higher-priced contracts, the clause was mild; it operated only in the period prior to the first delivery of gas. It stipulated that, if the buyer made any contract in District 4 prior to the first delivery of gas at any higher price, then that higher price was to be substituted. The lower-priced contracts contained stronger favored-nation clauses. But even these were weaker than the typical provision of this kind, since they were limited in operation to the gas field rather than to the larger area of an entire district.

It is possible, too, that the higher price level in the Texas Illinois contracts, as compared with the Transcontinental purchases in 1949, can be accounted for by differences in the strength of their favored-nation clauses. Assuming its validity, this possibility has important implications for the problem of market behavior. For this period at least, a new pipe-line project could avoid or weaken a favored-nation clause by offering a price concession: the pipe-line buyer was not faced with an all or nothing choice regarding such contract provisions.

Following the 1949–50 increase in field prices in these two supply areas, a period of stability at a lower price level is disclosed by the contract data. The condition extended through the end of 1951, during which time a price level of approximately 7.5–8.0 cents per MCF was maintained. Taken in conjunction with the small volumes characteristic of these contracts, the lower price level implies the existence of two markets for gas. One is a large-volume market involving purchase agreements negotiated by new or expanded pipe-line projects and requiring sufficient reserves to support the facilities for a fifteen- to twenty-year period. The price level in this market is generally well at the top of the prevailing price range.

A second market, with a lower price level, may have been established after 1950 for relatively small volumes of gas taken by established pipe lines with extensive gas gathering networks.

For example, most of the contracts of 1950 and 1951 in District 2 appear to be part of such a small volume market. Of these purchase agreements, twenty-five were arrangements in which the United Gas Pipe Line Company was the buyer; five were Tennessee Gas Transmission contracts. The typical price here was approximately 8.0 cents per MCF over a ten-year contract period. The volumes in the United Gas contracts were all indefinite; in the Tennessee Gas Transmission contracts, they were small. Of further interest—possibly reflecting buyer strength—the United Gas contracts contained no favored-nation clauses, and the buyer was obligated to pay only one-half of any additional taxes. For Tennessee Gas, the typical situation was to pay three-fourths of extra taxes and to include a favored-nation provision.

A similar pattern was also discernible in District 4. With but few exceptions, the twenty contracts covering the period from April, 1950, to September, 1951, appeared to establish the existence of a lower-priced small-volume gathering-system market. The predominant purchaser in District 4, however, was the Tennessee Gas Transmission Company. The prices in its agreements were between 7.5 and 8.0 cents per MCF, based on a twenty-year effective term. Furthermore, the volumes in these purchase agreements were consistent with the small-volume market hypothesis, with the exception of two instances where relatively large amounts of gas were sold at the 8.0 cents per MCF price.

The United Gas Pipe Line Company also acquired gas supplies in District 4 during this period. Its initial contracts were for a 6.0 cent average price over ten years, with no favored-nation provisions and no tax-sharing clause. Later purchases were at an 8.0 cent price and still continued the no favored-nation pattern, although the buyer agreed to pay one-half of taxes. In addition, one contract of this buyer is unusual for its exceptionally low price of 4.5 cents. In effect, it was a spot contract, the term running for thirty-day periods subject to renewal.

By the end of 1951, the relatively stable price level of the previous two years was under pressure. In District 2, for example, the Texas Illinois Natural Gas Pipeline Company completed a small-volume fifteen-year contract on November 1, 1951, at an average price of 9.75 cents. Its favored-nation clause, however, was still weaker than the typical proviso since it was limited to a single district and was only effective within a 40 mile radius of the buyer's primary pipe-line system.

The real break in the price level came with the entry of the Wilcox Trend Gathering System into the District 2 supply area. This company was an affiliate of the Texas Eastern Transmission Corporation, evidently created for the purpose of acquiring the gas reserves upon which a major expansion of the parent pipe-line company could be based.[2] Since it did not go outside of District 2 in its buying activity—at least as recorded in the contract sources—the discussion below is limited to that single supply area. At a later point, the analysis will return to District 4.

In a purchase agreement dated October, 1951, the Wilcox Trend Company raised the level of prices to approximately 12.0 cents per MCF, averaged over a twenty-year effective term. This contract also contained an exceptionally broad favored-nation clause (based on Texas and Louisiana fields) and raised the buyer's share of additional taxes to seven-eighths. Immediately following the Wilcox Trend contract, a group of contracts were negotiated by United Gas Pipe Line and Tennessee Gas Transmission which were virtually the last in the 7.0 to 8.0 cent price range.

During the first half of 1952, a price level above 12.0 cents per MCF was established in a series of ten contracts negotiated by the Wilcox Trend Gathering System.[3] These contracts were alike in containing a contract term of twenty years, a favored-nation clause, and a seven-eighths buyer tax-sharing clause. Furthermore, the 12.0 cent price recorded for them was the average price over a five-year effective term. If the price had been averaged over a

[2] Opinion No. 241, *Texas Eastern Transmission Corp.*, 11 FPC (1952), 435.

[3] These ten contracts were completed in the period between March and July, 1952. Actually, more than ten such agreements were found in the basic sources. In all these, though, the price and other terms were the same. Where contracts were for the same field or were completed on the same date, they were grouped together to provide only a single observation. Thus, Wilcox Trend negotiated twenty-six separate agreements in District 2 during this period, all having the same price and terms. Ten of these were utilized to represent the price level and trend in Figure 4.

twenty-year contract term, it would have approximated 13.5 cents per MCF.[4]

It would appear, then, using a standard of a twenty-year contract period, that a price level of approximately 13.0 cents per MCF was well set at the beginning of 1952. In view of the quantities involved, it may also be concluded that the Wilcox Trend contracts and the price pattern they demonstrate are to be considered a part of the small-volume gathering-system type of market. There are, however, apparent contradictions. For example, in District 2 a relatively large volume contract was negotiated by Tennessee Gas Transmission in March, 1952, at an average price of 12.3 cents over a twenty-year effective term. But in June, 1952, the Texas Eastern Transmission Corporation paid 16.3 cents for a smaller volume, over a twenty-year effective term. The apparent inconsistency is partly explained by geographical factors. Some gas fields are on the border line between Districts, and thus, while assigned to one, they may be more closely related to another in their price patterns. This was evidently the situation in the Texas Eastern contract. The price stipulated there was more in line with prices prevailing at the time, and being paid by Texas Eastern, in District 3.

Aside from the above-mentioned agreements, the only substantial deviation from the 13.0 cent price level in District 2 during 1952–53 occurred in a group of five contracts negotiated by the Texas Ohio Gas Company. This company, organized to build a pipe line to the Appalachian area, was unsuccessful in obtaining the necessary certificate to undertake construction and begin operations.[5] Nevertheless, the price and terms in the contracts negotiated by this company were to some degree representative

---

[4] The contracts provided for the following schedule of prices:

First year	11.40 cents
Increases 0.23 cents yearly until	15.73 cents
Subject to redetermination.	

From Opinion No. 241, cited above, it was learned that the price redetermination was to occur at the end of the first five years. On this basis, a 5-year effective term was selected with an average price of 11.86 cents over that period.

[5] Opinion No. 238, *Texas Ohio Gas Co.*, 12 FPC (1953), 23.

of the conditions under which a new pipe-line project would have acquired its gas reserves.

The contracts of the Texas Ohio Gas Company were notable in a number of respects. First, they were recorded at 17.6 cents over a ten-year effective term, but with an average price of 18.8 cents per MCF on a twenty-year basis. Second, despite their higher price, the contracts did not represent particularly large quantities of gas. Finally, all of the sellers were apparently small producers; none of the major oil companies or other large gas producers were involved in these contracts, either in District 2 or, as will be seen later, in their counterparts within District 4.

After the Texas Ohio contracts, the level of prices through 1953 was fairly steady at about 13.0 cents per MCF for small volumes. Among the buyers were the Tennessee Gas Transmission Company and the Texas Eastern Transmission Corporation. The contracts of the latter purchaser generally provided for an initial price of 11.4 cents, increasing .2 cent each year. On a twenty-year standard, their average price was 13.5 cents per MCF. All contained favored-nation and tax clauses.

Shifting attention to District 4, the price level and marketing pattern after 1951 in this gas supply area matched quite closely that established in the adjoining District 2. A jump to at least a 12.0 cent price level was recorded by the end of 1951. Initiating this price movement was a purchase agreement between the United Gas Pipe Line Company and the Sunray Oil Company, dated December, 1951. Although the contract was for a twenty-year legal term, it contained a five-year price redetermination clause. This proviso stipulated that, after the first five years and for each five-year period thereafter, the price of gas was to be fixed at the average of the three highest prices paid in District 4, but not below minimum charges which escalated upward from the initial price. The inclusion of a price redetermination clause of this sort was quite unusual in view of the patterns previously associated with this particular pipe-line buyer. It is suggestive of an important change in the balance of bargaining strength within the gas field market.

Meriting further comment is the price established in this

contract. On a twenty-year basis, the average price was 14.25 cents per MCF, the relatively high level of which contrasts markedly with the previous pattern in the supply area. It is partly explained by the fact that the contract was apparently a large-volume purchase, although the data given in the sources did not permit the determination of a definite volume.

Following this break in the District 4 price level, the Tennessee Gas Transmission Company signed a few contracts at the old 8.0 cent level, but soon after—between April and August, 1952—it was negotiating small-volume purchases at a 12.5 cent price. In this same period, the Texas Illinois Natural Gas Pipeline Company negotiated a contract at an average price of 14.1 cents for a five-year effective term. Like the United Gas Pipe Line contract, it provided for price redetermination each five years with specified minimums. On a twenty-year standard, the average price was a minimum of 15.5 cents per MCF. The significance of this contract may lie not only in its confirmation of the price level of the earlier United Gas Pipe Line contract but also in the acceptance of five-year price redetermination and favored-nation clauses by another large pipe-line buyer, who had previously avoided such provisions.

Furthermore, in 1952 the Texas Ohio purchase agreements were negotiated. These were similar to the contracts by the same buyer in District 2 and provided for a price of about 18.0 cents per MCF. Their terms were comparable, and—like the earlier agreements—the volumes were relatively small. Curiously enough, in the same month Tennessee Gas Transmission was able to contract for very large gas volumes at prices considerably below Texas Ohio prices. Moreover, the purchases by Tennessee Gas Transmission were made in the same general area and, in some instances, in the same counties as the Texas Ohio arrangements.

Thus, a contract dated August, 1952, between Tennessee Gas Transmission and Humble Oil and Refining Company, stipulated a maximum annual volume of 16.0 million MCF. The price, on a twenty-year standard term, was 12.62 cents. In like manner, a purchase agreement, in the same month, between Tennessee Gas and the Chicago Corporation, provided for the exceptionally large volume of 37.9 million MCF at an average price of 11.2 cents per MCF for approximately a twenty-year period. The gas fields in the second contract were the Stratton–Aqua Dulce fields in District 4. No indication that these contracts were renegotiations of earlier arrangements could be found, which would be the only plausible explanation for their low price and large volumes. The tentative conclusion is that they represented new gas supplies. If correct, the price pattern in these contracts is difficult to explain.

Despite the contradiction afforded by the two above-mentioned Tennessee Gas Transmission contracts, a price pattern emerged in District 4 during 1952–53 which adds support to the distinction between a large-volume and a small-volume field market. The latter was evidenced by seventeen contracts covering a period from October, 1952, to November, 1953, which were substantially identical in their terms, although they encompassed a large number of sellers and many separate gas fields. These, too, were virtually all Tennessee Gas Transmission purchases. The price level established by this contract group was approximately 13.0 cents per MCF on a twenty-year standard. In addition, they contained favored-nation clauses based on District 4, as well as conventional tax-sharing clauses. While definite gas volumes are not known for most of these agreements, since the contract sources provided only the information that volumes were to be "based upon estimates of recoverable reserves," it may be assumed that, in this supply area, the indefinite gas volumes represent small quantities.

These purchase agreements, with the uniform 13.0 cent price they established, are evidence at least for the existence of a distinctive type of field market. It is that characterized by a purchaser with an extensive gathering system and sellers owning small and scattered gas reserves. Whether a distinctive and lower level of prices prevails in such circumstances depends on the establishment of a different price level for a large-volume market.

In this connection, the price level in a large-volume new-project market for gas in District 4 during 1953 must be found in two unusual purchase agreements. These involved buyers which were not pipe lines with transportation facilities reaching into the supply area. Instead, they were basically gas distributors who, after making field purchases, arranged to have their gas supplies transported on a common carrier basis by the Tennessee Gas Transmission Company.

In the first of these contracts, completed in February, 1953, the Niagara Gas Transmission Company contracted for gas from the Phillips Petroleum Company. The legal term of the contract was twenty years, which is also assumed to be the effective term, in the absence of any indication of a price redetermination clause. Under this condition the average price was approximately 19 cents per MCF over a twenty-year term, the initial price being 17.1 cents on a 16.7 psi pressure base with approximately 1.0 cent price escalation each four years. Although no specific quantity is shown, the contract committed a large volume of gas to the buyer. It was one of a group of three contracts signed by the Niagara Gas Transmission Company—the others being in another gas supply area—the total volume of which was 22 million MCF per year. While this contract did not contain a price redetermination clause, it did provide for a third-party favored-nation clause. Under this arrangement, prices could be adjusted upward to the average of the three highest prices paid in District 4.

The second of the large-volume contracts in District 4 involved the Equitable Gas Company and a group of sellers, headed by the Humble Oil and Refining Company. Dated September, 1953, it was also a long-term agreement, the average price of which approximated 18 cents per MCF for an annual volume of 8 million MCF. The initial price in this contract was about 16 cents on a 16.7 psi pressure base, which increased 1.0 cent each four years to a maximum of 20.5 cents. A conventional favored-nation clause based on District 4 and a tax-sharing clause were also included. Although only these two contracts are available to substantiate the conclusion, in view of their importance and the previous price trend, it may be asserted that a price of 18.0–19.0 cents was the level in 1953 for a large-volume large-reserve market.

Completing the analysis for Districts 2 and 4, a summary of

the representative field prices which have been estimated is presented below:

REPRESENTATIVE FIELD PRICES: TEXAS GULF COAST—
DISTRICTS 2 AND 4

Large Volume	Cents per MCF (16.7 psi)
1945	5.0
1946	6.0
1947	7.0
1948	(no data)
1949 (first half)	7.5
1949 (second half)	9.5
1950	10.0
1951	10.0
1952	18.0
1953	18.0–19.0
Small Volume	
1950	7.0
1951	8.0
1952	12.0
1953	13.0

B. TEXAS GULF COAST—DISTRICT 3

The northernmost portion of the Texas Gulf Coast gas supply area is that included within the Texas Railroad Commission District No. 3. Being closer to interstate markets by approximately 300 miles than other sources and containing six interstate pipe-line purchasers, it is to be expected that patterns in the area would differ from the other Texas Gulf Coast supply areas. To a considerable extent this expectation is realized, although less in the timing of price changes than in price level. To establish the existence of this condition as well as to find further confirmation for some of the patterns already discerned, it is desirable to analyze District 3 as a distinct unit. Price levels for the supply area are given in Figure 6.

163

Table 26

ANALYSIS OF NATURAL GAS PURCHASE CONTRACTS

IN THE TEXAS GULF COAST GAS SUPPLY AREA—

TEXAS R. R. COMM. DIST. NO. 3, 1944–53

RANK OF SELLER BY ANNUAL GAS VOLUME	Annual Gas Volume M³CF	Number of Contracts	Number of Buyers
1. Sun Oil Co.	63.3	4	4
2. Shell Oil Co.	47.3	3	3
3. Magnolia Petroleum Co., et al.	43.1	3	2
4. Phillips Petroleum Co.	25.4	3	3
5. Stanolind Oil & Gas Co., et al.	23.3	2	2
6. American Republic Corp.	16.4	3	2
7. Texas Gas Corp.	16.3	1	1
8. New Ulm Corp.	16.0	1	1
9. The Texas Company	11.8	1	1
10. Sinclair Prairie Oil Co.	9.1	1	1
11. Tide Water Associated Oil Co.	8.6	2	1
12. Meredith Clegg & Hunt, et al.	8.0	1	1
13. Superior Oil Co.	6.8	1	1
14. Butcher-Arthur, Inc., et al.	6.5	2	1
15. Fairbanks Operators, Severally	6.0	1	1
16. Cities Service Oil Co.	5.9	1	1
17. Skelly Oil Co.	5.1	1	1
18. Floyd L. Karsten, et al.	4.4	1	1
19. Ohio Oil Co.	3.6	1	1
20. Republic Natural Gas Co.	3.2	1	1
21. BBM Drilling Co.	2.5	1	1
11 sellers reporting less than 2.0 M³CF of annual gas sales	9.7	11	
Subtotals	342.3	46	
18 sellers not included in above listing, having contracts with indefinite gas volumes	—	18	
Renegotiated and other indefinite gas volume contracts	—	9	
Totals	342.3	73	

Texas Gulf Coast Supply Areas

The structure of this supply unit is presented in Table 26. It is seen that there were fifty separate sellers in this market in the period covered. Twenty-one of these recorded annual gas volumes of 2.0 million MCF or more, while seventeen sellers had annual volumes of 5.0 million MCF or more.[6] In a pattern somewhat different from Districts 2 and 4, the large-volume sellers in this supply area were almost entirely the larger petroleum companies. Moreover, there was a sharper downward gradation in volume from the largest supplier to the smaller sellers.

On the buying side of the market, there were six pipe-line purchasers recorded for District 3, five of whom were also buyers in District 2. The sixth pipe-line company was the Trunkline Gas Company, which entered the supply area in 1948. In addition, the purchasers in District 3 included a proposed pipe-line project, the Piedmont Natural Gas Company, Inc., which was unsuccessful in securing a Federal Power Commission certificate, and one non-pipe-line purchaser—the Iroquois Gas Corporation.

Turning to the analysis of field prices, the price level in District 3 prior to 1947 was not much different from that already noted in Districts 2 and 4. If the first two contracts in this district are to be considered representative, the level approximated 5.0 cents per MCF. During 1947, no contract activity was recorded in the contract data sources for District 3. However, in that year considerable purchase activity was occurring in the adjoining East Texas–North Louisiana supply area, while agreements committing sizable gas reserves were being negotiated in Districts 2 and 4. It was not until 1948 that contracts sufficiently numerous to establish a level of prices were recorded for District 3.

The 1948 field price level in District 3 was approximately

[6] Some interesting elements of uniformity are to be found in a comparison of the three Texas Gulf Coast Districts, as is evident from the following:

Supply Area	No. of contracts	No. of contracts reporting volumes	No. of sellers	No. of sellers reporting volumes	No. of sellers reporting annual volumes more than 2.0 M3CF
District 3	73	46	50	32	21
District 2	86	42	62	36	19
District 4	81	45	50	35	21

9.0 cents per MCF over a twenty-year effective term, a level not reached until 1949 in the other two Texas Gulf Coast supply areas, though it had been achieved by the end of 1947 in the East Texas supply area. This variation in timing illustrates well the character of the price interrelationships between these different supply areas.

It was the activity of the Texas Eastern Transmission Corporation, previously an important buyer in the East Texas area, which was instrumental in raising the District 3 level to 9.0 cents. In a series of contracts between April and June, 1948, this corporation acquired gas supplies that provided an annual volume of more than 50 million MCF. The fields in which the gas supplies were obtained contained large gas reserves, and—except for the Sheridan field—they were geographically concentrated in the northeast portion of District 3, relatively close to the East Texas supply area. Consequently, both the geographical concentration and the location within the district minimized transportation costs to the buyer. The exception was the Sheridan field contract, but it involved a substantially larger volume than the other three purchase agreements.

The initial price, as well as the price escalation, was the same in all of these contracts. The price of gas was set at 7.5 cents per MCF for the first five years and escalated 1.0 cent in each of the three subsequent five-year periods over the twenty-year term of contract. The average price was thus 9.0 cents per MCF. All of these agreements contained similar tax-sharing clauses, in which the buyer portion was equal to seven-eighths of additional taxes. Favored-nation clauses were not included in three of these agreements. The Sheridan field contract with the Shell Oil Company, however, included a rather strong two-party favored-nation provision covering any future purchases of gas by Texas Eastern in either Texas or Louisiana.

The substantial upward impact on field price levels evidenced by these Texas Eastern contracts was a not uncommon occurrence in the Gulf Coast field markets during the postwar period. A new pipe-line project would be initiated or new pipe-line facilities would be extended into a supply area with the purchaser seeking a few large sources of gas to minimize the cost of pipe-line facilities. To obtain its requirements, the buyer would "break" the prevailing price level by offering a schedule of prices and contract conditions more favorable to sellers. The uniformity of terms in the various contracts of Texas Eastern could be readily explained on this basis.

A second pipe-line purchaser in District 3 during 1948 was the Transcontinental Gas Pipe Line Corporation. It negotiated a single large-volume contract with the Sun Oil Company, covering gas supplies in the North Markham and North Bay City fields. Like the 1947 contracts which Transcontinental had negotiated in Districts 2 and 4, this purchase was part of the initial gas reserves for the proposed pipe-line project. However, the price in the District 3 contract was higher by approximately 2.0 cents per MCF. The agreement had only a fifteen-year effective term, and, averaged over this period, the contract price equaled 9.5 cents per MCF. The contract also contained a two-party favored-nation clause. The contract sources did not disclose any further purchases by the Transcontinental Company in District 3, indicating that the effect of a favored-nation clause may be elimination of a pipe-line purchaser from a supply area after the buyer has negotiated a large-volume contract containing such a proviso.

In addition to the two pipe-line purchasers already mentioned, the Tennessee Gas Transmission Company was also a buyer in District 3 during the first half of 1948. Its contracts illustrated the diversity in purchase patterns that could prevail in a supply area at a given time. These contracts were not particularly small-volume agreements—the range was between 4.0 and 12.0 million MCF per year. The sellers were not distinguishable in the character of their operations, and the gas fields involved were not significantly different in size or location. In fact, with respect to two of the Tennessee Gas Transmission contracts, the gas fields were in close proximity to those involved in the Transcontinental purchase.

Yet despite such similarities, the Tennessee Gas Transmission contracts stipulated lower prices than other purchase agreements at the time, although actually the total consideration—including non-price elements—may not have been so different.

Basically, all of the Tennessee Gas Transmission purchase agreements included a 6.0 cent price for the first five years which then increased to 7.0 cents for a second five-year period. Prices for the last two five-year periods of the twenty-year term were not given and were to be set by negotiation. Consequently, for the ten-year firm period, the average price was no more than 6.5 cents per MCF. Assuming a continued escalation of 1.0 cent after ten years, the average price would be 7.5 cents per MCF for the twenty-year standard necessary to make these contracts comparable with the other supply agreements.

Although the Tennessee Gas Transmission contracts disclose a price level that is 2 to 3 cents lower than other agreements, one of their main features, which may have equalized the total consideration from the point of view of the sellers, was the shorter effective contract term. The possibility of upward price adjustment at the end of ten years could prove extremely attractive under circumstances where the amount of the increase was unpredictable but, in view of a rising price trend, was expected to be large.

A second feature which the sellers in the Tennessee Gas Transmission contracts were likely to have valued highly as an offset to a lower price were the relatively strong favored-nation clauses. These, along with other provisions, however, did vary somewhat and may have been due to the differential bargaining strength of sellers. For example, in two contracts, a conventional two-party favored-nation clause was provided with a relatively broad favored-nation area encompassing both Districts 2 and 3. These particular agreements, however, contained no tax-sharing provision. A third contract contained a favored-nation clause based only on District 3 but included a three-fourths buyer tax-sharing clause. Finally, a fourth contract, with the Sinclair Prairie Oil Company as seller, included a tax-sharing clause and a favored-nation provision which stipulated that "buyer was to meet the price of any transporter of gas for public consumption" in District 3. This was, in effect, a third-party favored-nation clause which was unusual for the time and the place. Its use in the above-mentioned contract represents the first appearance of such a clause in District 3.

It is clear, then, that the lower prices in the Tennessee Gas Transmission contracts were balanced by a considerable amount of contract price flexibility. Since long-term firm contracts were still being negotiated, this combination of price and non-price elements was presumably chosen by the pipe-line buyer. The purchaser may well have decided that immediate savings in the cost of purchased gas, which were not insignificant, would tend to offset future price increases. Moreover, the greater willingness of sellers to enter into contracts on these terms and to commit gas to the pipe-line system would have facilitated its rapid expansion. The buyer, in this case, may have had as much interest in the financial gains of pipe-line expansion as in minimizing long-term gas supply costs.

Similar to occurrences in other supply areas, District 3 illustrates the impact of a succession of new pipe-line projects upon prices and marketing patterns. The first of these was the Trunkline Gas Company, which ultimately became an affiliate of the Panhandle Eastern Pipe Line Co., supplying the latter's Michigan and Indiana markets. In contract activity covering the last half of 1948 and the first half of 1949, the Trunkline Gas Company negotiated three purchases in District 3, as well as three in the adjoining Southwest Louisiana gas supply area. With one exception, these were identical in price and other contract terms.

Thus, two of the District 3 agreements, as well as the three Louisiana contracts, stipulated a 9.0 cent price for the first year, increasing 0.2 cent each year for the next nine years, after which time negotiation was undertaken by five-year periods for the remainder of the twenty-year contract term. The exception— also the first District 3 contract—was an agreement between Trunkline and the Phillips Petroleum Company involving a relatively large volume from the Chocolate Bayou field. It provided for a price of 8.5 cents for the first year, increasing 0.2 cent for each of the next fourteen years, with negotiation based on stipulated minimums for the remainder of a twenty-five-year contract term. This contract, moreover, was less favorable to the seller than the other Trunkline purchases, since it contained, in addition to a slightly lower price, no provision for tax-sharing, and merely provided for a two-party favored-nation clause.

The remaining two Trunkline contracts in District 3 were negotiated in January, 1949, and were distinctive by their inclusion of the third-party favored-nation clause which had been present in earlier contracts completed in the Southwest Louisiana supply area. A relatively strong provision, it stipulated that the buyer would pay the same price to the seller as paid to any other seller or as paid by any other buyer to any other seller in an effective cost area. These contracts also raised the District 3 price level to approximately 11.0 cents per MCF from the previous level of 9.0 cents. While for a ten-year effective term the average contract price was only about 10.0 cents per MCF, if the twenty-year standard contract period were used and assuming a continuation of the 0.2 cent annual increase, then an average price of 11.0 cents per MCF would be obtained.

At the beginning of 1950, two new pipe-line projects sought gas supplies in District 3, resulting in a higher price level for large-volume large-reserve gas at approximately 12.0 cents per MCF. Balanced against other contract provisions, in particular the absence of third-party favored-nation clauses, it is probable that this price merely matched the 1949 level.

The buyers concerned were the Piedmont Natural Gas Company, Inc., and the Texas Illinois Natural Gas Pipeline Company. The former, seeking to serve markets in North Carolina and Virginia, was ultimately unsuccessful in securing Federal Power Commission certification. Still, its contracts, contingent upon certificate approval, were representative of price levels and contract patterns prevailing at the time. They stipulated average prices of 11.9 and 12.25 cents over effective terms of fifteen and twenty years, respectively. Conventional two-party favored-nation clauses were included, as were tax-sharing provisions.

A more authoritative indication of market conditions in this supply area was the two contracts of the Texas Illinois company. The larger resources of this project, its connections with Chicago utility interests, and the alternative supply sources available to it in Districts 2 and 4 evidence a buyer bargaining position as strong as any likely to be achieved. There is much to support the presumption that these contracts typify the results for the time of an arm's-length bargaining between equally strong market participants.

The more important of the two Texas Illinois contracts was with the Magnolia Petroleum Company, which also represented other sellers in the producing field. Of note was the large annual volume of 36.5 million MCF to be obtained from the Old Ocean field, one of the larger gas fields in the United States. The initial price was 11.0 cents for the first five years, escalating 1.0 cent in each subsequent five-year period of the twenty-year contract. In the last five-year period, however, the 14.0 cent price was a minimum, subject to negotiation. For the effective contract term of fifteen years, the average price was therefore 12.0 cents. A three-fourths buyer tax-sharing clause, as well as a two-party favored-nation clause, was included.

The favored-nation provision, however, was very limited in its scope and was no longer operative after the beginning of pipe-line operations, since it provided that only if the buyer paid a higher price in Districts 1, 2, 3, or 4 prior to first delivery of gas under the contract could the price be renegotiated. It is of some importance to the issue of competitive behavior in the gas field that, as late as 1950, a strong buyer could, with appropriate price concessions, still obtain a large-volume gas contract without a favored-nation clause and with a minimum degree of contract price flexibility.

The second Texas Illinois contract was negotiated with the Phillips Petroleum Company and represented an annual volume of about 10.0 million MCF from the Chocolate Bayou field. Detailed information on this agreement is limited, however, since it was not obtained from the same source as the other contracts.[7] The negotiation date of the contract is estimated to be near the

[7] Information on this contract was secured from Moody's *Public Utility Manual—1954*, 358, and from *Texas Illinois Natural Gas Pipe Line Co.*, 9 FPC (1950), 105. The exact date of this decision, which certificated the project, was June 13, 1950.

first part of 1950.

The term of the contract was twenty years from April 1, 1952, which—in the absence of other information—was assumed to be the effective contract term. No details were available concerning favored-nation provisions. The price stipulated in the contract, expressed on a 14.65 psi pressure base, was 9.0 cents for the first two years, increasing 0.44 cent each two-year period thereafter over the life of the contract. The average price for a twenty-year effective term, adjusted to a 16.7 psi pressure base, was estimated to be 12.5 cents per MCF, which is in general alignment with the level prevailing at the beginning of 1950.

Following the establishment of a 12.0 cent price level in District 3, field prices seemingly declined to approximately 8.0 cents per MCF. However, it may be well to call attention to the change in the character of the contract source materials for the period beginning in 1950. Prior to that time, the sources were the Kerr-Douglas contracts, which appeared to emphasize large-volume purchases. After 1949, FPC data compilations, which did not appear to be particularly selective with respect to volume, were used. There is, therefore, the possibility that a lower-priced, small-volume market could have been more clearly demonstrated before 1950, if a more extensive contract coverage had been available. On the other hand, there is a strong possibility that the gathering-system type of market might not have been very important then, in view of flush supplies obtainable at relatively low cost. It may have required the price increases of 1949 to make small-volume gas fields economical.

The two purchasers whose activity was dominant in the period 1950–51 were the United Gas Pipe Line Company and the Tennessee Gas Transmission Company. Their contracts were again characterized by small gas volumes, many sellers, and many small and scattered fields—all the features attributable to a gathering-system type of market. For example, the United Gas Pipe Line Company purchase arrangements in District 3 were similar to those made by this buyer in the other Texas Gulf Coast supply areas: no favored-nation clauses, except in one case; contract and effective terms of ten years or less, with average price of 8.0 cents or higher; and, in many instances, no tax-sharing clauses. The many contracts of the Tennessee Gas Transmission Company, extending through January, 1952, also exhibited great uniformity. These provided for twenty-year effective terms with a typical average price of 7.8 cents and included tax-sharing clauses and favored-nation provisions based on District 3.

Similar to price movements discerned in other supply areas, a new and higher level of prices was recorded in District 3 during the first half of 1952. It approximated 16.0 to 17.0 cents per MCF and was established over a period extending from April to August, 1952, in a group of contracts negotiated by the Texas Eastern Transmission Corporation. Marking the first re-entry of this pipe line into the District 3 market since 1948, these Texas Eastern contracts provided for an initial price of 14.25 cents, increasing 0.23 cent annually over a twenty-year effective term. The average price was thus approximately 16.5 cents. Moreover, virtually all contracts contained favored-nation provisions, apparently of a two-party variety, based in most instances on Texas and Louisiana gas fields, and all contracts included a seven-eighths buyer tax-sharing clause which was typical of Texas Eastern gas purchase agreements. These supply contracts, excluding certain renegotiations which did not appear to change quantities very much, did not secure for the Texas Eastern Company particularly large gas supplies.

The Texas Illinois Natural Gas Pipeline Company, however, was more successful in securing large gas volumes—a success apparently based upon the payment of an even higher price. Thus, out of a group of six contracts negotiated by Texas Illinois during a period from August, 1952, to January, 1953, five included the following price schedule, expressed on a 16.7 psi pressure base:

First five-year period	17.10¢
Second five-year period	18.24¢
Third five-year period	19.38¢
Fourth five-year period	19.38¢

Expressed on a 14.65 psi pressure base, the price for the first five years would have been 15.0 cents per MCF, with 1.0 cent escalation. The prices in the last three periods were minimums, subject to redetermination. On the basis of the actual five-year effective term, the price was 17.1 cents per MCF; on a standard twenty-year contract term, it would be about 18.5 cents per MCF.

Indicative of the substantial change in market conditions during 1952 is the fact that all except one of the Texas Illinois contracts contained a favored-nation clause which was apparently a two-party stipulation encompassing the District 3 supply area. It was absent only in the smallest volume contract. More significant, however, was the acceptance by the purchaser of five-year price redetermination with the considerable contract price flexibility afforded by such a provision.

While the Texas Illinois contracts were establishing a large-volume price level of approximately 18.5 cents, a second market for gas existed during 1952 at a 13.0 cent price. This price level was again associated with a small-volume gathering-system market, as evidenced by a group of Tennessee Gas Transmission contracts, covering the period from June, 1952, to February, 1953. Initial prices in these agreements were generally about 11.5 cents, with an average price of 13.0 cents over a twenty-year effective contract period, and—as before—all contained two-party favored-nation clauses with tax-sharing provisos.

A further indication of the character of the large-volume market for gas in District 3 is to be found in a gas purchase agreement negotiated by the Iroquois Gas Corporation, dated December, 1952. The interest in this contract results not only from its being among the first of the direct-distributor purchases in the gas fields of the Southwest but also from the price level which it established. Moreover, it received considerable attention in Congressional hearings concerned with the amendment of the Natural Gas Act.[8]

---

[8] *Hearings—H. R. 4560, 1692, 1696; Hearings—S. 1853, 697, 1444.* It may be noted that, in the legislative discussion, references to field prices in District 3 were made which substantiate the price level evidenced in the contracts. It was asserted that ". . . by later 1952 the current market price for pipe-line quality gas and reserves of the magnitude of Sheridan was well in excess of 15 cents per thousand cubic feet. Even smaller reserves were commanding 12.5 cents per

The Iroquois Gas Corporation, a distributor of gas in the Buffalo area of New York, arranged for a common carrier transportation of its gas purchases via the facilities of the Tennessee Gas Transmission Company, which was already supplying it with a portion of its gas requirements.[9] The need for a direct-distributor purchase of gas was occasioned by the unwillingness of the Tennessee Gas Transmission Company to supply additional gas to Iroquois, on the grounds that Tennessee Gas Transmission's attempt to contract for new gas would trigger favored-nation clauses in its older contracts.[10]

In the Iroquois contract, the seller was the Shell Oil Company, which also represented other owners in the Sheridan gas field. The contract had a term of twenty years and contained a favored-nation clause, based on District 3, and a tax-sharing provision. The initial price was set at 16.5 cents per MCF (on a 14.65 psi base) for the first three years, with 1.0 cent escalator increases in each subsequent four-year period to a final price of 20.5 cents. On the 16.7 psi base, the initial price would be 18.8 cents per MCF with 1.14 cent increases in the periods noted above. The average price over a twenty-year term would then equal 21.3 cents per MCF.

It is this twenty-one cent price which is shown in Figure 6, since the FPC contract sources gave no indication that a shorter effective term was valid. However, statements in the Congressional hearings on H. R. 4560 assert that the contract provides for a renegotiation of the price each four years, with minimum prices that are not less than the prices already stipulated or less than the average of the three highest prices paid for comparable gas in District 3.[11] Under these circumstances, the contract period within which prices would be firm is only four years. This is in line with the five-year effective terms in the Texas Illinois contracts of the same period.

thousand cubic feet." (It is presumed that these prices were at 14.65 psi.) See statement of W. B. Golush, Shell Oil Co., *Hearings—S. 1853,* 1446.

[9] See Opinion No. 261, *Tennessee Gas Transmission Co.,* 12 FPC (1953), 311, for the certification of the common carrier service.

[10] *Hearings—H. R. 4560,* 1692.

[11] *Ibid., 1692.*

This contract, with its peak price, marks the entry into the gas field market of a new type of buyer. Such a distribution company buyer, concerned with a particular final consumer market, would be better able than a pipe line to gauge the upper limit of the price it could and would be willing to pay for new gas supplies. Furthermore, it would not be restrained in its bargaining by the existence of old favored-nation contracts. Under the circumstances, prices in this kind of contract are likely to be above those which would prevail in a strictly pipe-line market.

A final indication of the price level and price pattern in the District 3 supply area was provided by a purchase agreement not included in the price chart. In a contract dated January 5, 1954, the Phillips Petroleum Company agreed to sell the Texas Illinois Natural Gas Pipeline Company additional gas from the Chocolate Bayou field.[12] These two concerns had previously negotiated a contract for gas supplies from this source in 1950, and that agreement was still in effect on its original terms.[13]

In the 1954 contract, the Texas Illinois Company paid a price of 15.0 cents per MCF on a 14.65 psi pressure base. Measured on a 16.7 psi base, the price was equal to 17.1 cents, or the same as initial prices in the longer-term 1953 contracts of this buyer.[14] The quantity of gas involved in this contract was exceptionally large for the supply area, ranging between a minimum of 30,000 MCF and a maximum of 60,000 MCF per day. On an annual basis, the maximum volume would be approximately 20 million MCF. The possibility of varying its daily purchases within a fairly wide range would be of great advantage to the pipe-line purchaser, since this supply could then be used to meet fluctuating peak requirements.

The distinctive feature of this contract, however, was its provision that the agreement was to run for only one year—to January 1, 1955—and thereafter until terminated on forty-eight hours notice. At the end of 1954, the contract was apparently renewed

12 Moody's *Public Utility Manual—1954*, 358.
13 *Ibid.*, 358.
14 The purchases may have been needed because of difficulties encountered by Texas Illinois in actually obtaining the gas volumes committed to it under older contracts in the La Gloria field. See *Hearings—H. R. 4560*, 76–77.

at the same price and for the same quantity but with the agreement to extend to January 1, 1956, and thereafter until terminated on forty-eight hours notice.[15]

To conclude the review of contract data in this particular supply area, the representative field prices which have been derived may be summarized. These are estimates and are adjusted to reflect an average contract price over a standard twenty-year contract period.

REPRESENTATIVE FIELD PRICES: TEXAS GULF COAST—
DISTRICT 3

Large Volume	Cents per MCF (16.7 psi)
1945	5.0
1946	5.0
1947	(no data)
1948	9.0
1949	11.0
1950	12.0
1951	12.0
1952	18.0
1953	18.0–20.0
Small Volume	
1950	8.0
1951	8.0– 9.0
1952	13.0
1953	13.0–16.0

[15] Moody's *Public Utility Manual—1955*, 743.

CHAPTER 6

Louisiana Gulf Coast Gas Supply Areas

AMONG THE IDENTIFIABLE GAS SUPPLY AREAS, two of the more important are to be found in the Louisiana Gulf Coast region. Not only has there been considerable postwar exploration for petroleum here, with the attendant discoveries of gas, but future oil and gas development through offshore drilling is likely to be centered in the area. Furthermore, the present importance of the region as a gas supply source is well evidenced by the concentration within it of the large-volume gas purchases negotiated by new pipe-line projects since 1952.

A. SOUTHWEST LOUISIANA

The first of the two supply areas which together constitute the Louisiana Gulf Coast unit is that encompassing southwestern Louisiana. The exact boundaries of the supply area are given in the appendix, and the field price observations obtained from the contract data are presented in Figure 7. And, in accordance with procedures followed previously, the structure of the supply area is summarized in Table 27.

The supply area, in this case, contained forty-seven sellers making sales in a total of eighty-three separate contracts. In spite of the fact that gas volume data are more complete in these contracts than in other areas, the number of large sellers did not differ greatly from that found in the other supply areas. Thus, only sixteen sellers had annual gas volumes of 5.0 million MCF or more. In this supply area, as in District 3, there was a preponderance of the major petroleum companies among the large sellers, although their size ranking in the two supply areas was not the same.

Nine purchasers were identified, of which four were pipe

Louisiana Gulf Coast Gas Supply Areas

Table 27

ANALYSIS OF NATURAL GAS PURCHASE CONTRACTS
IN THE SOUTHWEST LOUISIANA GAS SUPPLY AREA, 1944–53

RANK OF SELLER BY ANNUAL GAS VOLUME	Annual Gas Volume M³CF	Number of Contracts	Number of Buyers
1. The Pure Oil Co.	81.0	1	1
2. Marine Gathering Co.	39.5	2	2
3. Sohio Petroleum Co.	38.5	3	3
4. Southern Production Co.	36.0	1	1
5. Pan American Production Co.	32.3	1	1
6. The Texas Company	31.2	2	1
7. Shell Oil Co.	29.3	4	2
8. Superior Oil Co.	28.1	3	3
9. Magnolia Petroleum Co.	26.7	3	3
10. Union Oil Co., et al.	23.0	1	1
11. Sun Oil Co.	21.4	4	4
12. Union Sulphur & Oil Corp.	16.3	2	1
13. Hassie Hunt Trust	6.0	1	1
14. Grubb & Hawkins	5.9	1	1
15. Stanolind Oil & Gas Co.	5.1	3	2
16. Phillips Petroleum Co.	5.0	3	3
17. Natural Gas & Oil Corp.	4.1	3	2
18. O'Meara Brothers, et al.	3.2	1	1
19. Tide Water Associated Oil Co.	2.9	1	1
20. Gulf Refining Corp.	2.4	2	2
21. Fred W. Bates, et al.	2.2	2	1
22. Mar-Tex Realization Corp.	2.2	1	1
21 sellers reporting less than 2.0 M³CF of annual gas sales	21.2	24	
Subtotals	463.5	69	
4 sellers not included in above listing, having contracts with indefinite gas volumes	—	4	
Renegotiated and other indefinite gas volume contracts	—	10	
Totals	463.5	83	

lines active in the Texas Gulf Coast region. These included the Tennessee Gas Transmission Company, the Transcontinental Gas Pipe Line Corporation, Trunkline Gas Company, and the United Gas Pipe Line Company. In addition, an important buyer was the Texas Gas Transmission Corporation, contracting directly and through its two subsidiaries—the Texas Northern Gas Corporation and the Louisiana Natural Gas Corporation. Other purchasers were the Southern Natural Gas Company, negotiating a single large-volume contract; two direct-distributor purchasers—the United Fuel Gas Company and the Niagara Gas Transmission Company; and a relatively new pipe-line project—the American Louisiana Pipe Line Company—which entered the supply area in 1953.

Turning to an analysis of price levels, no buying activity was recorded in the contract data sources prior to 1948. Consequently, the first of the gas purchase contracts recorded were dated in the middle of that year and were agreements negotiated by the Transcontinental Gas Pipe Line Corporation. These contracts, one with the Sun Oil Company and the other with the Union Oil Company, provided for an average contract price of 9.5 cents per MCF on a fifteen-year effective term, a three-fourths buyer tax-sharing provision, favored-nation clauses, and a buyer obligation to pay the 1.0 cent Louisiana gas-gathering tax. Based on this information, a field price of 11.0 cents per MCF for the standard twenty-year term was estimated.

One of the above Transcontinental contracts negotiated with the Union Oil Company contained a third-party favored-nation clause. In a subsequent effort to remove this proviso, a new contract was negotiated with the seller during 1953, in which the favored-nation clause was modified, additional reserves dedicated, and a new price established. The new prices were set at 16.0 cents per MCF (15.025 psi pressure base) for the first five years, increasing 1.0 cent in each of three subsequent five-year periods.[1]

Immediately following the Transcontinental purchases, the Trunkline Gas Company entered this market in the middle of 1948, negotiating three contracts—the largest of which was with

[1] Moody's *Public Utility Manual—1955*, 54. See also *Hearings—S. 1853*, 1027.

the Superior Oil Company. Another seller was the Sohio Petroleum Company, the contract with which was completed as late as March, 1949. These purchase agreements were alike in providing for 9.9 cent average prices over ten-year effective terms, as well as third-party favored-nation clauses. In addition, the buyer was required to pay the first ½ cent of the Louisiana gas-gathering tax, and thereafter taxes were to be shared three-fourths buyer and one-fourth seller. Assuming a continuation of the escalation stipulated for the first ten years, and adding the ½ cent gathering tax, the average cost of gas under this contract for a twenty-year term would be approximately 11.5 cents per MCF. It is therefore possible to conclude that the large-volume price level in this supply area during 1948 was about 11.0 cents per MCF, a level higher than that recorded anywhere else.

During 1949, two other pipe lines negotiated large-volume purchases in the supply area. One was the United Gas Pipe Line Company, which completed an agreement in March, 1949, with the Magnolia Petroleum Company and other sellers for an annual gas volume of 36.5 million MCF in a contract which ran for ten years and year-to-year thereafter. An initial price of 9.0 cents was set for the first five years, escalating to 10.0 cents in the second five years with a .25 cent dehydration charge to be paid by the buyer. The buyer was also to pay the Louisiana gathering tax, in addition to one-half of any new taxes. Of particular note was the absence of any form of favored-nation provision. Adjusting for these various factors and assuming a twenty-year contract term, the total consideration in this agreement was approximately 11.75 cents. Strong buyers, in this case, were able to avoid the favored-nation provisos found in other contracts of the same place and period without the payment of a large price premium.

Price levels and market behavior in the large-volume market were further illustrated in an agreement between the Tennessee Gas Transmission Company and the Sohio Petroleum Company dated May, 1949. The contract term was twenty years, but the effective period was no more than eight years, because of a price redetermination proviso. Prices in the agreement were initially 9.25 cents, increasing 1.0 cent in each four-year period.

Beginning with the third period, however, "prices were to be re-determined and set equal to the average of the three highest prices being paid for like quantities by transporters of gas for public consumption within the pricing area but not less than those stated under the contract rate." The pricing area consisted of the various parishes that make up the Southwest Louisiana gas supply area as defined. In addition to the price redetermination provision, an ordinary two-party favored-nation clause was included, and the buyer was to bear the 1.0 cent gathering tax and three-fourths of additional taxes. Calculated on the standard twenty-year period used for purposes of comparison and including taxes, the average price was approximately 12.25 cents per MCF.

Aside from these early 1949 contracts, no other large-volume agreements for this gas supply area were recorded in the contract sources until almost a year later. At the beginning of 1950, the Tennessee Gas Transmission Company negotiated an agreement with the Marine Gathering Company, which was apparently a jointly owned affiliate of the Kerr-McGee Oil Industries and the Phillips Petroleum Company.[2] The price and terms of this contract, as recorded in the contract sources, were identical with the 1949 Sohio Petroleum Company agreement, except for the omission of the price redetermination clause. There was some indication that prices in the Marine Gathering contract could be redetermined at the end of eight years but, since this was not certain, a twenty-year effective term was assumed for it. Thus, the first of the large-volume 1950 contracts established a price level of 12.25 cents on a twenty-year term, including the 1.0 cent gas gathering tax. This was not different from the price estimated for the previous year and serves to confirm a 1949 price level of approximately 12.0 cents per MCF.

A short while after, however, in a contract with the Phillips Petroleum Company dated June, 1950, the Tennessee Gas Transmission Company paid a price which—with the inclusion of the gathering tax—approximated 13.78 cents on a twenty-year term. The unit prices and escalation periods of the agreement were the

2 See contract between the Marine Gathering Co. and the Niagara Gas Transmission Co., *Hearings—S. 1853*, 1608.

same as the two earlier Tennessee Gas Transmission contracts, but the measurement base of the contract had been changed to a 14.65 psi base from a pressure base of 16.7 psi, resulting in a price increase of approximately 14 per cent.

Since conversion from a 14.65 psi base to the 16.7 psi base used in the contract sources resulted in unit prices that were irregular, instead of falling on even values such as 11.0 or 11.5, it was possible to identify the agreements in the contract sources which were originally quoted on the 14.65 psi base. In the Southwest Louisiana gas supply area, prices were apparently first quoted on the 14.65 psi base at the beginning of 1950. In the other Gulf Coast supply areas, a wider use of the 14.65 psi base also dates from 1950. Furthermore, the transition from a 16.7 psi base to the 14.65 base in the various supply areas—including Southwest Louisiana—displayed no marked pattern of uniformity. Some agreements after 1950 were still being negotiated with prices expressed on the 16.7 psi base. By 1952 and 1953, however, the use of the 14.65 psi base was predominant.

Following the Tennessee Gas Transmission contract, the United Gas Pipe Line Company re-entered the market, concluding an unusual agreement with the Pure Oil Company in July, 1950. The contract provided for an exceptionally large quantity of 81.0 million MCF annually under stipulations such as the following:

> When seller's reserves are 2½ trillion cubic feet, buyer will take 81,000,000 Mcf; when seller's reserves exceed 2½ trillion cubic feet, buyer will take the above plus 85% of the ratio of 36½ million cubic feet for each billion over 2½ trillion cubic feet.

On the basis of 2½ trillion cubic feet of reserves, the annual volume in this contract would represent a thirty-year supply. It is possible that these gas reserves were part of an offshore supply, since they were generally located in the Eugene Island area of St. Mary Parish, Louisiana.

The contract was unusual in other respects: It contained no favored-nation clause and no tax proviso. Moreover, the contract

183

term was to run for twenty-five years, which was also the effective term, since no redetermination or similar provisions were indicated in the contract sources. The price agreed upon was 10.0 cents for the first ten years, 12.5 cents for the second ten years, and 15.0 cents thereafter. Averaged over the twenty-five-year effective term, the price was then 12.0 cents per MCF.

Two similar contracts for the same Eugene Island area were also negotiated by the United Gas Pipe Line Company in 1951. Both of these contained the same basic price and contract stipulations as the earlier arrangement. The first contract, dated in February, 1951, involved a seller group including the Newmont Oil Company, Continental Oil Company, and the Magnolia Petroleum Company and was evidently a large-volume agreement —although no specific quantity could be assigned to it. A second agreement, dated December, 1951, with the Sun Oil Company as seller, provided for a medium gas volume of 10.6 million MCF. As noted, the two contracts were identical with the 1950 agreement except for the inclusion of a one-half buyer tax-sharing clause. In the Newmont Oil agreement, the buyer was also to pay gathering taxes in effect on June 1, 1950.

In accounting for this group of contracts with their lower prices, long terms, and exceptionally large volumes, speculation suggests two possibilities: first, accessibility of the gas may have been such that costly gathering and transportation facilities would have had to be built by the purchaser; second, the beginning and continuation of the Korean hostilities may have induced the sellers to commit their gas for fear that new pipe-line projects would be indefinitely postponed because of anticipated steel shortages.

The contracts reviewed up to this point represented the large-volume transactions through 1951. Contract quantities suitable for new projects were not recorded again until late 1952 and 1953. Thus, these purchase agreements are a distinct unit of considerable importance for the market behavior history of this supply area. In reveiwing them, one feature stands out: the considerable diversity in contract terms and conditions. The extent of that diversity is well demonstrated in the following summary:

Date	Buyer—Seller	Average Price*	Favored-Nation	Tax Clause†	Effective Term
		(cents)			(years)
4/48	Transco—Sun Oil	11.0	2–P, FN	¾	15
5/48	Transco—Union Oil	11.0	3–P, FN	¾	15
6/48	Trunkline—Superior	11.4	3–P, FN	¾	10
3/49	Trunkline—Sohio	11.4	3–P, FN	¾	10
3/49	United—Magnolia	11.75	No FN	½	10
4/49	Tenn. GT—Sohio	12.25	2–P, FN	¾	8
3/50	Tenn. GT—Marine	12.25	2–P, FN	¾	8
6/50	Tenn. GT—Phillips	13.78	2–P, FN	¾	8
7/50	United—Pure Oil	12.0‡	No FN	None	25
2/51	United—Newmont Oil	13.0‡	No FN	½	25
12/51	United—Sun Oil	12.0‡	No FN	½	25

* Adjusted to a standard twenty-year contract period and includes gathering taxes.
† Represents buyer's share.
‡ Based on a twenty-five-year term.

No obvious uniformity can be discerned from this tabulation, either in the average contract price or in the next most important item, the effective contract period. With respect to the total consideration in each purchase agreement, it is even more difficult to find an overt pattern of uniformity. Even though small differences in price are likely to be critical, the total consideration must ultimately influence buyers in their choice among alternative selling offers.

If a system of noncompetitive collusive seller action were to be established in a natural gas field market, it would have to be based upon a high degree of uniformity in total consideration of contract price and contract provisions. In the absence of such uniformity, any individual seller would be uncertain that he possessed the same opportunity to negotiate a sale as others and that he was not being adversely affected by the undercutting of other sellers. The only alternative system of noncompetitive seller co-operation would be one based upon the assignment of market shares and quotas or the allocation of customers. Such a system would appear impracticable under the conditions characterizing gas field markets.

Consequently, a persisting uniformity in price—where price means total consideration—would be the relevant test of non-competitive behavior in natural gas field markets. By this standard, there was little or no evidence of noncompetitive behavior in the group of market transactions examined. Indeed, it seems that each transaction was formed by distinctive and individual bargaining forces, and the different results—for contracts closely related in time—point to rivalry and bargaining in an imperfect market. If noncompetitive seller action was a factor in this supply area, it would have to be confirmed by evidence other than the price results of the market transactions recorded. Noncompetitive price levels could be the product of certain structural features of the field market, but that is a question not under present consideration.

While significant large-volume transactions in this supply area were not found again until 1952–53, a small-volume market was recorded in the contract data beginning in 1950. This small-volume market, however, was somewhat unusual, since its price level was almost equal to the large-volume price prevailing at the end of 1949. Although the large-volume price subsequently rose, the small-volume price level remained stable through 1953. Both of these characteristics were at variance with the patterns discovered in other supply areas.

Representative field prices in the small-volume market are to be found in a group of purchase contracts recorded during the last half of 1950 and the first part of 1951, in which the buyer was the Texas Gas Transmission Corporation. Generally, a price level of approximately 11.5 cents per MCF over a twenty-year term was established in these contracts since the basic price schedule in virtually all agreements stipulated an initial price of 10.0 cents for the first five years, increasing 1.0 cent in each subsequent five-year period for twenty years. The effective contract term, however, varied markedly among the agreements as a result of different price redetermination periods. Apparently, the price redetermination period was an important bargaining counter in these contract arrangements.

Other features in these Texas Gas Transmission contracts included seven-eighths tax-sharing provisos, but, in most cases, the buyer was not obligated to pay the 1.0 cent gathering tax—although, in the last of these agreements, near the middle of 1951, market conditions evidently made it necessary for the purchaser to accept the gathering tax obligation. Furthermore, favored-nation clauses were commonly present. These clauses were seemingly two-party arrangements and were generally based either on a narrowly defined area within Southwest Louisiana or—more frequently—on a 50 mile radius from the point of delivery. In many cases, operation of the favored-nation provisions was postponed; they were not to go into effect until after January 1, 1952, the date when most gas deliveries were to begin.

A second buyer during 1951, negotiating ten supply contracts, was the United Gas Pipe Line Company. Its purchase activity, however, did not disturb the prevailing 11.5 cent price level. The slightly lower average price recorded in the United Gas contracts reflects a ten-year legal contract period. An additional feature was the absence of favored-nation clauses. These two features were typical of United Gas purchase contracts, both in this supply area and elsewhere.

After 1951, the lower-priced small-volume market was preempted by the Texas Northern Gas Corporation and the Louisiana Natural Gas Corporation, both of which were gathering subsidiaries of the Texas Gas Transmission Corporation. For the two-year period of 1952–53, the price level and the pattern of contracts negotiated by these buyers were held stable at the 11.5 cent level prevailing earlier. Most of their contracts had twenty-year effective terms, providing for a price of 10.0 cents for the first five-year period, escalating 1.0 cent in each five-year period thereafter. Other provisions were generally similar to the earlier Texas Gas Transmission contracts.[3] On the basis of these purchase contracts, it may be concluded that an 11.5 cent price level characterized the small-volume gathering-system type of market

[3] A group of seven contracts in the nature of spot market purchases was also negotiated. These were mostly on a year-to-year basis with a non-escalated price of 7.78 cents per MCF. An 8.0 cent price might be viewed as a prevailing spot price level for the period.

in Southwest Louisiana during 1952–53. This level of prices was remarkably stable over an extended period beginning in 1950— a condition which may have been due to the predominant activity of the Texas Gas Transmission Corporation and its subsidiaries.

The last section of this analysis of the Southwest Louisiana supply area relates to the large-volume transactions of 1952–53. As noted before, by 1952, the Louisiana Gulf Coast had become the most important supply source for new or expanded pipe-line projects. For that period at least, large gas reserves for such undertakings were apparently unavailable elsewhere, and—in view of its tideland potentialities—the area is also likely to remain one of the most important future sources of large gas reserves. Therefore, the large-volume purchase transactions in this supply area would have a special significance in the establishment of a field price level for new-project gas supplies.

The first supply contract to set the large-volume pattern during the period under consideration was dated January, 1952. It was not an arm's length transaction, since it was negotiated by the Southern Natural Gas Company with the Southern Production Company, an affiliate of the pipe-line buyer. Nevertheless, the transaction would be valuable as a reflection of market conditions. Under the purchase agreement, a large annual gas volume of 36.0 million MCF was committed for twenty years at an initial price of 11.4 cents, with elaborate provisions for a rapid escalation to 17.1 cents in the last nine years of the contract term. Since the agreement had no provisions for price renegotiation or for favored-nation adjustment, the effective contract term was twenty years, and the average price over this period would be 15.8 cents per MCF. It is to be noted that this contract was negotiated at the same time that the buyer completed a number of agreements of similar price and contract results with independent sellers in the Southeast Louisiana supply area.

Subsequent to this contract, the large-volume new-project market was represented in the purchase agreements negotiated by the United Fuel Gas Company and the American Louisiana Pipe Line Company. Both were completely new pipe-line projects—

the former negotiating its purchases between May and December, 1952, while the latter acquired its gas supplies during the last half of 1953. The great interest and importance attached to these purchase agreements warrant a detailed treatment of their content and background.

The United Fuel Gas Company, a part of the Columbia Gas System, Inc., which transports and distributes gas in the Appalachian area, was a direct-distributor buyer. Having no pipe-line facilities into the Gulf Coast gas supply areas, the United Fuel Gas Company intended to have a common carrier transportation service performed for it by the Gulf Interstate Gas Company.[4] The latter concern was not affiliated with United Fuel and was organized expressly to gather and transport the gas of the buyer to a point of connection with United Fuel's system in West Virginia.

Four of the United Fuel contracts were alike in all important respects.[5] Although legal contract terms were for twenty to twenty-two years, beginning with initial delivery or some cut-off date, prices were to be renegotiated after the tenth year, so that the effective contract term could not be considered greater than ten years. The total quantity of gas involved in the four contracts was 41.0 million MCF per year. While some of the individual contracts specified small amounts of gas, they may be viewed as part of the large-volume market, since they were evidently located so that economical use was made of whatever facilities would be needed to tap the larger volumes. It may be noted, too, that annual gas volumes were based on 1,000 MCF for each 8,000,-000 MCF of reserves. As more reserves were proven, volumes could increase. The contracts also contained "standard" favored-

---

[4] Opinion No. 251, *Gulf Interstate Gas Co.,* 12 FPC (1953), 116.

[5]
Seller	Date	Location
Pan American Production Co.	May 27, 1952	South Pecan Lake, Cameron Ph., La.
Texas Company	Nov. 8, 1952	East Mud Lake, Cameron Ph., La.
Magnolia Petroleum Company	Dec. 19, 1952	Gum Cave Field, Cameron Ph., La.
Sun Oil Company	Dec. 30, 1952	Ellis Field, Acadia Ph., La.

nation clauses. These were presumed to be two-party type provisos whose area coverage varied slightly in different agreements
but, in general, included those parishes of Louisiana which define the Southwest Louisiana gas supply area.

Concerning the pricing arrangements and price levels in
these agreements, an initial price of 17.78 cents per MCF at 16.7
psi was established, which escalated 0.44 cent each year for ten
years. Thereafter, prices were to be renegotiated at the beginning
of each five-year period but were not to be less than the contract
price for the preceding period.[6] In addition, an increase in price
was stipulated if the recoverable reserves committed in the contract were to increase.[7] Under these provisions, substantial price
increases—as much as 2.22 cents per MCF—were possible. The
provisos dealing with recoverable reserves varied slightly in terms
among the four contracts. Joined with some small variations in
the area coverage of the favored-nation clauses, these seemed to
be the only elements of bargaining differentiation among the
contracts.

Based on the ten-year effective term, the average price in the
United Fuel contracts was 19.75 cents per MCF. But added to
this was the obligation of the buyer to pay the 1.0 cent gathering
tax, as well as three-fourths of additional taxes. On a twenty-year
basis obtained by assuming a continuation of the same yearly price

[6] Measured on the 14.65 psi basis on which the contracts were originally
negotiated (and the basis on which their price terms are usually quoted in various
references, e.g., Congressional hearings), the initial price was 16.0 cents per MCF,
escalating 0.4 cent each year.

[7] The exact stipulation in the largest of the four contracts, the Pan American Production Co. agreement, was as follows: "Prices to increase 1.11 cents
per MCF if net recoverable reserves exceed one trillion ft. and 2.22 cents per
MCF if they exceed 1½ trillion ft." This Pan American contract was amended
on January 2, 1953. The effected changes were, on the one hand, to exclude the
"tidelands area" from the coverage of the favored-nation clause. On the other
hand, the seller received concessions that made price adjustments based on
changes in recoverable reserves both more likely and more favorable. The new
provision stated that prices were to increase 0.56 cent per MCF if reserves exceeded 750 billion cubic feet; 1.11 cent if over 900 billion cubic feet; 1.67 cent
if over 1 trillion, 124.5 billion cubic feet; and 2.22 cents if over 1 trillion, 349.5
billion cubic feet. It is evident that provisions such as these were valuable considerations, especially in this supply area, where the direction of reserve adjustments was likely to be upward as the region became more fully explored and
developed.

escalation, average prices would approximate 23.0 cents per MCF, including the 1.0 cent gathering tax.

The other United Fuel contracts attributable to the Southwest Louisiana gas supply area established an even higher price level.[8] Although four separate agreements are involved, they have been grouped together to form a single contract observation. Since all refer to the same supply source—the Erath field in Louisiana—they bear the same date and are otherwise identical except for annual gas volumes. The largest seller of the four was the Texas Company, and—for present purposes—the contract observation has been assigned to it.[9]

The Erath field contract differed from the other United Fuel contracts in only one respect besides price. Based upon the information available in the contract sources, it was apparently a twenty-year agreement with no provision for renegotiation. However, its favored-nation clause would have assured the Erath field contract the equivalent of any price adjustments obtained at the end of ten years by the other United Fuel supply contracts in Louisiana. The pricing provision of the contract provided for an initial rate—converted to a 16.7 psi base—of 22.23 cents per MCF, increasing 0.22 cent per MCF "for each of 19 consecutive years, and 26.22¢ MCF thereafter."[10] Over the twenty-year term, the average price was 24.45 cents per MCF; if a buyer obligation for the 1.0 cent gathering tax were added, the price would be approximately 25.5 cents per MCF.

A final aspect of the Erath field contract may be noted. Its

[8] The higher price in these contracts for gas from the Erath Field was explained on the basis "of the large volume of gas concentrated in that field and because we were able to negotiate certain contract provisions giving us flexibility of take, which do not prevail with respect to other Southwest contracts." See letter of Mr. George S. Young, Columbia Gas System, Inc., *Hearings—H. R. 4560*, 1698.

[9] The Texas Company supplied an annual gas volume of 17.1 million MCF; the Tide Water Associated Oil Co., 4.1 million MCF; the Humble Oil and Refining Co., 3.0 million MCF; and various minority owners, 0.5 million MCF, for a total annual volume of 24.7 million MCF. These volumes have been combined and shown as a single observation in Figure 7.

[10] On the 14.65 psi pressure base, on which the contract was negotiated, the initial price was 20.0 cents per MCF, escalating 0.2 cent each year to 24.0 cents in the twentieth year. See Opinion No. 251, *Gulf Interstate Gas Co.*, 12 FPC (1953), 116.

favored-nation clause, unlike the other United Fuel contracts, included in its area coverage the "tideland area bordering the Louisiana Gulf Coast." Since future large gas reserves are likely to be available only in offshore gas and oil fields, the proviso may have considerable value to the seller.

Shortly after the United Fuel contracts were completed, the Niagara Gas Transmission Company, Ltd. acquired—on February 6, 1953—a substantial volume of gas in an agreement with the Marine Gathering Company. In this instance, the purchaser was also a non-pipe-line buyer, while the seller represented the Phillips Petroleum Company and the Kerr-McGee Oil Industries. On the same date, moreover, the buyer had negotiated another large-volume contract in District 4 with the Phillips Petroleum Company.

The contract term in the Niagara Gas agreement was approximately twenty years, and the effective term was ostensibly the same, since no provision for renegotiation was recorded in the contract sources. A broad third-party favored-nation clause was included, however, which seemed to permit price adjustment at any time. The clause was "based on average of three highest prices paid by anyone."

Price in this contract was initially 18.2 cents per MCF, escalating every four years to a final level of 22.7 cents per MCF. Assuming a twenty-year effective term, average price was 20.5 cents per MCF. Since the contract sources gave insufficient detail, it is not known whether or not gathering taxes were to be borne by the purchaser.

The last group of contracts in the Southwest Louisiana supply area which evidenced the prevailing level of prices for large-volume gas in 1953 were those negotiated by the American Louisiana Pipe Line Company. This concern, an affiliate of the American Natural Gas Company and the Michigan-Wisconsin Pipe Line Company, was organized to transport gas from Louisiana to Detroit, the initial gas reserves for the project being obtained under the agreements to be reviewed.

The contracts were negotiated with various large petroleum producing companies.[11] The legal term of contract for most of these agreements was stated as twenty-three years from June 1, 1953. In two, however, it was specified as the "life of the field" or until all the committed reserves had been delivered. No specific data concerning gas volumes were available; the contract sources merely noted that annual volumes were to be based on recoverable reserves, although gas volumes were unquestionably large. For example, it is known that the recoverable reserves available from all Louisiana producers to the American Louisiana Pipe Line Company were equal to 2.6 trillion cubic feet as of September, 1953. This quantity exceeds an annual volume of 100 million MCF over a twenty-five year period.[12]

The American Louisiana supply contracts were negotiated at two price schedules not widely different from one another. Thus, in one group of contracts, an initial price of 20.28 cents was established for the first five-year period, increasing to 23.06 cents in the second five years, then to 25.84 cents in the third five years, and finally to 28.62 cents.[13] Taken on a twenty-year basis, the average contract price would be equal to 24.45 cents per MCF. Since the contract sources indicated that stipulated prices were to be minimum rates after the first five years, it may be inferred that the contract provided for five-year price redetermination

[11] Seller	Date	Location
Stanolind Oil & Gas Co.	6/1/53	Bayou Mallet Field, and others, La.
Stanolind Oil & Gas Co.	6/1/53	Lewisburg Field and South Jennings, La.
Superior Oil Co.	7/17/53	Cameron Ph., and offshore, La.
* { Gulf Refining Co.	10/26/53	} Krotz Springs Field, La.
{ Humble Oil & Refining Co.	10/29/53	
* { British-American Oil Producing Co.	11/6/53	} Cameron Field, La.
{ Kerr-McGee Oil Industries	11/6/53	

* Two separate contracts with same price, terms, and field.

[12] Opinion No. 276, *American Louisiana Pipe Line Co.*, Federal Power Commission (September 30, 1954).

[13] These prices were on a 16.7 psi pressure base. On a 14.65 psi base, prices were estimated to be 17.75 cents initially, increasing 2.5 cents in each 5-year period.

periods. Therefore, in charting the price of these contracts, an effective term of five years was assumed, with the price in the first period equal to the initial level of 20.28 cents.

The other American Louisiana contracts differed from the above with respect to price, establishing the following price schedule—at 16.7 psi:[14]

First five-year period	22.23¢
Second five-year period	25.01¢
Third five-year period	27.79¢
Thereafter	30.57¢

On a twenty-year basis, the average price would equal 26.4 cents per MCF. But, again, the prices were declared minima after the first five years, and, therefore, a five-year effective term should be assumed. In two of these agreements, term of contract was specified as "life of the field." This would tend to reinforce the inference that some price renegotiation rights were available to sellers. It is unlikely that such an indefinite contract period would otherwise have been accepted by the seller.

Concerning tax-sharing, the contract sources were vague, stating only that the buyer was to bear a "portion of increases in certain taxes." No direct information was given concerning the assignment of the 1.0 cent Louisiana gathering tax. From other sources, however, information was obtained which attributed a 20.5 cent price to the American Louisiana contracts.[15] This appears to be the 19.5 cent price—at 14.65 psi—plus the gathering tax. If the gathering tax is included, the American Louisiana contracts resulted in average contract prices—at 16.7 psi—over a standard twenty-year term of 25.5 cents and 27.5 cents per MCF. These levels represented an increase over the United Fuel schedules of a year earlier, which—on the same basis—equaled 23.0 cents

[14] Converted to a 14.65 psi base, these prices were estimated to be 19.5 cents per MCF, increasing 2.5 cents in each 5-year period.

[15] *Natural Gas Pipe Line Company of America, et al.*, Docket No. G–4280, Federal Power Commission, Decision of the Presiding Examiner (February 1, 1956), 45. Mimeographed copy.

and 25.5 cents per MCF. It is noteworthy that the higher-priced Erath field agreements of United Fuel were the same as the lower-priced group of American Louisiana contracts.

All of the American Louisiana contracts contained favored-nation clauses—whether two-party or third-party is not stated—which were based on an area that included offshore oil and gas territory. A common contract specification was as follows: "based on area in Louisiana south of lat. 31° N. of portion of Continental Shelf in Gulf of Mexico south of Louisiana."

In summary, at least two important groups of contracts were negotiated in the Southwest Louisiana gas supply area in the period between 1952 and 1953: the United Fuel Gas Company and the American Louisiana agreements. These were persuasive examples of the cost and the conditions under which large-volume large-reserve gas supplies were obtainable at that time, both for new projects and possibly for established pipe-line systems. From these contracts, it becomes clear that a price range of 23.0–27.0 cents and a more generalized price level of 25.0 cents per MCF is representative for the period 1952–53.

Furthermore, the 25.0 cent price must be viewed as a minimum cost to buyers for large-volume gas supplies. Sellers were assured of this average price over the legal term of the contract, since fixed price escalation operates automatically and there were no provisions for renegotiating prices downward. These prices were also minimum in view of the likelihood that price redetermination at the end of five or ten years would raise prices still higher. In effect, the cost of large-volume gas is, at the very least, the average contract price over the legal contract term—plus a substantial factor to account for the ease with which sellers may adjust prices upward during this period.

Field price levels estimated in this examination of market behavior in the Southwest Louisiana gas supply area may be presented in summary form. Again, price estimates have been adjusted to a standard twenty-year contract period and include the 1.0 cent gathering tax when this has been typically the obligation of the purchaser.

REPRESENTATIVE FIELD PRICES: SOUTHWEST LOUISIANA
GAS SUPPLY AREA

Large Volume	Cents per MCF (16.7 psi)
1945	(no data)
1946	(no data)
1947	(no data)
1948	11.0
1949	12.0
1950	12.0
1951	12.0
1952	23.0–25.0
1953	25.0–27.0
Small Volume	
1950	11.5
1951	11.5
1952	11.5
1953	11.5–12.5

B. SOUTHEAST LOUISIANA–MISSISSIPPI

The second Louisiana Gulf Coast supply area provided un-usual information in two respects: First, until very recently this source has not been particularly important as a supplier of gas supplies to the interstate pipe-line market. Second, based on the available contract data, only one buyer—the United Gas Pipe Line Company—was active during most of the postwar period. Only with the entry of the Southern Natural Gas Company in July, 1951, and the later entry of the United Fuel Gas Company was this exclusive buyer position changed. Consequently, the supply area under consideration—like the West Texas–Permian Basin supply area—illustrated the effect on field prices of a single dominant buyer.

The structure of this gas supply market can be readily dis-cerned from an examination of Table 28. Sellers are ranked by the annual volume of gas sales recorded in their contracts, where such information is known and available. However, the lack of specific volume information for a number of important contracts in the period 1951–52 may limit the validity of the rankings.

From the contract data in Figure 8, it is clear that the supply area was not an important source of gas reserves during the first

Table 28

ANALYSIS OF NATURAL GAS PURCHASE CONTRACTS

IN THE SOUTHEAST LOUISIANA–MISSISSIPPI

GAS SUPPLY AREA, 1944–53

RANK OF SELLER BY ANNUAL GAS VOLUME	Annual Gas Volume M³CF	Number of Contracts	Number of Buyers
1. Humble Oil & Refining Co.	28.2	6	2
2. Gulf Refining Corp.	22.6	1	1
3. California Co.	20.6	2	2
4. Forest Oil Corp.	19.7	1	1
5. The Texas Company	13.0	2	1
6. Kerr-McGee Oil Ind., Inc.	12.3	1	1
7. Shell Oil Co.	10.9	4	1
8. Tide Water Associated Oil Co.	10.2	1	1
9. Fohs Oil Co., *et al.*	8.6	3	2
10. Cabot Carbon Co.	6.4	1	1
11. Union Producing Co.	3.9	1	1
12. Union Oil Co. of California	3.6	1	1
13. Mikton Oil Co.	3.3	2	1
14. Helis, William, *et al.*	2.4	1	1
3 sellers reporting less than 2.0 M³CF of annual gas sales	1.4	3	
Subtotals	167.1	30	
16 sellers not included in above listing, having contracts with indefinite gas volumes	—	17	
Renegotiated and other indefinite gas volume contracts	—	9	
Totals	167.1	56	

period of postwar pipe-line expansion; sizable gas volumes were not recorded until 1951. Furthermore, the fact that the United Gas Pipe Line Company was—for all practical purposes—the only buyer until 1951 makes feasible a more general analysis of field prices and contract patterns in this supply area.

Concerning term of contract, ten-year effective contract periods were almost uniformly present until 1951. The longer effective terms thereafter were attributable to the two other buyers in the supply area. A similar uniformity characterized the other provisions typically found in a natural gas purchase contract. Favored-nation clauses were absent from all of the United Gas Pipe Line contracts, as well as from Southern Natural Gas agreements. Only the single United Fuel Gas Company contract contained a two-party favored-nation proviso. The United Gas Pipe Line Company was to pay—in most of its contracts—no more than one-half of additional and new taxes. Only in a few instances did it agree to pay existing severance and gathering taxes.

The presence of a single buyer in this supply area also had its effect upon price levels. A considerable stability and uniformity in price is evident from an examination of Figure 8. This is clearly the case for the contracts recorded before 1948. The general price level established by these agreements was between 4.0 and 5.0 cents per MCF, and the volumes involved were typically small. By the beginning of 1949, a marked price shift occurred. The contract sources recorded an abrupt increase to about a 10.0 cent price level. The change was established in two contracts: the first with the Humble Oil and Refining Company and the second with the Shell Oil Company. In both, a non-escalating price of 10.0 cents per MCF was set for a contract period of ten years. In the case of the Shell Oil agreement, which was a renegotiation of a 1944 contract having an original rate of 4.0 cents, the buyer was also to pay the 1.0 cent gathering tax.

Many other contracts negotiated during 1949, some of which involved sizable gas volumes, sustained the new price level. Although generally twenty-year agreements, they had effective terms of only ten years. Prices were either 7.0 and 8.0 cents or 9.0 and 10.0 cents for the first and second five-year periods; thereafter, prices were to be the "average weighted price in the area." In the agreements recording sizable volumes, there was also a buyer obligation for the 1.0 cent gathering tax. Taking these various factors into consideration, the representative field price on a twenty-year standard for 1949 may be estimated at 11.0 cents per MCF.

In the period after 1949 and to the middle of 1951, when a second marked price level increase occurred, only two price levels prevailed: one, a price of 10.0 cents per MCF for gas purchased in Louisiana; the other, an average price of 7.75 cents for gas purchased in various counties of Mississippi. The 10.0 cent price was, in all instances, a straight price without escalation over a ten-year contract term. A large number of these agreements were renegotiations of earlier 4.0 and 5.0 cent contracts.

The 7.75 cent agreements were for gas purchased in various small fields of southern Mississippi. Contract terms were twenty years, but prices were not specified after ten years and were, instead, to be established by "mutual agreement." Initial prices were set at 7.5 cents per MCF for the first five years, increasing to 8.0 cents in the second five-year period, with the resulting average price of 7.75 cents. A characteristic of these contracts was the many individuals and small non-petroleum company sellers involved. For example, one contract observation was a consolidation of eleven identical agreements involving different sellers.

The relatively lower and more stable price levels which prevailed in this supply area were definitely attributable to the fact that only the United Gas Pipe Line Company was active here. Confirming this conclusion was the substantial rise in the level of field prices which accompanied the Southern Natural Gas Company's entry into the supply area in 1951. Four contracts were completed by the Southern Natural Gas Company in a period extending through February, 1952, all of which were for relatively large volumes and were negotiated at approximately the same price. Contract periods in three of the four purchase agreements were for twenty-five years. In the fourth, a term of twenty years was stipulated. None of the agreements contained favored-nation clauses, nor was there any other indication in the contract sources that the prices were not firm for the full contract period.

In the three twenty-five-year agreements, prices were set at 13.34 cents for the first five-year period, increasing in subsequent five-year periods by 1.1 cent to a final price of 17.78 cents. Average price over a twenty-five-year effective term was, therefore, 15.56 cents per MCF. Added to this was an obligation to pay up to 1.3 cents per MCF of gathering and severance taxes. In the remaining contract, with a twenty-year term, prices were initially 11.11 cents per MCF, escalating each year to a final price of 16.67 cents. In this case, the average price over a twenty-year effective term was 15.78 cents per MCF, plus gathering and severance taxes of 1.3 cents. Tax-sharing of additional taxes was also required in all the agreements. The stipulation was one-half buyer in the two earliest contracts of this groups. It increased to two-thirds buyer in the later agreements. In general, the Southern Natural Gas contracts established a large-volume price level of approximately 16.0 cents per MCF, including tax payment obligations.

Following the upward price "break," the United Gas Pipe Line Company negotiated what appeared to be a large-volume agreement in December, 1951, with the Humble Oil and Refining Company. In this contract, an unusually large volume of "98,517,-000 Mcf/yr., subject to ratable taking" was recorded in the contract sources. Because of evidence suggesting the unreliability of the volume information in this contract, this amount was not shown in the price chart. Instead, a classification "indefinite" was assigned.

Assuming it to be a large-volume contract, as appears likely, the agreement was important in establishing patterns, as well as in showing the impact of a second buyer upon the position of United Gas Pipe Line. The agreement provided for a twenty-year contract term, which was also taken as the effective term. Prices were initially 13.34 cents per MCF in the first five years, increasing to 15.0, 16.67, and 18.9 cents in each of three subsequent five-year periods. Average price over twenty years was therefore 15.83 cents per MCF. This was not increased by any buyer obligations for existing gathering taxes, although new and additional taxes were to be shared one-half buyer and one-half seller.

Although no favored-nation clauses are recorded for this contract, a provision having a similar effect in permitting price adjustment was included. It was the stipulation that prices in the agreement were subject to a wholesale price index. This may be taken to mean that contract prices were tied to a published price index and were automatically adjusted to reflect general price level fluctuations. Finally, the approximate 16.0 cent price established in this contract accords with the Southern Natural Gas agreements, and it may be taken as the large-volume price from the middle of 1951 through the beginning of 1952.

For the remainder of 1952 two contract observations were available to establish price levels and patterns in this supply area. One of these was unique, since it represented offshore tidelands gas. Thus, in a contract negotiated between the United Gas Pipe Line Company and three sellers—the Phillips Petroleum Company, Kerr-McGee Oil Industries, Inc., and the Stanolind Oil and Gas Company—a large but indefinite annual volume was contracted for from the "Ship Shoal area, Gulf of Mexico off shore from Terrebonne Parish, La." The annual gas volume in this agreement, under given circumstances, could have equaled or exceeded 82 million MCF.[16]

The period to be covered by this contract was twenty-five years, with seemingly firm prices over this term, since no favored-nation, renegotiation, or other adjustment clauses were recorded. Initial price was to be 9.0 cents per MCF for the first ten years, 11.25 cents for the second ten-year period, and 13.5 cents for the remaining five years. Average price over the twenty-five-year effective term was thus 10.8 cents per MCF.

This contract was of special interest for two reasons: first, the relatively low price per unit of gas; second, the long-term commitment without known provisions for adjustment. Both of these

[16] Contract sources gave the following information: "Minimum: 32,850 Mcf/yr. each billion cu. ft. of reserves up to a total of 2½ trillion. If developed reserves exceed 2½ trillion cu. ft. basic annual minimum for such excess shall be 31,025,000 cu. ft. for each billion cu. ft. excess. In both cases, Buyer's obligation contingent on Seller's ability to deliver 11/0 of daily avg. of basic annual quantity, and in the latter case up to 82,125,000 Mcf plus 23/17 of such daily avg. when basic annual min. exceeds 82,125,000 Mcf. Provision for reduction in minimum annual quantity."

reflected the special circumstances of utilizing offshore gas, and both may become characteristic of offshore gas supplies, at least in the beginning stages of their development. The lower price for this gas undoubtedly reflected the substantially higher costs and greater risks for the buyer associated with its gathering. A longer term of contract with firm prices may also be needed to render such costly facilities economical.

The point may be more readily illustrated by the following diagram, in which the line PP' represents the going price of on-shore gas, including some normal gathering cost. Curve CC' represents the special cost of gathering from an offshore source. Because of the large investment required and its heavy fixed charges, the unit cost of gathering offshore gas would tend to fall sharply with an increase in the total quantity of gas which is transported via the facility. Given the capacity of the gathering line, the effective contract term would determine the quantity of gas which would be transported during the life of the facility.

The buyer would evidently not pay a price for gas greater than the difference between the going price of onshore supplies and the special cost of offshore gas, e.g., the difference between the line PP' and curve CC' at any point on the quantity scale where the difference is positive. But unit costs of offshore gathering would fall with increased quantity, which implies a longer effective con-

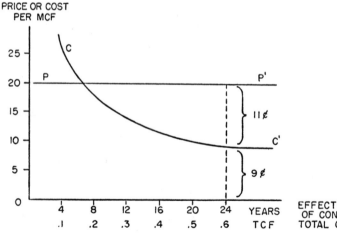

tract term. Some effective contract terms would be too short to justify any positive price, e.g., less than eight years. On the other hand, the price which buyers would pay increases as the effective term of the commitment becomes longer, e.g., approximately 11.0 cents for a twenty-five-year contract period. Unless sellers expected the price of onshore supplies to increase markedly—for the PP' line to rise above 20.0 cents—they, too, would find the longer effective term more advantageous. Therefore, it may be expected that offshore gas supplies would tend to have longer effective contract terms and lower unit prices, both reflecting the special gathering costs in utilizing this supply source.

Another large-volume contract exemplifying the 1952 price level in the Southeast Louisiana supply area was a direct-distributor purchase, dated October, 1952, and involving the United Fuel Gas Company. This agreement—a part of the group already analyzed in the Southwest Louisiana supply area—specified prices and contract conditions which were not different from its companion contracts. Its average price was approximately 20.0 cents per MCF over a ten-year effective term, with a 1.0 cent gathering tax obligation. The contract has a special interest because the gas field to which it relates was an onshore field in Terrebonne and La Fourche parishes, Louisiana, close to the off-shore gas supplies analyzed above. The United Fuel contract may therefore be considered representative of the price for large-volume onshore gas in the later part of 1952.

If this is correct, then average prices between 20.0 and 22.0 cents per MCF presumably characterized the large-volume market in Southeast Louisiana during 1952–53. But only one contract observation was recorded at these levels, and the contract sources did not extend beyond this agreement into 1953. Consequently, such a conclusion must necessarily be tentative. However, there was some confirmation of this price level in a contract not recorded in the price chart. This agreement, dated July 7, 1954, covered a gas purchase in southern Mississippi and involved the Transcontinental Gas Pipe Line Corporation as buyer and the Sun Oil Company as seller.[17] The initial price was 20.0 cents per

[17] Portions of the contract are reproduced in *Hearings—H. R. 4560*, 721–23.

MCF for the first five years, increasing to 22.0 cents in the next five-year period—no pressure base given. The contract price was subject to redetermination each five years, with new prices based on the average of the three highest prices paid for comparable quantities of gas in an area encompassing southern Mississippi and southern Louisiana east of the Mississippi River. A two-party favored-nation clause covering the same area was also included in the contract.

In summarizing the features of this gas supply area, little can be added to information included in the body of the analysis. A statement of the existence of a relatively high degree of price uniformity bears repetition. That this was due to the structural circumstance of a single buyer rather than any seller action seems unquestionable. However, the sharp increase in the field price level in 1948—to a point not far from other supply areas—indicates that the dominant buyer did not possess an unlimited power over price. The United Gas Pipe Line Company may well have been influenced and restricted in the exercise of its market power by the possibility of attracting new buyers into the market—a possibility which was realized in 1951 and which resulted in a substantial upward shift in the price level.

Representative field prices of the supply area, summarized below, were adjusted to reflect a twenty-year standard contract term. In view of the short legal contract terms which were typical before 1949, adjustment to the twenty-year standard was necessarily approximate. Furthermore, the prices before 1949 may have been more relevant for small-volume purchases. At least, there were no clear price distinctions based on volume until 1950.

REPRESENTATIVE FIELD PRICES: SOUTHEAST LOUISIANA–
MISSISSIPPI GAS SUPPLY AREA

Large Volume	Cents per MCF (16.7 psi)
Prior to 1945	4.0
1945	5.0
1946	5.0

Louisiana Gulf Coast Gas Supply Areas

1947	5.0
1948	6.0
1949	11.0
1950	11.0
1951 (first half)	11.0
1951 (second half)	16.0
1952 (onshore)	20.0–22.0
1952 (offshore)	11.0
1953	(no data)

Small Volume

1950–51 (Louisiana)	10.0
1950–51 (Mississippi)	8.0

PART III

Monopoly in the Gas Field—An Evaluation

THE MAIN ARGUMENT used to justify an extension of public price control to natural gas field markets centers on the claim of monopoly. In effect, it is asserted that there is within these field markets an absence of those competitive forces necessary to provide a protective barrier against a producer-seller exploitation of buyers. This monopolistic market condition, it is further argued, lies beyond the effective reach of antitrust legislation or comparable forms of public control. Consequently, the inevitable conclusion reached is that utility regulation—a developed and tested community response to a large and ineradicable monopoly condition—should be applied.

By providing the most widely accepted rationalization for public control, the issue of monopoly acquires a critical importance in the development of public policy in natural gas production. Unfortunately, a rational consideration of this issue has been hindered by inadequate factual information. It has been, of course, an objective of this study to contribute—in part at least—to the removal of this deficiency by an investigation of natural gas field markets during the critical 1945–53 period.

Therefore, while previous chapters have explored the pertinent factual aspects of gas field markets, the remainder of the study is to be devoted to a synthesis and evaluation of these data. To aid in this task, presentation of a conceptual basis for determining the competitive condition of field markets is needed. Following this, the major factual results of Parts I and II are to be evaluated for their bearing on the question of monopoly and competition in the gas field. Finally, the conclusions of this study on the gas monopoly issue are to be offered, with a policy proposal for dealing with the field price problem.

CHAPTER 7

Criteria for Field Market Monopoly

Essential to any meaningful discussion of the gas monopoly issue is a clarification of both the notion of monopoly and the criteria which can be used to measure its presence in natural gas field markets. Such a clarification will, at least, lead to a definition of terms. But it is also hoped that a general economic analysis of monopolistic market power and its possible bases in natural gas field markets will make more comprehensible the evaluation presented later.

The first step is to consider and to exclude from the definition of monopoly those price effects arising from natural limitations upon supply. Because this has not always been done, considerable semantic confusion has surrounded the term "monopoly" when used in reference to gas field markets.

In its most widely understood meaning, monopoly relates to the noncompetitive behavior of individuals and organizations, as well as to the noncompetitive industry-market structures which are the product of deliberate effort and conscious design. But the term "monopoly" has frequently been used in a broader fashion to encompass those environmental factors—such as the limited availability of a natural resource—which, through their restrictive effect upon supply, give price results that appear to be monopolistic.

The necessity for distinguishing between the two usages is essential. First, the price effects arising from natural limits upon the supply of a resource, the discovery of which is increasingly difficult and costly, can be found in competitive markets. The existence of prices well above the long-run costs of many producers and the persistence of profit returns to resource owners substantially in excess of a compensatory minimum are fully consistent with the most competitive of industry structures and can prevail in spite of the most intense forms of competitive rivalry. Thus, in the case of natural gas production, much evidence dealing with prices and profits, cited in support of an asserted monopoly condition, does little more than reveal the presence of strong elements of natural scarcity.

Second, public policy, while reasonably well formed with respect to monopoly returns, has not been as clearly formulated with regard to scarcity returns; it has not, in the main, sought the elimination or the social appropriation of scarcity returns or economic rents. In view of these differences and their importance, it would seem to be in the interests of clarity to differentiate between the two situations. Accordingly, for purposes of this study, the concept of monopoly excludes the effects of a natural limitation upon the expansion of supply.

A. CONCEPT AND CRITERIA OF MARKET POWER

Even with this qualification, a further definition of monopoly is required. Thus, among traditional and popular views, monopoly has been conceived as a single firm in exclusive control of a given product or as an agreement among sellers to fix prices. The difficulty with such notions is their narrowness. If strictly adhered to, they would include only the infrequent and, under contemporary circumstances, the unlikely monopolistic situations. Therefore, a broader conception, in which monopoly is to be viewed as an undue power to control a market, is necessary.

Seller market power rests on the ability to manipulate price, to regulate output in the short run, and to restrict entry as a means of limiting supply in the long run. These elements of market power, in turn, are to be found in one degree or another in all markets, even in those which might normally be regarded as competitive. As an example, where a seller is large, although not necessarily dominant, an important power over price exists through an ability to affect the industry-wide output, and such large size also has an adverse effect upon entry.

Furthermore, these elements of market power differ in their

comparative force. The possession by a producer-combination of a power to fix price, not supported by a control over output, results in only short-run monopoly returns. The establishment of a high price would become self-defeating as each producer sought to maximize his own returns by enlarging output. The increased supply could result in prices lower than those which would have been obtained in the absence of the price control attempt.

Similarly, the ability of existing sellers to fix a price and to maintain it by restricting output may represent a lower degree of monopoly power than if such power were combined with control over entry. For under such circumstances, the attraction of large profits would lead to the creation of productive capacity by new entrants and thus undermine the existing program of output restriction. There seems little doubt that the power to prevent entry and to control the rate of industry expansion is the strongest of market powers and socially the most pernicious.

It is, of course, exactly at this point that natural limitations upon supply can blend with a condition of seller monopoly. For the natural limitations which prevent the production or expansion of supply at costs no greater than those incurred by existing sellers is a ready-made restriction upon entry. In industries where these conditions prevail, a control over price alone may have a greater monopoly effect than elsewhere.

Elements of market power, appearing in a variety of forms and combinations, exist in all real-world markets and lead to a concept of seller monopoly which relates it to an excessive degree of market power. To use such a concept, however, requires not only that the sources of market power be identified but also that criteria be defined which make it possible to measure the degree of market power. Even more necessary is a determination of the degree of market control which is to be considered socially objectionable or, as in the present case, which is to result in detailed public regulation.

The measurement of market power can be accomplished by utilizing various criteria of competition, since these yardsticks for ascertaining the presence of competitive forces also serve to indicate the absence of a large and exploitative seller market power. Included among such criteria of competition is a standard based on market structure, a standard related to seller behavior, and a standard founded upon economic performance.

Competitive structure refers to those features of a market which operate to oppose and make difficult the maintenance of a monopolistic market control. These structural features also function to achieve their competitive effects with a minimum need for public intervention. One such structural feature, possibly the most important, centers upon the number of participants in an industry or market. It leads to a concentration test for ascertaining the existence of a competitive industry-market structure.

Monopolistic market control is likely to be absent in a competitively structured industry because sustained market control requires agreement and co-ordinated action in the matter of price and output. Where many are involved, this is difficult to achieve and to conceal. Generally, too, with many producers there are wider differences in costs and consequently market strength, in financial needs, and in judgments on current and future demands. There is a greater probability of "individualists" and nonconformists without whose co-operation the control scheme fails. These factors, leading to varied business decisions and policies, give assurance that competition and not monopoly will prevail.

Furthermore, the condition of many uniformly sized producers introduces the least resistance to new entry and the increase of capacity. It is the competitive expansion of productive capacity by new entrants which is the factor most inimical, in the long run, to any scheme of capturing and retaining market control. In this connection, the importance of minimizing publicly sponsored entry retardants such as licensing is clear. Similarly, the allocation of restricted production quotas to individual producers by some public agency is a structural feature which, whatever its other benefits, is not consistent with a competitive market condition.

A second standard of competition is that related to seller behavior. Although difficult, it is not impossible for the producers in an industry containing many firms to secure a high degree of market power. This can be accomplished through collusive agreement to adopt monopolistic prices and outputs or, through tacit co-operation, to avoid competitive actions. In either case, behavior becomes the key to testing the presence or absence of competition.

In general, the standard of competitive behavior requires the absence of an agreement among sellers which seeks to establish uniform policies with respect to price, production, or entry. It also requires the absence of efforts to establish such policies indirectly by an agreement among all or some sellers to adhere to certain practices which affect price, output, or entry. In both situations, it is to be assumed that such privately determined policies maximize private advantage and are therefore likely to be economically inefficient and exploitative.

Since any standard of competitive behavior must ultimately depend upon the absence of seller collusion, the main practical difficulty involves the identification of such collusion. Only the most naïve or the most careless of arrangements would be discovered. As a consequence, efforts to apply such a standard are usually limited to a search for inferential evidences of monopolistic agreement. These might be obtained by analyzing the nature of changes in the level and pattern of prices, or they might be found in an improbable uniformity of seller actions and responses. Indirect evidence of monopolistic behavior might also be derived from an examination of marketing practices where it could be demonstrated that these are inconsistent with competitive rivalry.

A highly important complement to the criteria of structure and behavior is the standard of competition founded upon the economic performance of an industry. This approach looks directly to the consequences of a competitive economy which are presumed to justify such a form of economic organization rather than to the conditions which are expected to give rise to those consequences. Its basic presumption is that the industry-market conditions which can give workable competitive results are too varied and complex to permit classification into generally applicable rules of structure and behavior. Its rationale is simply that the ultimate concern of society in the matter of monopoly is to prevent an excessive deviation from the results of competition.

Vital to a comprehension of the standard of competitive performance is an answer to the question "What are the socially desirable results to be expected in a competitive economy?" Two of the more important may be identified. One outcome of competitive organization is the optimum use and allocation of existing economic resources. A second is the distribution of income so that the owners of productive services receive no more than a minimum compensatory return—an income just sufficient to cover all costs and sacrifices—including entrepreneurial risk and initiative.

With respect to the first outcome, a competitive economy generates forces which press in the direction of an efficient use of economic resources. Each business firm is subject to the manifold pressures arising from a comparison with rival units in an impersonal market place. The choices of consumers give differential gains to these economic units along a scale which is correlated with efficient economic performance. These gains result both from the effective management of resources and a superiority in selecting and initiating the activity in which they are to be used. At the other extreme, seriously inefficient performance is ultimately removed by losses which cannot be long sustained by private business.

As for the distributive effects of a competitive economy, these arise as individuals respond to the prospect of a more-than-compensatory income return from the use in a particular employment of their productive services. Under competition, at any given time, the price which a good or service obtains is a reflection of its relative scarcity. Whenever, because of relative scarcity, prices are greater than the costs which would be incurred, a strong pecuniary incentive arises to expand the stock of that good or service. A major role of competitive economic organization is to keep open the opportunities for response to such incentives. The ultimate effect is a decrease in the relative scarcity of the good and—by reason of the resulting decline in price—a reduction to minimum compensatory levels of income returns realized from its production.

This fundamental distributive result of competition, however, presupposes the possibility of acquiring those productive elements, such as machines, materials, and skills, which are essential to an enlargement of the desired output. Where the required expansion of productive elements encounters a physical or cost limit, as in the case of many natural materials, the income returns received by existing resource owners which are above compensatory levels are not reduced. They persist indefinitely unless some technological advance increases the yield of existing resources or makes available a lower-cost substitute. When a non-reproducible resource is also a depleting resource, these income returns would continually increase as relative scarcity increased. Thus, even a high degree of competition in natural gas production may not lead to the distributive results expected of competition.

The allocative and distributive results associated with competitive economic arrangements have a wide social acceptance. The desirability of efficiency in the use of economic resources is evident, assuming that it is or can be made consistent with the achievement of other social values. There is also much obvious merit in an arrangement which seeks to distribute income according to an individual's contribution to the well-being of others—a goal most likely to be achieved when the product of effort is valued impersonally by others in an unrigged market.

That this compensation should be at the minimum necessary to induce individual effort is, as much as anything, the result of an inability to define any other magnitude. In practice, there is no limit to a maximum compensatory income when judged by the income recipient; the range below is indeterminate, when fixed by others. Only a minimum compensatory income can be objectively defined in an impersonal market. If it is not obtained, evidence is soon made apparent in the form of unproduced goods and unrendered services.

When markets are rigged—are made personal or are subject to a monopolistic control—something more than a minimum economic return is obtained. Consequently, aside from its effects upon the efficiency of resource utilization, the major social objection to monopoly resides in the advantages it affords for securing a more-than-compensatory share in the social income.

This same reasoning may also explain and possibly rationalize a social antipathy to the private retention of those income returns above competitive levels which can accrue from the ownership of scarce natural resources. This objection may prevail even if such resource owners have not tried to augment their returns by the devices of seller monopoly. An element of inequality in income opportunity is recognized; those commanding other types of productive services are subject to more rigorous competitive pressures than individuals protected by the shield of natural scarcity.

From this general discussion, it is seen that, granted unimpaired competitive forces, a continual downward pressure operating to eliminate income returns in excess of competitive norms is exerted on price. Therefore, a principal indicator of competitive performance is a tendency for price adjustment to costs of production where these are a summation of minimum compensatory payments for all necessary productive services. This tendency suggests one of the most direct tests of monopolistic market power—the persistence of prices in excess of long-run costs.

Unfortunately, the utilization of such a test presents serious practical difficulties. There is the difficulty of securing complete cost and revenue data which would permit the measurement of profit returns, as well as the problem of deciding what constitutes an excessive return for a given industry. Moreover, the fact that returns above costs are being received at any given time does not necessarily imply monopoly. Instead, the industry may be in the period of adjustment during which returns above cost are generating the changes leading to the competitive norm. Finally, the returns above cost may be the outcome of natural limitations upon supply, rather than the outcome of monopoly, and separation of the two would not be a simple matter.

All together, these factors limit severely the possibility of utilizing a standard of competitive performance in the area of natural gas production. Other more theoretical tests, based upon the performance standards of a purely competitive market, present an even smaller possibility of practical application. Main reliance must therefore be placed upon the standards of competitive structure and behavior, with their respective tests of concentration and uniformity in seller actions.

Apart from the question of competitive standards, there is still the problem of defining the degree of market power which is to result in social action. On this matter, there is little doubt that art and judgement will have to prevail, for the concept of monopoly which has been offered is based upon the premise that elements of market power are found everywhere and that their exploitative potential is restrained only by the existence of certain structural and behavior conditions. These conditions are not always present in a form or combination which achieves maximum competitive results. Realism supports this view; most markets are characterized by sizable seller market power only partially checked by competitive forces.

Thus, real-world markets are not inherently competitive; the mere presence of identifiable market power does not necessarily require public action. This shift in emphasis is important. It nullifies to a large extent the traditional criterion for public action—the elimination of any and all forms of seller market control. In its place, a determination must be made of the degree of market power which is to actuate public intervention. For this reason, a broad area of judgment seems unavoidable.

B. BASES FOR MARKET POWER IN THE GAS FIELD

The foregoing discussion of market power has proceeded on the assumption that monopolistic returns depend upon the ability of sellers to control price, output, and entry relative to total supply. While a control of total supply constitutes the strongest and most lucrative foundation for the exercise of market power, it is also one of the most difficult to achieve. Where natural gas production is concerned, it would require a dominance over total gas reserves. However, particular markets may have character-istics which can provide the base for a partial—but nonetheless substantial—seller monopoly power.

In the case of natural gas field markets, a partial or limited market power can be derived from the following: first, the pres-ence of substantial buyer exit-costs, once commitment to a given supply area has been made; second, the existence of differential supply costs between developed and undeveloped gas-producing areas; and third, the prevalence of certain marketing practices, such as long-term purchase contracts, price redetermination, and favored-nation clauses.

It may be noted that, in dealing with these bases for market power, no attempt is made to determine whether or not they have been actually exploited by gas producers. The objective is simply to create an analytical framework within which the problem of monopolistic market control in the gas field can be more ration-ally considered.

Large buyer exit-costs, one of the bases for market power, are a product of the technological requirements of the industry. A sizable investment in pipe-line facilities is required to connect a gas supply area to consumer markets, and additional expendi-tures for gathering and field equipment are needed to reach a par-ticular seller. As the designation clearly suggests, buyer exit-costs are the costs facing a committed pipe-line buyer if the price in-creases of a present seller are considered exploitative and the buyer anticipates shifting to a new source of supply. Their mag-nitude is determined by losses from the abandonment of existing field facilities and the expenses involved in the construction of new gathering lines and similar equipment. They may also require the extension of pipe lines or, in extreme instances, the abandon-ment of all or part of the transportation pipe line.

Thus, even one seller acting alone may possess a consider-able market power based upon the buyer exit-costs involved in relocating within a gas supply area. Still greater market power could be obtained if an important gas supply area were dominated by a few producers, since the affected pipe-line purchaser would have only the prospect of entering an entirely different supply area. Consequently, field prices above competitive levels could be established and maintained, the level of which would depend entirely upon the proximity of alternative gas supply sources.

While market power may be possessed by gas producers as a result of buyer exit-costs, certain restrictions upon its exercise are noteworthy. First, it is operative only with respect to committed pipe lines and is really large only if it presents the buyer with the prospect of abandoning mainline transportation facilities. This prospect is not likely, except in cases where a pipe-line purchaser is dependent upon a single supplier or where the supply area is controlled by a few or a colluding group of producers. If multiple supply sources have been tapped by the pipe line, the output of any one producer may be dispensed with at no great cost to the buyer.

Furthermore, there has been widespread use of long-term purchase contracts in gas field markets. If these are firm price agreements having a duration sufficient to amortize the affected investments, they are fully protective of buyer interests. Even when these supply contracts permit price adjustments, as in the more recent arrangements, such adjustments are—in most cases— limited to changes in the general market value of gas; they do not result in the direct exploitation of any single buyer's exit-costs.

It may be noted, however, that use of long-term purchase contracts, while a protective device with respect to buyer exit-costs, may have other and broader effects leading to gas field prices above competitive levels. The real importance of buyer exit-costs may not be their effect upon the market strength of buyer and seller in individual transactions but their role as a generalized market imperfection. By immobilizing committed pipe-line buyers as a group, these costs can ratchet a market-wide level of field prices to a point well above competitive norms. But these effects will be explored at a later stage of the analysis.

A second base for seller market power is to be found in the existence of cost differentials between developed and undeveloped gas-producing areas. Thus, at any given time, it is not likely that large increments in the supply of natural gas can be obtained, except at supply prices above prevailing levels. Such increases would reflect the added expenses of securing gas from known but undeveloped reserves—cost presumably being the main reason for their nonutilization earlier.

Differential supply costs, such as those under consideration, can be the product of differences in drilling and production expenses caused by geological factors; or they can result from differences in gathering, processing, and field compression expenditures which reflect the physical characteristics of supply. For example, significant cost increases result when relatively small, isolated gas reserves are tapped, requiring an extensive gathering network; or when the quality of the gas, e.g., high sulphur content, makes special processing installations necessary; or when offshore gas reserves impose unusual costs. Furthermore, from the buyer's point of view, not the least of the factors causing differential supply costs is the location of gas supply. Geographical factors requiring larger or smaller investments in transportation facilities can lead to a considerable variation in the effective cost of gas from alternative supply sources.

Natural gas supply is, therefore, characterized by major differences in costs of production and utilization, and a movement from established gas supply sources to untapped supply sources is likely to entail a cost "jump" of some magnitude. This condition could be a basis for market power. For example, the market demand for gas may be such that only the most advantageously located gas fields, for a given point of consumption, are currently in production. Assuming this producing area to be controlled by a combination of sellers, monopolistic prices could be set. However, the level of these could not exceed the costs to existing and prospective buyers of gas from alternative supply sources. If undeveloped gas reserves, only slightly less advantageously located, were to overhang the market, seller market power would not be serious. But, if the cost differential were large, the combination of sellers could secure sizable monopolistic returns.

These returns, moreover, are not to be mistaken as rents for differential advantages of location; they are true monopoly returns. It was assumed that the developed producing area was capable of meeting all existing demands for gas at prices which, if competitively determined, would be below the cost of gas from other sources. Therefore, some restriction on sales would be necessary to raise the price above competitive levels. The function of the monopolistic seller combination, of course, is to achieve this restriction of supply.

To clarify the point further, the price of gas, in any given producing area, may possibly include returns above cost which are due to realized differential advantages. If the prices include only these, they are consistent with the existence of a competitive market. But there is no reason why—as a result of monopolistic combination—the price could not be raised above such a level and monopoly returns added to scarcity returns, subject to a limit set by alternative higher-cost gas supplies. In short, returns attributable to differential advantages—potentially available to sellers in a given producing area but not yet obtainable under competitive conditions—can be largely but not completely realized through seller combination.

Differential supply costs, therefore, can be important for an analysis of market power in the gas field. Like buyer exit-costs, this base for market power depends for its force upon the cost of the supply options available to purchasers. However, it is broader in its influence, including buyers not yet committed to a particular supply area. It is also evident that a combination of sellers could exploit both sources of market power and secure monopolistic returns greater than that obtainable from either singly.

Seller market power can also be the outcome of certain marketing practices. Interacting, these practices can lead to price levels above competitive norms, and achieving these price levels requires no more than a general seller adherence to the market devices in question.

The derivation of a noncompetitive level of field prices from a "mechanism" combining long-term purchase contracts, favored-nation clauses, and price redetermination provisos can be described in this manner: Long-term purchase agreements, by tying up gas reserves and contractually eliminating them from current markets, engross a portion of the existing total supply of gas. If these contracts contain two-party favored-nation clauses, the additional gas needs of the buyers involved must be met from uncommitted gas outside the favored-nation area. Were this not done, the established pipe-line buyer would risk "triggering" price increases on all or much of his contracted gas to obtain what might be a relatively small increment to that supply.

Thus, given the use of long-term purchase contracts, new buyers seeking to enter field markets are unable to compete for committed gas supplies; they must concentrate their demands upon uncommitted gas reserves. And, given the favored-nation clause, old buyers are not even able to meet gas requirements for expansion from all of the uncommitted gas reserves.

As a consequence of focusing new demands upon a limited portion of total supply, prices are lifted above competitive levels. The new level of prices, however, does not immediately apply to reserves committed earlier, and the function of the price re-determination clause is to transmit these back to the old contracts. This is readily accomplished, since most redetermination clauses provide for new prices equal to the average of the three highest in the price redetermination area.[1]

The above discussion has been concerned with a brief de-scriptive presentation of the bases—other than a dominance over total supply—from which seller market power in the gas field can conceivably be derived. As such, it was intended to serve as a point of departure for the technical analysis given below.

The physical and technological features characterizing the production and utilization of natural gas lead to substantial vari-ations in the costs of alternative gas supplies. These cost differ-ences are inherent, and, consequently, at any given time a rising long-run supply function characterizes the aggregate of known gas supply sources.[2] In addition, the rising supply function postu-

[1] In another industry where natural limits on total supply exist, namely, the newsprint industry, somewhat similar marketing practices evidently prevail. Thus, long-term contracts running from five to fifteen years characterize the sale of newsprint, with price redetermination clauses tying the price of news-print to the average price of two or three of the largest producers. See *The Newsprint Problem*, House Committee on the Judiciary, 83 Cong., 1 sess., (1953), 20.

[2] Basic changes in total gas reserves, such as the discovery of new supply areas, are not reflected in the postulated supply function. In this respect, such

lated is not continuous. Instead, the cost "jumps" or "steps" among various supply sources are likely to be pronounced. The conditions described are illustrated in Figure A, where the long-run supply functions for alternative gas supply areas are shown. Costs, in this case, exclude rents arising from the differential advantages of particular supply areas for any given use of gas.

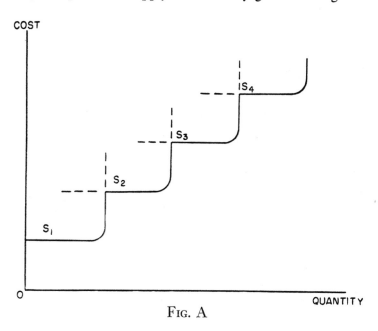

Fig. A

In Figure A, a low-cost gas supply source, such as a field or supply area, with advantages of location, is represented by S_1. Alternative supply areas with higher costs of production and utilization are represented by S_2, S_3, etc. As the S_1 supply area becomes fully developed, a stage is reached where the supply function turns up sharply. At this point, although additional gas is still obtainable for additional cost outlays, the technological features of gas production are likely to result in a very rapid in-

changes are like technological innovation, the effects of which on supply price are generally assumed constant simply because the effects are so uncertain. If new gas supply sources are discovered, the supply function merely shifts and changes shape, depending upon the cost level characterizing the new supplies.

crease in marginal costs. Once the cost "jump" is made to the most economical alternative supply area—S_2—the supply function becomes relatively flat and remains so until the ratio of labor and capital inputs to natural resource inputs again starts to rise. The resulting cost increase is rapid, until a new supply area—S_3—is made economic. A steplike supply function for natural gas—in which the supply areas are arranged in an ascending order from low-cost to high-cost supply sources—is thus derived.[3]

It is further assumed that the various supply areas, each with a distinct cost structure, are also differentiated according to ownership. Separate sellers are to be found in different segments of the supply function. Consequently, the same range of costs are not experienced by all and a distinction between high-cost and low-cost producers is possible.[4]

The virtue of the type of supply function postulated is its usefulness in demonstrating that a partial monopoly power may be obtained from a control over a portion of the total supply. Thus, a monopolistic market power can be based upon a dominance over low-cost supplies.[5] Generally, the degree of market power obtained is dependent upon the size of the cost "step" buyers must take to reach uncontrolled gas supplies. More accurately, it is also determined by demand elasticity and the elas-

<hr/>

[3] The kind of total supply function being postulated in this analysis is analogous to the "particular expenses curve" of Alfred Marshall (see *Principles of Economics*, [8th Edition Macmillan and Co., Ltd., 1920], 810, n. 2). A "particular expenses curve" differs from a normal supply curve in that the former "take(s) the general economies of production as fixed and uniform throughout." The assumption of such a condition is necessary in order to obtain the same results from a "particular expenses curve" as from a normal supply curve. However, this assumption cannot be made for a "commodity that obeys the laws of increasing return." It can be made, and it may, at times, be convenient to do this, for commodities subject to decreasing returns. (See *ibid.*, 812.)

[4] The cost function for each supply area is similar to that of a conventional supply curve; in fact, each supply area could be viewed as an "industry" consisting of many firms with uniform long-run cost structures. The relationship of one supply area to another is like that of industries whose products are close technical substitutes but which have different production and utilization costs.

[5] "Monopolistic market control," as well as all the variations of that term, is defined as the ability of sellers to establish prices and outputs different from those which would prevail in competitive markets. The magnitude of the deviation is not considered.

ticity of the uncontrolled portion of the supply function. The second factor, in turn, is influenced by whether or not the supply function is continuous; thus, other things equal, market power would be increased if the function were discontinuous. The nature of the market control referred to, as well as the effects of discontinuity, are illustrated in a preliminary fashion in Figures B and C.

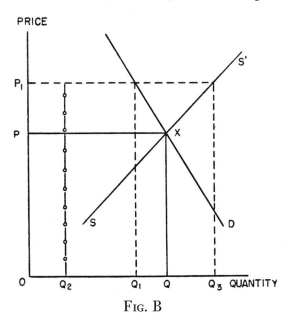

FIG. B

In Figure B, a continuous supply function is assumed. Competitive price and output are then equal to P and Q, respectively. Only the low-cost portion of the supply, represented by SX, is monopolized. If an attempt is made to raise the price to P_1, a reduction of output to Q_1 occurs. But the increase in price makes available higher-cost supplies in the amount of QQ_3, and the quantity supplied by the original sellers falls to Q_2, where Q_2Q_1 equals QQ_3.

The case of a discontinuous supply function is shown in Figure C. Here the increase in price to P_1 reduces sales of the monopolistic combination of low-cost producers to Q_1, but not farther, since additional supplies are forthcoming only at a price

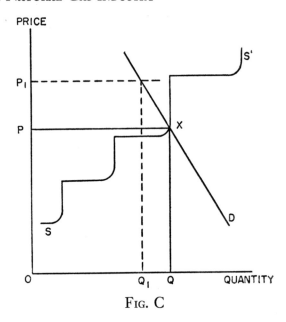

FIG. C

in excess of P_1. A discontinuous supply function therefore enhances the market power to be obtained from a control over low-cost supplies. The discontinuity causes the supply function to become almost perfectly inelastic over certain price ranges. It is further evident that the size of the cost "jump" determines the price range over which inelasticity prevails, and thus the range of price within which monopolistic power may be exercised.

In this connection, the exact price and output which maximizes producer returns from a control over the SX portion of total supply can be ascertained by application of the usual profit-maximizing principles. This is illustrated in Figures D and E, respectively, for the continuous and the discontinuous cases.

Referring to Figure D, SX is again that portion of total supply which is controlled. The average revenue curve which faces the sellers controlling this part of the total supply is represented by AXD, since, if this group were to set any price above the competitive level, sales would be lost to the uncontrolled sellers. Loss of sales would continue until a point were reached, at a price equal to A, where the price-raising, output-restricting group

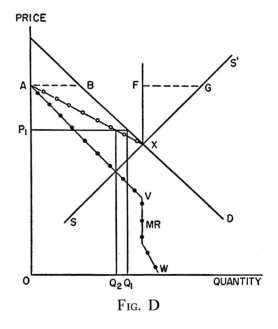

FIG. D

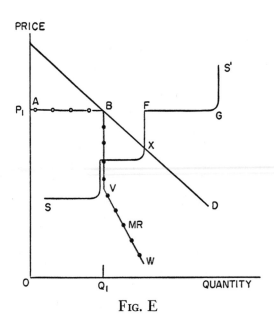

FIG. E

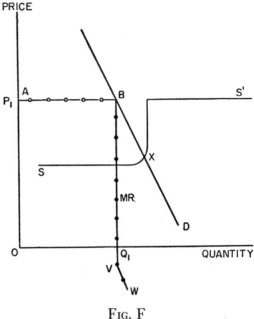

FIG. F

would have zero sales—AB being equal to FG, the quantity supplied by high-cost producers. The marginal revenue for this average revenue function is represented by AVW. Since the supply curve SX is also a marginal cost function, the group of low-cost sellers taking joint action will establish a price of P_1 and sell a quantity of Q_2. The total quantity sold, however, equals Q_1—the additional amount Q_2Q_1 being supplied by the high-cost sellers.

The maximizing price in the discontinuous case is just equal to cost in the alternative gas supply area. This would always be true if the demand function were inelastic, as represented by a negative marginal revenue, over the relevant price range (See Figure F). It could also occur—even if demand were elastic—if the cost "step" were not too large (See Figure E). But if demand is very elastic, the maximizing price would be less than the cost of gas from an alternative supply area (See Figure G). If this highly elastic demand condition does not prevail—or is believed not to prevail—a "working rule" can be formulated: the maximizing price for a partial monopoly is just equal to the costs of an alternative, uncontrolled supply source.

A monopolistic market power can also be obtained from a control over the higher-cost portion of a total supply, but an increase in demand is required for its implementation. The variations of the case are shown in Figures H and I. For simplicity of analysis, assumption of a continuous supply function is restored. In Figure H, it is assumed that the low-cost supply is competitively held and is freely available to new buyers. Figure I assumes a similar competitive condition, but the low-cost supply is committed by long-term contracts and is not available to new buyers.

In Figure H, the high-cost, uncommitted portion of supply—XS′—is monopolized. Demand increases from D to D_1. In this case, an increase in demand is viewed as a uniformly proportional increase in quantity response over the range of existing prices. A competitive price, if established, would be fixed at P_1, reflecting an increase—caused by the demand change—over the older competitive price P. But a monopoly of the high-cost supply confronts that part of the new D_1 demand which cannot be serviced

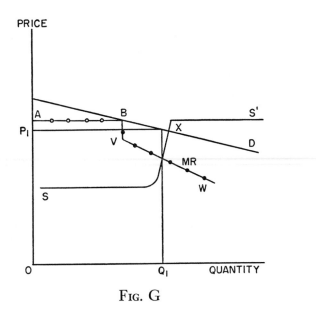

F<small>IG</small>. G

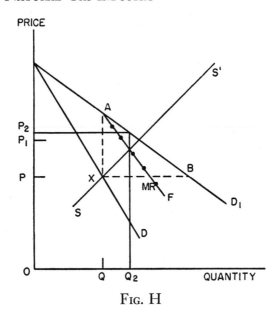

FIG. H

by low-cost producers. Thus, the average revenue function facing the partial monopolist is the AB portion of the D_1 demand curve, or the AB portion of any new demand curve intersecting the perpendiculars—AX and BX. If the relevant marginal revenue function is drawn—line AF—it is price P_2 which maximizes the returns of the high-cost monopoly. Quantity Q_2 would be forthcoming, OQ of which is supplied by the low-cost competitive sellers who also secure the benefit of the monopolistic price.

If the low-cost supply, however, is not available to meet the demands of new buyers, then a considerably enlarged market power can be derived from control of uncommitted supply sources. The condition is illustrated in Figure I, in which it is assumed that the increased quantity which new buyers wish to take must come entirely from the high-cost portion of the supply function. Old buyers continue to purchase quantity OQ at price P.[6] The average revenue function of the monopoly which con-

[6] This does not mean that so-called old buyers cannot increase their demand for gas. Such a demand increase, however, along with that of new buyers, must be met from the uncommitted portion of the total gas supply.

trols uncommitted supplies then becomes CB. This represents the quantity which new buyers are willing to take at various relevant prices, such quantities being measured from point Q on the quantity scale. Because of contract restraints, the increase in demand must be entirely met from the XS' portion of supply. The demand function becomes CBD$_1$. The marginal revenue function is represented by CF, and the price set by the monopoly for its portion of the supply is then equal to P$_3$.

This price is higher than both the price which would prevail if all supplies were competitively held and the price that would be established if old supplies were freely available to meet new demands. An interesting aspect, however, is the fact that—despite the higher price—a quantity larger than Q$_2$ in Figure H is marketed. This is the result of the effective price discrimination which is operative in the market. The low-cost sellers, bound by their contracts, continue to receive only the competitive price prevailing before the demand increase.

However, such sellers will ultimately increase their prices as contractual restraints expire, and, in the absence of any further

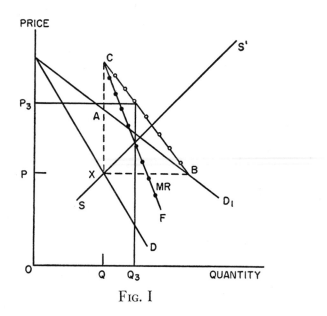

FIG. I

demand increase, some purchasers and some demands will be eliminated. A general reallocation of supply occurs, in the course of which the P_3 price and the Q_3 quantity decline to the P_2 and Q_2 level of Figure H.

The foregoing has demonstrated the market power which is implicit in a control over low-cost supplies; it has also established the monopolistic market control which can reside in a dominance over higher-cost uncommitted supplies. In addition, the domination of any portion of total supply can, under appropriate circumstances, give rise to monopolistic market control. This case is presented in Figure J.

In this instance, four gas supply areas are assumed, each being monopolized—or controlled—by a combination of their respective producers and each having distinctive cost positions. When the level of demand is D_1, the S_1 supply area will provide the market requirements, and the maximizing price and output will be set at P_1 and Q_1. If demand increases to D_2, the S_2 supply area will

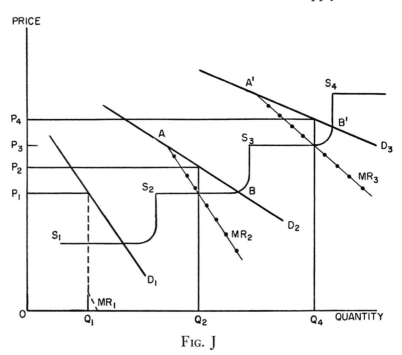

FIG. J

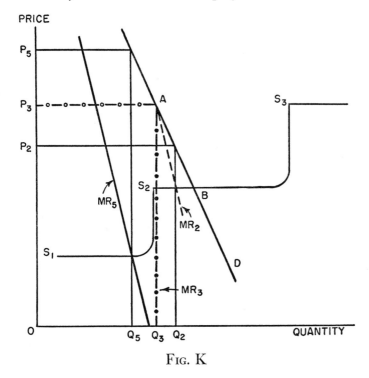

Fig. K

be brought into the market. If the S_2 supply area acts independently of S_1, it is faced with the AB portion of D_2. S_2 cannot fix a price higher than P_3 without losing all sales to the S_1 supply area.

The maximizing price set by S_2, acting independently, will therefore be P_2. This monopolistic price will also be secured by the S_1 supply area, even in the absence of any collusion between S_1 and S_2. For, as demonstrated in Figure H, the S_1 supply area could be competitively structured and yet a monopolistic price might prevail, since the supply area on the margin of development will be price-determining. Thus, whether competitive or monopolized, the S_1 supply area need take no action toward effectuating the P_2 price.[7]

[7] There is the possibility that S_1 could take the maximum output of S_2, as given, and adjust price to a level higher than P_2 (but only up to the limit of P_3), absorbing the necessary curtailment of total output. However, this is not likely, since the total revenue from the sale of S_1's entire output at a price set by S_2

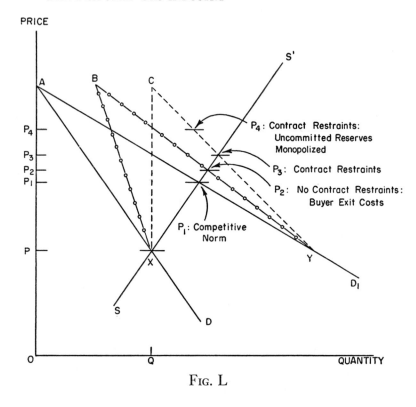

FIG. L

Given a further increase in demand to D_3, the situation just described will be repeated. But supply area S_3 will now be on the margin of development, and a dominant seller here will establish a monopolistic price equal to P_4. In the long run, this will become effective for all lower-cost supply areas.

The presumption so far has been independence of action among the various supply areas. The different price results of joint action may also be presented; the possibilities are shown in Figure

would probably give larger returns than the sale of a portion of the S_1 production at a higher price, depending on the market share which would have to be accorded to the S_2 supply area. Success in such a policy would require a relatively inelastic demand function. But if that part of the demand function facing S_2 is inelastic, the S_2 supply area would, on its own initiative, be setting a price just equal to the cost of the S_3 supply area, or price P_3. Since this is the maximum price that S_1 could charge, that area would have no interest in taking independent action.

K. Thus, if S_1, S_2, and S_3 act together or are dominated by the same sellers and the demand function is such that no demand exists at the costs of any supply area beyond S_3, a full monopoly price would be obtained. The relevant marginal revenue would be MR_5, and the monopolistic price would be equal to P_5. If only S_1 and S_2 form a coalition, they can accept as their joint average revenue function the line marked off as P_3AB in Figure K. In this case, the marginal revenue function would be MR_3, and the maximizing price would be fixed at P_3. The last and lowest monopolistic price would be P_2, where the monopolists of each supply area act independently.

Up to this point, some degree of seller monopoly in the supply of gas has been assumed. But, even in the absence of any monopolistic conditions, prices above competitive norms can be established as a consequence of market imperfections, such as large exit-costs for committed buyers. A similar and stronger price effect results from the prevalence of long-term purchase agreements which place contractual restraints upon the reallocation of previously committed supplies.

Utilizing graphic techniques previously developed, these possibilities are demonstrated in Figure L. AD represents the initial demand of uncommitted buyers and SX the portion of supply devoted to meeting this demand. AD_1 represents a net increase in demand that has been combined with the initial AD demand. Given the absence of buyer exit-costs, as well as contract restraints on supply, P_1 becomes the ruling price and the competitive norm.

With buyer exit-costs, the initial demand AXD changes to BXD, reflecting the greater inelasticity of demand after buyers have become committed.[8] Increments in demand must now be added to the BXD function, and BYD_1 represents an increased demand. P_2 then becomes the ruling price, assuming no contractual restraints upon the reallocation of supply.

[8] If exit-costs are so large that committed buyers can release no part of their supply over a relevant price range, then CXD would represent the initial demand after buyer commitment. In the absence of contract restraints, some release and reallocation of committed supply is more realistic, and the demand function would lie somewhere between AXD and CXD.

In a similar manner, CXD becomes—in effect—the demand of committed buyers, obtaining an OQ supply under long-term contractual arrangements. At least, increments to demand must now be added to the CXD function, and the new enlarged demand is represented by CYD_1. Consequently, P_3 becomes the ruling price, under a condition of contract restraints, with or without the presence of buyer exit-costs. As previously shown in Figure L, P_4 represents price, assuming contract restraints and a monopoly of the uncommitted supply XS'. Finally, continuing the assumption of contract restraints, if the increase in demand were matched by an even greater increase in supply—as in the case of new discoveries—prices could be established below a competitive norm and below the price of previously committed supplies (see Figure M).

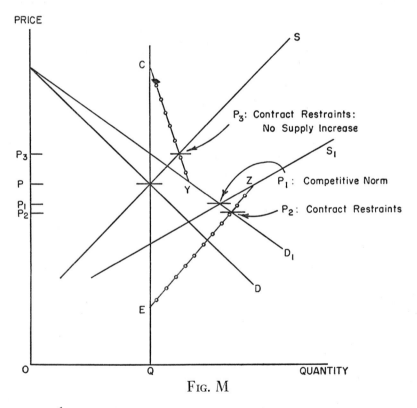

FIG. M

Criteria for Field Market Monopoly

The more important implications and conclusions of this analysis may be summarized in the following:

1. A control over a portion of the total supply of field gas can, under the conditions characterizing natural gas production, give rise to partial monopoly power.
2. Dominance over low-cost gas supplies, sufficient to meet current market demands, results in a monopolistic market control limited only by the cost "jump" to alternative gas supply resources.
3. Dominance over uncommitted gas supplies also results in market power sufficient to permit the establishment of noncompetitive prices as market demand increases.
4. The monopolistic market power resulting from a control over uncommitted gas supplies is enhanced by market practices such as long-term contracts, which—by preventing a reallocation of committed gas supplies—enables establishment of a higher monopolistic price than would otherwise be the case.
5. Where a number of gas supply areas can be distinguished, the one on the margin of development is price-determining. A monopoly condition here can result in monopolistic prices, the benefits of which are also obtained by other gas supply areas. These latter supply areas need not be dominated, nor is there any necessity for joint producer action within or between these supply areas.
6. Monopoly returns and monopolistic prices, however, are increased by joint producer action, and the larger the number of supply areas brought into a coalition—from lowest to highest-cost—the greater the monopoly price.
7. Finally, even in the absence of monopolistic conditions in natural gas field markets, noncompetitive prices—prices above competitive norms—can be established as a result of contract restraints on the reallocation of committed gas supplies or—without this factor—as a consequence of large buyer exit-costs.

237

CHAPTER 8

Monopoly and Field Market Structure

A MARKET CONTAINING numerous sellers of sufficient size to offer effective supply options to buyers is structured in the direction of competition. This condition generates much of the force and pressure leading to competitive action and rivalry. In contrast, a high degree of seller concentration constitutes a structural condition inimical to competition in at least two respects: First, the existence of few sellers leads more readily to an appreciation by all that the greatest long-run gain of each is likely to be obtained by maximizing industry-wide profit. Once individual market shares are reasonably well defined, there is little interest on the part of a particular seller to follow an independent and competitive course of action.

Second, a market containing few sellers is able to secure and maintain uniformity of practice without the need for direct seller agreement. Granted producer acceptance of the rule that industry-wide profits are to be maximized, a limited number of sellers, with all it implies of personal relationships and easy, frequent communication, makes the needed uniformity of behavior more easily attainable. Even worse, the condition may lead to small tacit diversities in seller actions which do not affect the ultimate goal but which make detection by inference from persistently uniform behavior almost impossible.

These general possibilities have their application in natural gas field markets. Seller concentration here is one of the surest means for achieving a large market power, and a structural condition which facilitates co-operative seller action is also needed to exploit even a lesser market position. The degree of seller concentration in field markets is clearly critical, if not decisive, for the question of monopolistic market control.

Monopoly and Field Market Structure

A. GENERAL CONCENTRATION LEVELS

The first of the measurements of concentration which was made in this study dealt with concentration in the ownership of gas reserves. Such a measure provides the broadest view of the competitive potential of industry structure in the case of natural gas production. Control over gas reserves, including those not yet committed, is needed if the most lucrative source of market power —a control over total supply—is to be exploited.

A highly useful and complementary measurement, however, is the degree of concentration in the current field sale of gas. Sales concentration complements reserve concentration by giving an approximate picture of the level of concentration of gas reserves or supplies which have already been committed. It indicates the extent to which a structural condition inimical to competition has prevailed in the past and thus the extent to which current field prices or recent changes in them may have been subjected to monopolistic pressures.

A detailed analysis of concentration in gas production was undertaken and substantiated in Chapter 1. Determining the approximate level of reserve concentration was made difficult by the incompleteness of available data concerning reserve holdings. It was necessary, therefore, to begin with a calculation of the minimum level of reserve concentration and, by various techniques, to obtain plausible approximations of reserve concentration.

In measuring sales concentration, attention was focused upon sales to interstate pipe lines. Since it was possible to demonstrate that the level of concentration in sales to interstate pipe lines did not differ greatly from that of total interstate and intrastate sales, this limited view raised no serious problems. Determining the proper level of sales concentration was, however, complicated by the possibility of alternative concentration bases. These bases differed in their geographical dimension, e.g., whether they were to cover the entire United States or were to be limited to sales made in the Southwest. They also differed in whether or not they were to include that part of the total gas supply of interstate pipe lines which came from the latter's own production.

From this information, approximations of the level of concentration characterizing natural gas production can be obtained —approximations which provide a general reference magnitude for evaluating monopolistic potential. Although strictly applicable only to 1953, the determined concentration levels can also be considered representative for some time after that year, since structural market conditions do not change rapidly.

The concentration ratios given below apply to a market unit of the entire United States, including pipe-line-owned reserves and production. Such a market unit, encompassing the total gas supply in the United States, is considered more appropriate than others for use in developing a reference standard of concentration; it includes virtually all of the alternatives of competitive significance available to pipe-line buyers.

ESTIMATED CONCENTRATION AMONG INDEPENDENT
GAS PRODUCERS—1953

	Reserve Holdings	Sales to Interstate Pipe Lines
5 Largest Producers	30%	25%
10 Largest Producers	45%	33%
25 Largest Producers	60%	50%

A comparison of these estimated ratios indicates that reserve concentration is slightly higher than sales concentration. The validity of this difference gains strength from the fact that even the minimum level of reserve concentration exceeds sales concentration for the first two size groupings of producers. However, the deficiencies in data concerning reserve holdings and the relative closeness of the two ratios make hazardous any firm conclusion other than that the reserve and sales concentration levels are approximately the same.

Still, the possibility that reserve concentration is the greater of the two ratios is sufficiently strong to justify a consideration of its implications for the question of concentration among uncommitted gas reserve holdings. In a broad sense, the level of sales concentration which has been presented also measures the

degree of concentration among committed gas reserve holdings
—at least among those committed to interstate pipe lines. Furthermore, there is evidence that sales concentration in an interstate
pipe-line market is not greatly different from that prevailing in a
market unit which includes the total marketed production of gas.
Consequently, a concentration level for total reserve holdings
which is greater than that obtained for sales—the latter reflecting
the concentration condition for committed gas reserves—implies a
higher degree of concentration among uncommitted gas reserves.

If this analysis is valid and reserve concentration exceeds
sales concentration, it is possible to conclude that concentration
among uncommitted gas reserve holdings—and thus new gas supplies—may be even greater than that indicated by either of the
two concentration measurements presented. The importance of
the level of concentration among uncommitted gas reserve holdings is great, and it derives from a previous analysis which has indicated that a partial—but nonetheless burdensome—monopoly
power can be based upon a dominance over uncommitted gas supplies. But such a conclusion is not to be hazarded from this study,

	Marketed Production or Purchases TCF	Gas Reserves Owned or Committed TCF	Reserve-Production Ratio
Interstate Pipe-Line Gas Supplies			
Pipe-Line-Owned	1.2	28.1	23.4
Independent Producers	4.2	96.7	22.7
Subtotal	5.4	124.8	23.0
Field Use	1.8	—	
Other Uses	1.2	—	
Total	8.4	211.5	
Reserves Outside Interstate Pipe-Line Market		86.7	

and other data dealing directly with concentration among uncommitted gas reserves are not available.

There is even a substantial lack of knowledge about the amount of uncommitted gas reserves. Virtually nothing is known about reserve commitments outside the interstate pipe-line market. Available data can be summarized quickly in the tabulation below. These amounts are taken from various tables in Chapter 1 and relate to the year 1953.

In the above tabulation, the total production of 8.4 TCF is equal to Bureau of Mines marketed production for 1953. Field use of 1.8 TCF is derived from the same Bureau of Mines source. The gas supply data for interstate pipe lines come from the Federal power Commission, while the 1.2 TCF in the "Other Uses" classification is a calculated residual amount. This 1.2 TCF presumably represents intrastate and, to a considerable extent, non-pipe-line uses of gas. It may also be noted that the interstate pipe-line gas supply of 5.4 TCF exceeds interstate shipments of 4.2 TCF recorded in Bureau of Mines data. The difference evidently results from sales of large quantities of gas in the producing state by pipe lines which are also engaged in interstate transportation—for example, the United Gas Pipe Line Company.

Although approximately 87 trillion cubic feet of gas reserves were outside the interstate pipe-line market in 1953, the proportion of these which were uncommitted gas reserves can only be estimated. If the same reserve-production ratio of 23.0 were applied to the 3.0 TCF of gas produced for sale or use outside the interstate pipe-line market, then about 18 TCF would represent uncommitted reserves. This amount, however, is to be viewed as a minimum, since it is unlikely that reserves equal to twenty-three years production would be committed, for example, to field use.

Having determined the concentration ratios which are to serve as a reference standard for the degree of concentration in field markets, there remains the task of evaluating their significance for the issue of gas field monopoly. The question is: Granted that the estimated sales concentration ratios reflect current structural conditions in the interstate pipe-line market and that reserve concentration ratios indicate longer-term competitive possibilities, can it be concluded that these concentration levels establish the existence of an objectionable degree of seller market power? Also, do they establish this condition as being so large and so innate that the detailed and continuous intervention of a public regulatory authority is needed?

The answers must be founded upon judgment, for no specific and widely accepted criterion exists to mark an objectionable level of concentration. But some aids to judgment may be available. Thus, the level of concentration which characterizes the American economy outside of natural gas production might be one bench mark. It would at least represent conditions which, until this time, have been socially tolerable. However, this general level suffers from the logical defect of circularity and can be further criticized because it ignores the distinctive features associated with the business of natural gas production—features which may require a lower level of concentration if competitive results are to be achieved. Nevertheless, the yardstick of comparative concentration is persuasive and may facilitate the present task of evaluation.

The concentration level which is typical in manufacturing may be determined from an analysis of data relating to concentration of employment in 247 industries for 1950. An alternative measurement for an earlier period is also available in the form of concentration in the value of goods produced, a measure which is equivalent to sales concentration. This information is available for 356 manufacturing industries covering the year 1947. A frequency distribution of these concentration ratios, taken for only the four largest companies, was prepared, and the results are given in Table 29.

From this material, it is seen that for both 1947 and 1950 a concentration ratio of approximately 40 per cent for the four largest companies is to be considered typical—one-half of the industries in the tabulation had concentration measurements greater than this, and one-half had less. The median values were 37.7 per

Table 29

DISTRIBUTION OF CONCENTRATION RATIOS IN MANUFACTURING
INDUSTRIES, CALCULATED FOR 4 LARGEST COMPANIES—
1947 AND 1950

Concentration Ratios	NUMBER OF INDUSTRIES	
%	*1947*	*1950*
0 to 9.9	24	9
10 to 19.9	46	36
20 to 29.9	71	41
30 to 39.9	48	27
40 to 49.9	42	33
50 to 59.9	40	27
60 to 69.9	29	24
70 to 79.9	26	17
80 to 89.9	18	11
90 to 99.9	11	7
Not available	1	15
Total	356	247
Median Ratio	37.7%	40.9%

Source: Report on Changes in Concentration in Manufacturing, 1935 to 1947 and 1950, Federal Trade Commission (1954).

cent and 40.9 per cent for 1947 and 1950, respectively. Furthermore, in both groups of data, there was some peaking of the distribution in the concentration ratio class of 20.0–29.9 per cent.

If these concentration values are accepted as representative and if the yardstick of comparative concentration is generally acceptable, there is little support here for a conclusion of excessive concentration in natural gas production. The concentration levels estimated for current sales in the gas field and for reserve ownership—25 per cent and 30 per cent, respectively, for the five largest producers—are less than the median values of Table 29. Actually, the ratios for the natural gas producing industry are overstated relative to the data with which they are being compared, since they are values for the five largest producers rather than the four largest companies. Made comparable, the concentration ratios for gas production would be smaller. For example, the sales concentration ratios for the four largest sellers would fall somewhere within the range of 18–24 per cent, depending upon the concentration base selected. Perhaps a sales concentration ratio of 20 per cent for the four largest producers would be an acceptable estimate.

It is evident that the level of concentration in natural gas production is not excessive by comparison with manufacturing industry. The structural condition of natural gas field markets, by these tests, does little to support a claim of gas producer monopoly. Other factors, however, might require a lower level of concentration in gas production.

In many manufacturing industries, high levels of concentration are not completely destructive of competitive results, since it is possible for new firms to enter the industry—a factor which acts as a restraint upon existing producers. Thus, the exploitative potential of seller concentration is limited by the fear of stimulating the construction of excess productive capacity, which in turn may lead to a prolonged period of depressed conditions in the industry. Since natural limitations retard the expansion of productive capacity in natural gas production, it may be argued that the preservation of competition here requires a lower level of concentration than in other industries.

It has already been established that concentration in gas production is less than that typical of manufacturing industries. How much lower it must be to represent competitive conditions can only be determined on a judgment basis, which tends toward the conclusion that concentration is not excessive in gas production, even in light of special factors affecting entry. Two facts concerning entry should be noted. Thus, many manufacturing industries which have high levels of concentration—about 60 per cent or more for the four largest companies—also have severe restraints upon entry either because of large capital needs or because of requirements for product promotion and distribution. Evidently, the economic consequences of such a condition have not as yet been sufficient to warrant full-scale regulatory action.

Moreover, whatever the level of concentration, gas field

markets contained a relatively large number of sellers. For example, the twenty-five largest producers accounted for only about 50–60 per cent of total sales or reserve holdings. Many additional sellers would be included if as much as 75 per cent of total sales were taken as a measurement base. Given so many producers, a considerable degree of seller co-operation would appear necessary before natural limits upon supply could be fully exploited.

B. SUBMARKET CONCENTRATION

If it is difficult to find a monopolistic structure in an over-all view of natural gas field markets, it may nevertheless be present in local or regional submarkets. Concentration measurements over a national market are frequently misleading as an index of market power, since buyers may not have effective options outside a small local area. In natural gas production, the measurement unit utilized thus far has been a national market, or a unit which is the same thing for all practical purposes—the southwestern gas-producing area of the United States. Although this market unit may contain the effective supply options available to new pipe-line projects, the competitive choices available to established pipe lines may fall within a more restricted area.

The level of concentration within gas supply submarkets is important for two reasons: First, committed pipe-line buyers can be seriously affected by this level. If sizable exit-costs are encountered in the abandonment of existing supply areas, buyer demand for replacement gas supplies is confined to the smaller submarket and is conditioned by the degree of concentration in this local market. Second, even uncommitted buyers can be adversely affected by submarket concentration caused by differential supply costs. As developed earlier, this situation is a possible source of market power and does not require a monopolistic structure in the total market. Exploitation depends only upon a sufficiently high level of concentration in localized gas supply submarkets.

Consequently, the degree of concentration in submarkets may evidence a noncompetitive condition of some importance—

perhaps enough to justify public action—even though the over-all field market for gas does not have a clear-cut monopolistic structure. An effort to ascertain the level of concentration in various submarkets was undertaken earlier in this study. Although the data for the investigation differed from those upon which the over-all sales concentration estimates were based, the concentration ratios for a comparable market unit were remarkably similar. This relative identity has the effect of substantiating the reliability of the concentration measurements made for the submarkets.

An analysis of concentration in localized gas supply areas indicates a higher level of concentration than cited thus far. In six of the eight gas supply areas, concentration ratios were about 50–60 per cent for the five largest producers and about 80 per cent for the ten largest producers. The highest level was found in the Panhandle-Hugoton gas supply area, where the five largest sellers accounted for 80 per cent of reported annual gas volumes; the lowest concentration level was applicable to the East Texas–North Louisiana supply area, where a concentration ratio of 40 per cent for the five largest producers was recorded.

These concentration ratios, however, may overstate the true monopolistic potential in these local markets. Actually, each of the supply areas contained a substantial number of sellers who were competitively significant, for they presented good competitive options to buyers and could act independently of one another if they so desired. Thus, in virtually all of the supply areas there were at least fifteen producers disposing of annual gas volumes of 5.0 million MCF per annum and twenty or more sellers disposing of annual gas volumes in excess of 2.0 million MCF.

The manner in which concentration ratios may overstate the degree of monopolistic power can be further illustrated in the Panhandle-Hugoton supply area. The high concentration level in this local supply source reflects the dominant position of the Phillips Petroleum Company, which was responsible for approximately 40 per cent of recorded annual gas sales. In spite of this predominance, at least five other sellers of considerable size, as well as sixteen sellers recording gas volumes of 5.0 million MCF or more, were operative in the area.

Relative dominance by a single seller or small group of sellers may have a smaller monopolistic influence in the gas field than in markets such as those served by manufacturing industries. In manufacturing markets, pricing and selling are highly repetitive over short time periods. Dominant size of one seller may be a strong lever influencing smaller rivals, since the latter must continually face the possibility of that dominance being deliberately used to destroy them.

By way of contrast, under conditions characterizing the field sale of gas, a completed transaction is valid for the term of the purchase contract. Fear of retaliation or of initiating a "price war" is minimized as a factor restraining price competition. Actually, price competition might expectedly be intensified under these conditions—particularly among relatively small producers with meager financial resources. Once a pipe-line purchaser meets gas supply needs for a new project in a particular area or for an expansion of existing facilities, that buyer may not be in the market again for a considerable period of time.

Consequently, the mere size of a dominant seller in gas field markets—unlike manufacturing—may not be an important instrument for imposing price conformity upon smaller rivals. Disparities in the size of producers may have less of an adverse effect upon competition in the gas field than elsewhere, and relatively small producers can provide effective competitive alternatives to pipe-line buyers. For example, a major pipe-line expansion—and even a new project—could have been economically undertaken in the period after 1945 on the basis of an annual gas volume of 80–100 million MCF. Thus, a seller offering 10–20 million MCF per annum would have been a primary source of supply, a volume of 5 million MCF would have been important, and 2.0 million MCF would by no means have been unimpressive.

In addition to the factors mentioned, the relatively high concentration levels recorded in individual supply areas may be inadequate measurements of competitive structure for another—and perhaps more important—reason: They are not suitable market units for testing competitive structure because they do not include all of the more immediate supply options available to pipe-line buyers. Aggregations of these supply areas, designated as submarkets, are judged to be more appropriate in this respect.

By way of illustration, the three supply areas in Texas, defined by the Texas Railroad Commission's Districts 2, 3, and 4, constitute a meaningful market unit in accordance with the above criterion and may be designated the Texas Gulf Coast submarket. Similarly, the two supply areas in southern Louisiana can be grouped together and identified as the Louisiana Gulf Coast; the West Texas and Panhandle-Hugoton supply areas can be considered another submarket. The East Texas–North Louisiana supply area is sufficiently large and distinctive to stand alone.

The supply areas combined in this fashion are close enough geographically to minimize the exit-costs of committed pipe-line buyers if they should choose to shift within them. Their proximity also suggests small differences in supply costs. It is concluded that these designated submarkets are the most suitable units for testing the presence of an effective competitive structure in markets smaller than those representing a national unit.

The concentration levels in these submarkets—adapted from Table 14—are summarized below:

CONCENTRATION IN GAS SUPPLY SUBMARKETS

	5 Largest Sellers (per cent)	10 Largest Sellers (per cent)	15 Largest Sellers (per cent)
Texas Gulf Coast	40	60	70
La. Gulf Coast	40	60	80
East Texas–North La.	40	60	70
All Gulf Coast and East Texas–North La.	25	40	50
Panhandle-Hugoton– W. Texas	60	75	80
All Southwestern Gas Supply Areas	32	46	55

As the various supply areas were aggregated into larger submarket units, the level of concentration diminished. This result was not inevitable and would not have occurred if the dominant sellers in each supply area had been the same. However, in the analysis of submarket concentration, significant diversity of dominant sellers was found among the different supply areas. This condition—competitive in its implications—was responsible for the decline in concentration levels.

Combining submarkets in the Gulf Coast gas-producing area resulted in an added substantial reduction in concentration levels —again the outcome of seller diversity among market units which individually have the same concentration level. However, the inclusion of supply areas with high concentration levels—the Panhandle-Hugoton and West Texas–Permian Basin supply areas— to secure a Southwest regional market unit led to an increase in concentration levels. These results lead to a conclusion of substantial importance: In a major regional supply unit, structural conditions are more competitive than in a larger and more inclusive market unit of which it is a part.

The lower concentration level in the Gulf Coast and East Texas submarket was clearly effective for pipe lines originating in this producing area. Since postwar expansion of interstate pipe lines was—to a large extent—based upon this supply source, the competitive structure of the postwar field market for gas was greater than that inferred from concentration measurements of the entire southwestern gas-producing region. In short, for an important group of pipe lines, the effective degree of structural competition among sellers in the gas field markets is understated by the usual over-all concentration measurements.

It is interesting, too, that in the Panhandle and West Texas submarket, where seller concentration is very high, the monopolistic potential of this condition was largely offset by unique conditions on the buying side of the market. In West Texas, only one interstate pipe-line buyer was operative for an extended period of time; in Panhandle-Hugoton, most pipe-line buyers possess substantial gas reserve holdings of their own.

Generally, the level of submarket concentration is not so high that it is likely to result in a large market power based either upon differential supply costs or buyer exit-costs. An exception might be made for the Panhandle-Hugoton–West Texas supply unit, although in this case it is offset by a stronger-than-average buyer position. In the case of the Gulf Coast submarkets, purchasers usually have pipe-line facilities which traverse the entire producing area. For these purchasers, the competitively significant supply unit is the Gulf Coast–East Texas submarket. Only if a buyer were faced with the necessity of shifting from this supply source to an entirely different producing area would any large exit-costs be involved. The probability that such a market power could be exploited is slight, since the degree of seller concentration in the Gulf Coast–East Texas submarket is even less than the concentration level for a larger regional market unit.

On the basis of available information concerning concentration in national, regional, and local submarkets, it is difficult to conclude that a structural condition exists in natural gas field markets which generates strong tendencies toward monopolistic pricing and behavior. While some market power may undoubtedly arise from structural conditions in certain gas supply areas smaller than the defined submarket units, the power does not appear sufficient to warrant an extended system of price control.

C. CONSERVATION CONTROLS AND COMPETITION

An important structural aspect of natural gas field markets relates to the competitive impact of producing-state conservation controls. Among these devices are unitization, well-spacing, control of gas-oil ratios, the establishment of gas production allowables, and minimum field price regulations. All of these are probably justifiable as conservation measures or as means of assuring equitable treatment to individuals, but—at the same time—they may have noncompetitive effects. The objective here is to note these effects and to form some judgment concerning their magnitude for the monopoly issue.

Unitization permits the owners of a gas field to combine for a joint effort in development and marketing of gas production. By diminishing the number of potentially independent sellers, structural competition is reduced. More important, the pressure to produce and market gas competitively, to avoid losses or to gain benefits from drainage, is eliminated. Well-spacing and limitations upon gas-oil ratios have the effect of restricting production: the first device through limitation of the number of wells which can tap the gas field; and the second by preventing a high ratio of gas production, which would reduce reservoir pressures in oil pools. Both provisions may have clear-cut justifications in the control of physical waste, but they also have a noncompetitive effect by preventing an expansion in the rate of production from a given field in response to the economic incentive of a high price.

The conservation control which has the strongest potential noncompetitive effect is the setting of production allowables, since the power to restrict output is a power to raise prices. But such allowables are generally set on the basis of the nominations of existing buyers and, because of this, may have a lesser effect than if the conservation authority were free to initiate a reduction in the total supply. The fixing of minimum field prices for gas production, as practiced by some producing states, operates to limit the area within which buyer and seller bargaining can occur. If set too high, the minimum price might actually become an effective maximum and be in excess of that which would prevail as a competitive price.

In evaluating the impact of these conservation controls upon natural gas field markets over the period 1945–53, the following is noted: These conservation controls are very probably less of a market force than is commonly assumed, since they are not applicable in all parts of the southwestern gas-producing region. The most restrictive of such controls—the setting of production allowables—is not, as in the case of oil, co-ordinated over a large part of the producing region, nor is it even on a state-wide basis in Texas.

A system of gas production allowables is most highly developed within the Panhandle-Hugoton supply area. The strongest noncompetitive effect upon prices seems to arise from the limitation the system imposes upon pipe-line-owned production. It cannot be greatly expanded as an offset to a rising field price level. Actually, the setting of production allowables may force a reduction of pipe-line-produced output, with the result that these pipe-line buyers must compete for a relatively small amount of excess allowables.

Minimum field price controls have not been widespread enough to be considered a basic factor influencing field prices. Again, the controls are almost exclusively found in the Panhandle-Hugoton supply area, and, in this instance, they are not applicable to the Texas portion of the supply area or any other Texas gas production. Without minimum field price regulations for Texas gas production, the effect of this type of conservation control upon the general level of field prices is negligible.

Furthermore, in the Oklahoma and Kansas portions of the Panhandle-Hugoton supply area, the minimum prices established have been true minima in the sense that they were set below an existing price level and well after that level was established. In these states, the minimum field price regulation appears to have the purpose of relieving gas producers of an obligation to fulfill low-priced contracts which were negotiated during a prewar and early postwar period.

Another consideration of importance to an evaluation of conservation controls is that they do not add markedly to the monopoly power of individual producers or small groups of sellers. With the exception of unitization, these controls are much more general in their impact. If they are a strong influence upon field prices—which is questionable—the influence is exerted for the benefit of all producers, and it is independent of competitive conditions in field markets.

The problem becomes one of deciding whether or not state conservation controls are managed exclusively in the interest of gas producers or, as an alternative, whether or not the gains of resource conservation to the community are sufficient to counterbalance any unwarranted benefits which producers might receive. However, this problem is present regardless of the degree of private monopoly among gas producers. Thus, it is not really a proper consideration in an evaluation of monopoly in the gas field.

Putting this argument aside, though, it does not appear that the present pattern of conservation controls in the producing state has bettered the market position of gas producers. Certainly it cannot be said that conservation controls have had any major role in the rapid postwar rise of field price levels. Granted they may have had some restrictive effect upon gas supply relative to the quantity which would have been forthcoming in their absence, but, among other factors operating upon price, this would have been minor.

Moreover, the nature of the conservation controls are such that they operate more to prevent a decline in the field price structure than to provide a mechanism for shifting it upward to monopolistic levels. Prorationing, for example, even if widespread in the gas producing region, would operate to prevent the price level from falling rather than to initiate an upward movement, since it would reduce output to buyer demand at a given price. This does suggest that market power among producers, combined with prorationing, could be a highly efficient system: the former would act to raise the price level, and the latter would function to maintain it. But prorationing is not widespread in natural gas production, and the question being reviewed is whether or not the requisite degree of private monopoly power exists. It may be concluded that conservation controls alone have not been an important factor affecting field prices in the period under consideration.

CHAPTER 9

Monopoly and Field Market Behavior

W̲HILE COMPETITIVE FORCES are generated by a structural condition of numerous sellers, they can be counteracted by non-competitive behavior. Difficulties in securing the needed co-operation, however, increase with the number of sellers, since the possibility of large individual gains from competitive behavior becomes greater, and problems of co-ordination mount. Still, with a firm belief in the long-run advantage to be derived, the most competitively structured industry may feature the quintessence of noncompetitive behavior.

To realize monopoly returns, noncompetitive behavior must perform in two arenas. It must act initially to raise prices to monopolistic levels and thereafter adjust them to new monopolistic positions as cost and demand circumstances change. It must also act, in the face of a variety of downward pressures, to maintain such prices at existing monopoly levels. These requirements can be met by a collusive agreement among sellers which determines a particular price; they can be secured by tacit co-operation—such as "price leadership"—by a dominant seller; or, where sellers are numerous and circumstances highly variable, they may be at least partially achieved by collusive or tacit adherence to particular marketing practices.

It is not likely that direct evidence of seller collusion would be readily obtainable, and proof of tacit agreement is inherently difficult to ascertain. Similar problems would be encountered in proving that adherence to particular practices was the outcome of agreement. As a consequence, if the competitiveness of seller behavior in the gas field is to be evaluated, it must be based upon inferential evidence. The primary clue to noncompetitive behavior is the existence of uniformities in seller actions under circumstances where such uniformities are inconsistent with the realistic functioning of a competitive market.

This base for evaluating seller behavior is by no means a weak foundation. The action of establishing monopolistic prices—while necessary—is not a sufficient condition for securing monopoly returns; these prices must be sustained. To accomplish this, the manifold downward pressures on price must be resisted, usually by the maintenance of a considerable uniformity in seller pricing actions. Uniformity, moreover, must be extended beyond price if the system of seller co-operation is to be kept intact. For, without a general uniformity, rivalry can erupt in non-price forms, and —once out of control—such rivalry can quickly destroy the psychological bases for co-operation. Minimum variety in seller actions diminishes the opportunity for rivalry—or at least the narrower and less destructive of monopoly gains are the channels into which it can be diverted.

Uniformity of pricing and other actions is also vital as an instrument for assuring all sellers an equal opportunity to secure monopoly profits. Unless buyers are rendered indifferent in a choice among sellers by persisting identity of prices and terms, some sellers will be more fortunate than others in the completion of transactions. It would require exceptional faith in the good sense—if not the goodwill—of a business rival for the unsuccessful seller not to believe that the ground rules of co-operation were broken. This possibility is greatly accentuated in markets—such as those for field gas—where negotiations over price and terms are protracted and unpublicized. The buyer may pit one seller against another, and only faith or the settled uniformity of basic terms and conditions could then assuage the uncertainty of particular sellers concerning their equal opportunity.

A. Price Uniformity and Concerted Seller Action

The existence of uniformities in seller actions, inconsistent with the realistic functioning of a competitive market, is to be the primary test of noncompetitive behavior, and the most pertinent uniformity is that of price. Application of a price uniformity test, however, is greatly complicated by the fact that, over the period to be covered, there has been a large increase in the demand for gas, resulting in a rapidly rising price level. Between 1945 and 1953, there was a 300 per cent increase in the quantity of field gas acquired by interstate pipe lines; this growth was matched by about a 300 per cent increase in the general level of field prices in the southwestern gas-producing region. An absence of that form of price uniformity known as price inflexibility necessarily exists. Nevertheless, price uniformity among sellers at a given time or price uniformity between distinguishable supply areas is possible even with a rising price level and can provide useful inferences regarding competitive behavior.

The analysis of field prices contained in Chapter 2 has given some indication of inter-supply area price relationships. In general, the analysis did not uncover patterns of price uniformity among the various supply areas which would suggest concerted seller action or indicate the presence of a strong price leadership mechanism. Actually, the timing of inter-supply area price movements was highly suggestive of competitive responses between these markets. The detailed field price analysis demonstrated the existence of a steplike change in supply area price levels. The rise of prices in one induced a buyer shift to another supply area, resulting in an increase of prices in the latter, while an absence of purchase activity characterized the higher-priced supply source. Generally, the timing of the price changes in the various gas supply areas appeared to be far more consistent with shifting demand pressures than with a hypothesis of monopolistic seller agreement.

In addition to inter-supply area patterns, there is the matter of uniformities within individual supply areas. A basis for conclusions is to be found in the extended survey of market behavior in the gas field contained in Part II. From that analysis, one fact became obvious: the consideration in a field purchase transaction is a complex "mix" of price and contract conditions. The characteristic feature of field market contracts was not one in which price was the only important factor, with minor roles assigned to contract conditions; instead, price and terms were often combined in a manner which suggested that a low or high contract price was being offset by a favorable or unfavorable non-price condition. Consequently, price uniformity in the field market must really mean uniformity in the total consideration embodied in a purchase contract. This could be achieved by either an agreed-upon balance of price and terms for the multitude of combinations possible or an identity in price and other contract provisions.

There is no evidence to indicate the employment of the first method for establishing effective price uniformity. It would, in fact, be extremely difficult to implement since it would entail an almost formal consultation among numerous sellers. Even consulting sellers would have difficulty deciding what combinations of price and contract conditions constituted identical total considerations, since much would depend upon the circumstances facing individual producers.

Instances of price uniformity, in which both price and contract terms were identical for successive purchase agreements, were found at different times in many supply areas. Where uniformity persisted for any extended period, it was in gas supply areas—such as the West Texas–Permian Basin and Southeast Louisiana—which contained only one or two pipe-line buyers. In these cases, it is reasonably certain that contract uniformity came from the buyer and not the seller. Pipe-line buyers were, in effect, "posting" the price and contract terms at which they would purchase. Many contracts containing identical price and contract provisions would then be negotiated.

A similar buyer-determined contract uniformity was also found for shorter periods in other supply areas—such as the Texas Gulf Coast. Here, established pipe lines with extensive gathering networks appeared to "post" prices, presumably as a means of dealing with numerous small sellers. That this uniformity was not seller-determined is also evident from the fact that, at the same time and in the same supply area, two or more pipe lines would be offering a different "mix" of price and contract terms.

Aside from these cases, a considerable degree of contract uniformity was noted in the purchase agreements of new pipe-line projects—especially after 1951. These were not infrequently identical in their most important respects, including a precise uniformity in contract terms other than price stipulation. This uniformity could also have been the product of buyer initiative. Thus, rather than bargain with producers individually, a new project desiring large gas reserves might attempt to "break into" the field market by means of a uniform contract offer containing a higher price and advantageous terms. Sellers would then be under pressure to "sign up" before the buyer's needs were met. Alternatively—and possibly the more likely situation—once the terms of a key contract were made reasonably definite by negotiation, the pipe-line buyer would find it simpler to offer the same terms to others to fill out supply needs.

Although these two possibilities are plausible and become more so as uncommitted gas reserves become less plentiful, unless it can be ascertained that uniformity was buyer-determined, the presumption of concerted seller action or localized price leadership must be entertained. Except in cases of buyer-determination previously listed, a complete and precise uniformity of price and contract terms was so uncommon a feature of field markets that its existence presses heavily toward a conclusion of noncompetitive seller behavior.

It is of some interest that the type of uniformity treated here —virtual identity of price and contract conditions negotiated by a particular buyer acquiring gas reserves for a new project—was especially noticeable in the Louisiana Gulf Coast submarket. On the basis of this evidence, it might be claimed that the substantially higher price level established in this supply area during 1952–53 was the outcome of a monopolistic agreement among producers. But it is also possible that producers of the Louisiana Gulf Coast were simply the beneficiaries of a growing scarcity of reserves suitable for new projects—a scarcity which was accentuated by an earlier commitment of such reserves located in other supply areas. Moreover, the higher price level in the Louisiana Gulf Coast area after 1951 may have reflected more fully its advantages of location relative to other supply areas.[1] These factors, as well

[1] See letter of Mr. George S. Young, The Columbia Gas System, Inc.,

as the possibility of buyer determination, make difficult a quick conclusion that the differentially higher price level was obtained by a noncompetitive seller agreement, implemented by a collusive contract uniformity.

The analysis of field market transactions covering the period 1945–53 did not disclose a condition of contract uniformity which could sustain an inference of monopolistic seller agreement. In a number of supply areas, the condition of contract uniformity was clearly buyer-determined, and, in others, the possibility of buyer determination was strong. In general, the evidences of contract uniformity do not lend much support to a conclusion of collusive pricing behavior among gas producers.

This conclusion relies heavily upon the evidence of uniformity, and some question might be raised about the overvaluation of a uniformity of price and terms as a test of noncompetitive behavior. For example, could there not have been co-operation among producers for the establishment of monopolistic field price levels in a manner not requiring detailed contract uniformity?

Uniformity would be important for reasons already mentioned which relate to the preservation of the system of monopolistic co-operation—an importance which would be increased by the fact of highly informed pipe-line buyers and large-volume purchases. Small differences would bulk large and it is presumed that pipe-line buyers would accept that seller offer which was most advantageous, however slight the concession might appear. Without a high degree of similarity in contract price and terms, some aggressive sellers would be more consistently successful than others—a situation obviously not conducive to the maintenance of co-operation.

---

relative to the cost of gas obtained from the Louisiana Gulf Coast Area, included in *Hearings—S. 1853*, 1808, given in part below:

> During the first quarter of 1955, the price of our south Louisiana gas to us by Gulf Interstate Gas Co. at Huntington, W. Va. was 30.08 cents per thousand cubic feet. This price includes, of course, the price we paid for the gas in south Louisiana. The short haul from south Louisiana as compared with south Texas justifies a field price higher than the south Texas prices.
>
> I think I should point out that this gas is costing us less at the present time than gas from some of our other sources.

Aside from this consideration, there is little support in the purchase contract data for a hypothesis that gas producers may have co-operated in some loose and general manner to establish monopolistic field price levels. For example, the inter-supply area price relationships disclosed by the purchase contract analysis do not sustain such a proposition; actually, price differences among the supply areas were frequently inconsistent with rational producer action under that hypothesis. Such price differences should have followed a pattern which rendered buyers indifferent in choosing among supply areas; inter-field price relationships should have reflected the differential advantages of field location. However, the field price data did not demonstrate any consistent relationship of this character.

Over the period 1945–53, there were notably different judgments among gas producers regarding the future course of field prices. If the general level of field prices had been under seller control, the actions of some producers in committing large gas volumes to interstate markets prior to substantial rises in the level of those prices would be difficult to explain. For example, it would be hard to account for the behavior of those sellers—including some in the Louisiana Gulf Coast supply areas—who negotiated relatively large-volume contracts in 1951, just before the 1952 field price increases.

If collusive monopoly had ruled among gas producers, the price "jumps" of 1952–53 should have occurred in 1948–49. At that time the largest volume of gas reserves in the Southwest was being committed to pipe-line markets under long-term contracts which contained virtually no contract price flexibility. There is great difficulty in justifying the notion that producers accepting a 9.0 cent per MCF price in 1949 did so to benefit those who, three years later, were to receive 18.0 cents per MCF—even if the ultimate effect was to raise general field price levels.

A scheme of monopoly generalized to the extent that some producers make sacrifices which give greater benefits to others— although all gain in the long run—would be most plausible in an industry of few large firms, where seller orientation is toward long-term gains and the superiority of joint profit maximization is firmly rooted. Such an industry structure was not characteristic of natural gas production during the period 1945–53. Consequently, monopolistic co-operation would have to be far more specific in price and contract terms if all producers were to make equal sacrifices, and if they were to secure roughly equal monopoly returns.

Of some importance to the proposition of a generalized monopolistic co-operation among gas producers is the fact that, in the extended legislative hearings on various gas bills, no serious effort was made to evidence such a condition. In spite of implied assertions of monopolistic agreement in the gas field, little or nothing which might substantiate such claims was offered. To illustrate, in the hearings held on the Harris bill, frequent reference was made to a producer objective of raising field prices to a 25 cents per MCF level, with implication of a collusive arrangement to accomplish this.[2] At one point in the hearings it was asserted that "we have been told that it is the objective of the oil companies who own these reserves to get the price up to 25 cents."[3]

Upon being pressed for the source of this information, the witness was unable to provide it. In a subsequent letter, he referred to a number of bases for the assertion, including the following:

> My present belief is, however, that my first advice arose in a conversation which I had with a chief executive of a large pipe-line whom I visited a year ago in order to attempt to find out where gas prices were going. My question to him was, "Was there a plateau which would be reached?" and he asserted that the only figure he had heard discussed among producers was 25 cents a thousand cubic feet; although it was the intention of this pipe-line to resist an increase to any such figure.[4]

Whether or not this evidences producer collusion is most uncertain; even the vague references to price objectives are not persuasive of effective monopolistic behavior, in the absence of evi-

[2] *Hearings—H. R. 4560*, 1179, 1188, 1382, 1439.
[3] Testimony of Mr. Charles H. Frazier, representing the Philadelphia Gas Works, *ibid.*, 798.
[4] *Ibid.*, 799.

dence revealing concerted action or a mechanism to achieve it.

At other points in the legislative hearings, implied references to possible communities of interest between pipe-line purchasers and gas producers were also made. It was frequently asserted that an absence of effective bargaining incentives on the part of pipe-lines existed.[5] While this argument did not explicitly claim any collusive relationship between pipe lines and sellers, it would have little or no purpose unless such relationships between buyer and seller were implied. It seems quite improbable that a pipe line would disregard its own interest in maintaining low supply costs. Passing on higher field prices to distributors can be slow and costly to pipe lines, as well as destructive of potential market growth and financial security for those pipe lines heavily financed with bonds.

Persuasive evidence of communities of interest which might limit a pipe-line buyer's interest in hard bargaining was not presented in the hearings. In one controversial situation, any collusive relationship between buyer and seller was specifically disclaimed.[6] However, if these communities of interest did exist, they would most likely take the form of interlocking directorates, although less tangible connections between pipe lines and producer interest groups might prevail.

A few individuals, who are closely associated with the gas-producing segment of the industry, are also directors of interstate pipe-line companies.[7] Furthermore, some of the postwar pipe lines are oriented toward the Southwest, for the promotional drive and some of the financial backing for these undertakings came from that gas-producing region. However, based on information derived from Congressional hearings and financial reporters, the extent of interlocking directorates is not large, and it can hardly be said that representatives of producing interests dominate pipe-line boards of directors.

The factor of orientation is too vague to be decisive. If it

[5] As an example, see the statement of the Public Service Commission of Wisconsin, *ibid.*, 1732.

[6] See testimony of Mr. James R. Durfee, Chairman of the Public Service Commission of Wisconsin, relative to the Phillips Petroleum Co. and Michigan–Wisconsin Pipe Line Co., contract, *ibid.*, 1740.

[7] *Ibid.*, 1874.

263

were a competitively important factor, pipe-line companies and their stockholders would have to gain more from a rising field price level than they would lose from an increase in supply costs. Even for pipe lines owning their own gas reserves—necessarily excluding most postwar projects—this situation would be doubtful. In short, it is difficult, on the basis of available evidence, to support a claim that noncompetitive communities of interest which materially affected natural gas field prices existed between pipe lines and gas producers.

B. MARKET PRACTICES AND COMPETITIVE SELLER BEHAVIOR

In addition to direct seller agreement, there is also the possibility that monopolistic price results can be obtained indirectly through seller adherence to certain market practices designed to have noncompetitive consequences. Such field market practices—referred to collectively as escalator clauses and appearing as contract provisions in natural gas purchase agreements—include tax-sharing, fixed price escalation, inflation adjustment, and favored-nation provisos, as well as stipulations permitting price redetermination or renegotiations.

The form and prevalence of these contract clauses have been dealt with at length in Chapter 3 and need not be repeated. Generally speaking, such contract provisos have one common feature which is pertinent at this point: they make possible price changes in what are otherwise long-term gas supply arrangements. However, effectiveness in this connection differs markedly. Tax-sharing and fixed price escalation permit only relatively small price changes, while two-party favored-nation clauses make contract price changes discretionary with the buyer. Only price redetermination clauses or third-party favored-nation clauses give any large measure of contract price flexibility.

Moreover, not all of these market practices were widely used. For example, spiral escalator or inflation adjustment clauses, as well as third-party favored-nation clauses, were rather infrequent. Consequently, these provisos—in addition to tax-sharing and fixed price escalation clauses with small price effects—need not be treated in detail. The escalator provisions which must be analyzed for their monopolistic implications include only the two-party favored-nation clause and the price redetermination clause.

Besides these two contract provisions, a characteristic feature of field markets has been the purchase of gas under long-term contracts. Although rarely viewed in such a light, this particular market practice can have a considerable price effect, since the practical result of the device is to tie buyer and seller together to prevent the reallocation of committed gas supplies. The demand for new gas supplies must thus focus upon uncommitted gas reserves—which can lead to higher prices for these reserves in comparison with prices which might be received if all gas supplies were brought to bear upon the market.

The three market practices which have the greatest relevance for the question of competition in the gas field include the favored-nation device, the price redetermination stipulation, and the long-term purchase contract. In assessing these, the general approach will be to determine whether or not they are consistent with the responses of non-co-operating sellers in a competitive market—as well as determination of whether or not they are so widely and uniformly adhered to that an inference of monopolistic seller agreement may be supported. Generally, the task is to discover whether or not these market practices represent a designed system, the purpose of which is to co-ordinate the actions of many sellers in a manner which raises and maintains field prices above competitive levels.

Ironically enough, the main pressure for the use of long-term purchase contracts—probably one of the major imperfections in gas field markets, leading to higher prices—has not come from the gas producer. It has come from pipe-line buyers desirous of assuring the availability of gas supplies in order to finance their projects, with considerable pressure exerted by regulatory authorities seeking to protect consumers against premature abandonment. Even when contract prices were not firm, and in spite of the realization that they might soon increase, pipe-line buyers have sought long-term purchase agreements. At least gas supply problems would thereby be resolved, on terms comparable to those paid by others.

With respect to price redetermination or practices conducive to contract price flexibility, the interest of sellers in some mechanism which would raise contract prices—as field prices rise —is not difficult to appreciate. As noted, gas reserves are typically committed to a particular buyer in long-term contracts—a practice which, aside from regulatory and financial requirements, is made necessary by the large capital expenditures characterizing long-distance pipe lines. The economic feasibility of such projects depends upon an assured gas supply sufficient for the lengthy amortization period required for recovery of capital investment. Here, indeed, is the hard core of the field pricing problem: pipeline buyers need the certainty of long-term gas supplies; gas producers, on the other hand, find their interest in avoiding firm price commitments, especially when they have reason to expect a rising level of field prices. The practical resolution of this conflict in the course of purchase contract negotiations has undoubtedly fostered many field market practices. By providing contract price flexibility, the price redetermination clause and—to a degree —the two-party favored-nation proviso serve a basic interest of gas producers. Meeting basic needs, these practices are thus not necessarily inconsistent with independent seller action, and they could have developed within the framework of a competitive field market.

From another point of view, both of these devices—as well as other practices which affect contract prices—are part of the total consideration given and received by participants in the market transaction. The inclusion of a two-party favored-nation clause or the broadening of its area coverage and the inclusion of a price redetermination provision or the shortening of the redetermination period are not essentially different from price increases, and they are dependent upon buyer and seller bargaining strength. In fact, the analysis of market behavior in Part II has established that these practices developed rather slowly and in a pattern which was highly correlated with the growing seller strength in the market. There is much reason to believe that they have been a product of the same forces which have resulted in substantial field price increases—forces which are not necessarily monopolistic.

It can be asserted, then, that price redetermination and favored-nation clauses are as much a part of the total consideration in a purchase transaction as the price schedule; adding or eliminating, strengthening or weakening these constitutes indirect price changes. The importance of this fact for assessing the competitive significance of these market devices is considerable. Practices which are not a part of the price bargain—in the sense that they do not directly affect the consideration given and received in a transaction—are much more suspect as artificial elements in a market, and their mere prevalence might support an inference of noncompetitive seller behavior.

In view of the above discussion, an assertion that the market practices being considered are per se monopolistic devices—entirely the result of seller collusion and incapable of being sustained except by such producer action—is an erroneous simplification of conditions prevailing in natural gas field markets. These practices are consistent with a workably competitive market. This does not mean, however, that they could not be used to achieve monopolistic results or—like any advantageous price increase— that they could not have been the product of seller collusion. But to establish these possibilities as facts requires something more than reference to the prevalence of these practices, since their prevalence cannot be considered any more evidence of monopolistic behavior than the prevalence of a given price.

Conferring important benefits upon sellers, these contract clauses are integral parts of the price structure, and they could logically be expected to become widespread. For example, if most producers are receiving about 10.0 cents per MCF plus a two-party favored-nation clause—other contract provisions given—any particular seller will insist upon the same or better. Once established in a supply area, a two-party favored-nation clause—like other practices which represent indirect price gains—will soon become widely adopted. A reverse illustration is found in the Panhandle-Hugoton supply area, where the favored-nation clause was never common and has not therefore become part of the prevailing price structure.

Better evidence that the favored-nation clause is the outcome of monopolistic seller behavior would be a refusal by producers to accept a price increase in lieu of a favored-nation clause—in which case seller collusion to propagate the practice might be presumed. The assertion that pipe-line buyers have had no choice but to accept such contract clauses has appeared in Congressional hearings.[8]

In support of this proposition, the testimony of various pipe-line purchasing executives before the Federal Power Commission has been cited, in which these individuals were questioned about the reason for a necessity of accepting favored-nation clauses in gas purchase contracts. The response, in one instance, was as follows:

> Generally speaking . . . the reason those favored-nation clauses were included in the contract was because we could not get the gas without them. In other words, they have come to be within the last 6 or 7 years a requirement of every producer when he is selling gas . . .
>
> Now, of course, that has been brought about by competition for the gas supplies in the particular area that we operate in, and in other areas, too, for that matter.[9]

In a second instance, it was stated in response to a similar question:

[8] Testimony of Senator Paul H. Douglas of Illinois, *Hearings—S. 1853*, 1593:

> The inclusion in gas purchase contracts of "favored nation" and "renegotation" and other escalation clauses also demonstrates the existence of a condition in the producing fields under which producers dominate the gas market.
>
> These clauses, which did not become prevalent until about 1947, place burdens upon the pipe-line buyers which they would be unwilling to assume if they had a free choice in the matter.
>
> . . . .
>
> On the other hand, there is evidence in proceedings before the Federal Power Commission showing that pipe-line companies had no choice, if they wanted natural gas, but to accede to the demands of producers that such clauses be included in the gas-purchase contracts.

[9] Cited in *Hearings—S. 1853*, 1594.

268

Answer. I would say that you have to have those in here for the same reason we had to pay 10 cents.
Question. Well, didn't Oklahoma Natural recognize that by the inclusion of such clauses a very dangerous situation was being created as to potential increases in their cost of purchased gas?
Answer. Well, you have to weigh that danger against the danger of not having any gas supply, and you come to the conclusion that you have to accept that rather than to not have gas at all.[10]

From both of the above testimonies, the conclusion has been drawn that, because of monopolistic influences, the buyer had no option but to accept the favored-nation clause. But there is also an equal—if not a stronger—basis in the statements for the inference that it had to be accepted as part of the going price structure. Nowhere is it made explicitly clear that the favored-nation clause could not be avoided, even by tendering a higher price. Most pipe-line buyers, in any case, would probably have preferred the future possibility of a price rise, especially where it would be within their control as with a two-party favored-nation clause, to the actuality of an immediate price increase.

Furthermore, there is some evidence that producers have been willing to trade price increases for the elimination of certain contract clauses. It is seen in the following, where reference was made to testimony given before the Federal Power Commission by the representative of a large gas producing company:

Mr. Howard B. Shelton, Vice-President and General Manager of Sohio Petroleum Production Company, testified on September 15, 1955, that his company had never entered into a twenty-year contract without a favored-nation provision and would not dispense with such provisions *unless he could make a contract commencing at a sales price of twenty-five cents per Mcf* . . . Mr. Shelton testified that if he could not get this price . . . then he would insist upon some renegotiation provisions or favored-nation provisions in the gas-sales contract.[11] [Emphasis added.]

10 *Ibid.,* 1594.
11 Paul H. Douglas, "The Case for the Consumer of Natural Gas," *Georgetown Law Journal,* Vol. XLIV (June 1956), 566, 597.

Some evidence that a higher price could secure the elimination of favored-nation restrictions was also found in the purchase contract data analyzed in Part II. In one case, too, it was seemingly the policy of one of the largest pipe-line buyers to engage in a reverse trade, offering price flexibility provisions in exchange for lower contract prices.

Generally, in the matter of a producer insistence upon favored-nation or redetermination clauses without regard for compensatory price concessions, there does not appear to be sufficient evidence to support readily an inference of seller collusion. A second approach, then, would be to search for evidences of uniformity in the use of these market practices since, as in pricing, a widespread uniformity would be an unlikely product of the type of bargaining transaction which characterizes the field market for gas.

In this connection, the distinction between prevalence and uniformity must be stressed; the former does not imply the latter. It is again a simplification to suggest, for example, that all favored-nation clauses are alike or that they differ only in unimportant details. Thus, two-party favored-nation clauses may be prevalent in most gas supply areas, but they are not necessarily uniform in their content.

The element of uniformity which is most important relates to the contractual definition of the favored-nation area—the area over which buyer action in acquiring gas at a higher price initiates a similar price change in the old contract. From a producer's point of view, a favored-nation clause—the coverage of which is limited to a single gas field or to a short radius from the point of production—is not likely to be very valuable or to represent much benefit. The extent of the favored-nation area, therefore, becomes a matter of bargaining between buyer and seller. And, like pricing, a system of monopolistic co-operation would require each seller's adherence to a uniform favored-nation area, since the buyer would plainly prefer that the seller be willing to accept the most circumscribed of these.

The examination of available contract data has disclosed, for the most part, an absence of uniformity in this vital feature of the favored-nation clause. This lack of uniformity unquestionably characterizes the submarkets which constitute the effective areas of competition. However, within individual supply areas, a larger uniformity element existed, with some tendency to make the favored-nation area conterminous with the involved supply area or the district. In part, this is explained by the fact that the district unit represents a well-known and precisely defined area, which would tend to minimize disputes in the interpretation of the clause. Nevertheless, since uniformity suggests the possibility of seller co-operation in the use of the favored-nation clause—at least within a given supply area—the monopolistic potential of the practice should be explored in detail.

In the case of price redetermination, there is also the need to distinguish between prevalence and uniformity. Various price redetermination clauses are quite different, depending upon the length of the price redetermination period, as well as the method of redetermination. The fact of the matter is that the length of the price redetermination period was a basic bargaining element in natural gas purchase contracts. Buyers wished to lengthen that period; sellers wished to shorten it; and, like price, changes which tended toward the advantage of buyers or sellers reflected changes in bargaining power. A pattern conforming to the above was clearly evident in the purchase contract data. At the beginning of the 1945–53 period, price redetermination was either absent or did occur only after fifteen years. With a strengthening producer bargaining position, the price redetermination period had been established, by 1953, at five years.

Furthermore, if price redetermination clauses were eliminated, gas producers would presumably use their bargaining power to negotiate contracts whose legal terms were no greater than what would have been the price redetermination period. Consequently, the mere prevalence of such contract clauses is small evidence of noncompetitive seller behavior. Only if such provisions were highly uniform in form and content, might a monopolistic condition be inferred—as might be done if prices displayed an unreasonably rigid pattern. Such a degree of uniformity did not seem to characterize field markets during the period 1945–53. Actually, there was probably less uniformity in the details of this contract provision than in almost any other.

C. MONOPOLISTIC POTENTIAL OF FIELD MARKET PRACTICES

Of the two market practices examined, a degree of uniformity which might have significance as an indicator of monopolistic behavior could be found only for the favored-nation clause. However, it must be stressed that, while such clauses were prevalent throughout the southwestern supply region, the competitively important element of uniformity, namely, the geographical scope of the favored-nation area, did not extend beyond individual supply areas. Since any single supply area would not normally encompass all the supply options available to a pipe-line buyer, this fact would tend to restrict the effects of uniformity in the favored-nation area, assuming that it had its origins in seller collusion.

Still, if favored-nation clauses operative within individual supply areas are a monopolistic device, their potential in this respect warrants examination. There is also the possibility that a combination of field market practices can have noncompetitive effects. This, too, requires consideration.

Apart from a limited role in bringing about future contract price adjustments, two-party favored-nation clauses can be explained, first, as an effort by gas producers to protect themselves against the discrimination inherent in the lack of open pricing in gas field markets. Pipe-line buyers can play one seller against the other and contract for gas from the weakest seller first, moving up the price scale until supply requirements are met. The two-party favored-nation clause removes any incentive the buyer might have to practice such discrimination. It is more than possible that this effect of the device may well have been responsible for its rapid spread after 1947—representing one direction in which gas producers, acting independently, could make use of a growing bargaining power.

While the favored-nation clause may prevent discrimination by the purchaser and have the effect of equalizing the bargaining position of different sellers, it can also diminish competition. The favored-nation clause requires the pipe-line buyer to pay the same price at a given time to all sellers within the favored-nation area. This action can be noncompetitive in its consequences, not only because it eliminates price bargaining, but also because it leads to a type of price leadership.

To illustrate, a uniform favored-nation clause may be widely used in a particular supply area. Under such a condition, the strongest seller, in effect, sets the price in the supply area. If all small producers insist upon a favored-nation clause, they know that any price they accept would not ultimately be less than that which the largest or strongest seller would obtain. Thus, a local price leadership condition with respect to any given buyer is made possible.

But this price leadership condition is weakened in many ways which also reduce its monopolistic potential. For example, a buyer may be purchasing in a supply area containing a substantial number of relatively small producers and a single large seller. It is assumed, furthermore, that there are no forms of co-operation other than the favored-nation clause. If the buyer can meet his needs without purchasing from the large seller, the price leadership effects of the two-party favored-nation clause are minimized; the strongest of the small producers then leads, and the price which he is able to set governs.

If the buyer is unable to meet his total supply requirements from among the smaller producers, he may have to accept a higher price demanded by the large seller, this price becoming applicable to all other contracts. But the buyer has a choice of meeting only that part of his supply needs which can be obtained from small producers and seeking the rest in some other supply area, or at least outside the favored-nation area. It is evident, therefore, that the extent of the favored-nation area is critical, since it sets a limit upon the buyer's option.

However, if the buyer finds it necessary to stay within the supply area and also to meet some gas needs from the largest and strongest seller, the situation shifts. Since there is no price advantage in dealing with small producers, the buyer may meet all of his requirements from the large seller; there may actually be small factors of convenience or economy to warrant such a choice. Small producers could actually be placed at a disadvantage by their insistence upon a favored-nation clause. It is conceivable that this explains the absence of a favored-nation practice in the one supply area—the Panhandle-Hugoton—which contained a single large seller and many relatively small producers.

The analysis may be advanced a step farther by eliminating the assumption of no direct seller co-operation. In this case, the monopolistic effect is enhanced if there are a few large producers controlling perhaps as much as 50–60 per cent of the available supply. This oligopolistic structure, or the direct co-operation which fewness facilitates, may lead each seller to demand about the same price. Then, if the buyer must purchase any part of his requirements from even one of these sellers, the favored-nation device makes this the ruling price for all others. In effect, there exists a condition of collective price leadership.

In the type of situation arising under the favored-nation device, however, the price leader would tend to make fewer sales than others or—in the case of collective price leadership—some of the price-leading group might lag in sales behind the others. There is nothing in the favored-nation device which allocates sales among producers, and market sharing would be difficult. Consequently, the seller with aggressive price-raising tendencies risks uncompleted sales; in effect, he raises and holds the price "umbrella" under which others secure the benefit. The large seller may reject this role and react competitively, unless it is anticipated that the policy would maximize long-term gains. But the uncertainties are so great, particularly in view of the non-repetitive character of sales in gas field markets, that such a policy may well be a gamble.

Although the favored-nation clause leads to uniformity in the contract prices which are ultimately effective, it does not necessarily imply a uniformity of initial asking prices on the part of sellers; the final uniformity occurs only after the buyer has determined how far he wishes to go along the rising curve of seller prices. Thus, the latest large-volume contracts in the Louisiana Gulf Coast area display a considerable uniformity in price and in other contract features. But it cannot be concluded from the fact of price uniformity that an advance collusive seller agreement was present. The very presence of favored-nation clauses prevents this conclusion. The asking prices might have been quite variable among different sellers but the final contract price results are identical in purchase agreements of any single buyer. The same cannot be said of uniformity in other contract elements. Unless the favored-nation clause is broadly phrased, it need not lead to uniformity in features other than price.

Based upon the foregoing presentation, it can be concluded that the favored-nation clause per se has little or no competitive significance outside individual supply areas. However, within such supply units it can have a significant monopolistic effect, to the extent that it facilitates a type of price leadership whereby the largest or strongest seller sets a price which is automatically effective for all other sellers within a given favored-nation area.

The biggest gap in such a system, however, is the buyer's ability to venture outside the favored-nation area—assuming that this area is not large enough to encompass all of his feasible supply options. The analysis of purchase contracts through 1953 has proved that the typical favored-nation area was no larger than a single supply area and, in many cases, even smaller. On the other hand, the supply options available to buyers are, at the least, encompassed within the larger submarket units, which embrace several supply areas. This fact limits sharply the monopolistic price effects which might arise from the favored-nation clause.

In the preceding discussion, market practices in the gas field have been viewed individually. However, there is the possibility that a combination of these practices would have price effects that would be, at the least, noncompetitive. "Noncompetitive" in this usage means that the asserted price effects would not necessarily be dependent upon features of structure and behavior in the field market which would be considered monopolistic. These price effects are noncompetitive in the sense that they differ from those which would prevail in the absence of these market practices, if there is an otherwise competitive field market.

The noncompetitive effects under consideration are general in nature and can be the result of a combination of long-term contracts, favored-nation clauses and price redetermination provisos. They may arise in the following manner:[12] Long-term purchase contracts first engross a portion of the existing supply of gas. If these contracts also contain two-party favored-nation clauses, there is a tendency for the additional gas needs of old buyers to focus upon the uncommitted gas supply in other producing areas. At the least, a situation arises in which all new demands for gas must be met from uncommitted gas supplies. In short, buyers are not able to compete for old gas supplies, and—given the favored-nation clause—some buyers cannot even compete for all of the uncommitted gas reserves.

As a consequence of focusing new demands upon a more limited supply, current prices are raised above competitive levels, e.g., that price which would prevail in the absence of these practices and assuming the market otherwise competitive. These noncompetitive prices are then transmitted back to committed gas reserves by price redetermination clauses, which establish new prices equal to the average of the three highest in the price redetermination area. The speed with which the new price level is passed back depends on the length of the price redetermination period and the scope of the price redetermination area.

These noncompetitive effects obtain even in the absence of seller behavior and seller structure which might be considered monopolistic. But, if monopolistic seller behavior characterized those producers having uncommitted gas reserves or if a more concentrated market structure prevailed in the supply area containing these reserves, the noncompetitive prices would be higher.

In general, the procedures governing this mechanism for establishing a noncompetitive field price level are few and simple: The first and most important is to remove a part of the total supply from the market by long-term contract; the second is to focus and concentrate new demands upon the reduced supply by two-party favored-nation clauses; and the third is to transmit

[12] A technical analysis of these price effects was given in Chapter 7, the results of which are restated here in summary form.

the new price level back to the old supply by price redetermination or similar contract price adjustment clauses.

Of the three devices which make up the mechanism, the two-party favored-nation clause is least necessary. Even in its absence, new demands can be brought to bear only upon uncommitted supplies, and its place in the system is simply to concentrate that demand. The key marketing practice is the long-term contract; without it the aforementioned consequences do not flow, and, even if it were the only practice in force, noncompetitive prices could still be obtained by the owners of uncommitted gas. Of course, without price redetermination, no benefits would be secured by those committing old supplies under contract.

That such a mechanism may have actually operated in the gas field market can be partly illustrated from inter-supply area price relationships after 1952. Thus, the Louisiana Gulf Coast supply areas—where most of the uncommitted reserves were found—recorded a considerable price premium for large-volume gas. In contrast, price levels for other supply areas were substantially below the Louisiana Gulf Coast level, although they did show a lagging upward adjustment.

Granted that the combination of marketing practices can result in the establishment and perpetuation of noncompetitive prices, the question arises of whether or not the mechanism was the outcome of conscious design and concerted action of gas producers. Unfortunately, the type of data available to this study is not well suited to resolving this question. The effects of the mechanism are generalized and are postponed in a manner which makes the usual test of uniformity inapplicable. Actually, uniformity in details of the practices is not necessary; it is enough that long-term contracts, favored-nation clauses, and price redetermination be prevalent. Even from the fact of prevalence, nothing certain can be concluded concerning collusive origins. As has already been fully demonstrated, the two key elements in the mechanism —the long-term contract and price redetermination—could easily have evolved without concerted seller action.

Since prevalence and uniformity of the market practices do not provide sure bases for judgment, support for a conclusion that the mechanism had monopolistic origins would have to come from direct evidences of seller collusion. If collusion was the force behind the system, discovery and proof of this fact would be beyond the resources of this study. But what are the probabilities? If the marketing practices were developed, their use stimulated, and the adherence of many sellers encouraged with a conscious anticipation of future monopolistic benefits, the situation would constitute an outstanding example of monopoly by indirection. Its relative complexity, the postponement of benefits, the large number of sellers whose co-operation would be needed, and the uncertainty of monopolistic gains to any particular producer—particularly the seller committing gas reserves when supplies were still plentiful—lead to a conclusion that the system did not have collusive or monopolistic origins, although these conditions do not exclude such a possibility.

Many lines of analysis have been followed in evaluating market behavior and practices in the gas field. All lead to conclusions which do not greatly strengthen a hypothesis of monopolistic seller behavior during the period under consideration. Thus, the existence of collusive or concerted seller action within a broadly defined gas field market—or even within submarkets and supply areas—could not be substantiated, at least by the test of price or contract uniformity. Generalized forms of seller co-operation, not requiring price-contract uniformity, appeared improbable, and evidence to sustain such a possibility could not be derived from the purchase contract data or other sources. The same held true for asserted communities of interest between pipeline buyers and gas producers.

A claim that prevalence of certain market practices was due entirely to monopolistic seller market power requires proof that they could not have been expected to develop as a result of independent seller action. Actually, the analyzed purchase contract data demonstrate quite clearly that these practices could easily have been responses to conditions which are characteristic of gas field markets.

Nevertheless, some of these market practices might have a monopolistic potential which would encourage their use. However, practices which introduce contract price flexibility, such as price redetermination, are simply price elements in the purchase transaction and do not, alone, constitute a means of manipulating price structure.

More significant in this respect were favored-nation clauses. Their principal monopolistic effect was to make possible a price leadership system whereby the price demanded by the strongest seller, whose gas supply was needed by the purchaser, became the ruling price. This effect, however, did not extend beyond the favored-nation area, which was rarely larger than a single supply area. Since supply options available to pipe lines generally included more than one supply area, it could be concluded that the favored-nation clause had a relatively slight effect upon field price levels.

Consideration was also given to the possibility that a combination of market practices—especially the long-term contract joined with a price redetermination device—might yield noncompetitive price results. The combination of these market imperfections did have such effects, although there was little evidence that the system was part of a deliberate monopolistic design.

Finally, of considerable importance for the whole problem of field market practices was the pattern by which these contract devices came into widespread use between 1945 and 1953. Development was not of a character which supports a presumption of monopolistic seller action. A basic conclusion derived from the investigation of market behavior in Part II was that these contract devices evolved gradually, becoming more advantageous to sellers in form and detail as individual bargaining positions were strengthened by a growing demand for gas. Had collusive monopoly been responsible for these market practices, introduction would have occurred earlier, over a shorter period of time, and in forms which—from the beginning—would have been more protective of seller interests.

A Policy Proposal

In the course of this study, many paths have been followed to search out the elements of monopoly in natural gas field markets during the critical period 1945–53. The general problem for which an answer has been sought is whether or not a monopoly condition exists which necessitates public intervention of a character generally associated with the system of utility regulation. As far as the facts and analyses of this study have been able to show, the requisite condition of monopoly is difficult to find. It is not that the investigation has been unable to discover any element of market power, or that regulatory intervention of any kind is unnecessary. Rather, it is a case where the degree of market power on the seller side of the field market simply does not appear great enough to warrant the application of public price controls.

If field price regulation—on a utility cost standard or otherwise—is to be sanctioned, it must be founded on something besides a claim of monopoly behavior or excessive concentration among gas producers. Of course, such a conclusion is necessarily limited to the factual foundation upon which it rests; it is conceivable that other evidence may exist, particularly concerning seller collusion, which might lend support to an opposite conclusion. However, the probabilities are not encouraging. Seller collusion leaves its imprint in the market it is seeking to control; vestiges would have been found in the market transactions analyzed.

Furthermore, confusion has arisen from the error of ascribing to monopoly those price effects which are the product of either field market imperfections or inherent natural limitations upon gas supplies. Both conditions can exist independently of monopolistic seller behavior or structure; both can conceivably be used to justify field price regulation. Market imperfections might be so refractory that they could be dealt with only through price control. Scarcity values might be so large that their social appropriation through administrative price fixing would be sought. But, whatever the merits of these possibilities, not to distinguish them from monopoly merely adds to confusion. They present problems for which quite different solutions can be found.

Since the conclusion reached in this study on the question of gas monopoly bears heavily upon important public policy decisions, its main supports might well be restated. At the outset, it should be noted that, although natural gas field prices rose markedly in the postwar period, it would be an extreme simplification to attribute that rise only to seller influences; an equally marked increase in demand was experienced. For example, it was estimated that between 1945 and 1953 there was a 300 per cent increase in the field price of gas entering the large-volume pipeline market. But it was also shown that, for the same time, there was approximately a threefold increase in the annual volume of gas absorbed by the interstate pipe-line market. An increase of this magnitude must surely have exerted considerable upward pressure upon field prices.

Still, such data do not deal with the essential question: Did gas producers possess a market power which led to greater price increases than those which might have been expected from the growth in demand? The question could certainly be answered negatively for the period 1945–50. Based upon a review of market transactions, there was little doubt that an arm's-length bargaining, in which the bargaining advantage was more than likely weighted on the buyer's side, characterized field markets at that time. Generally speaking, a workable competition was clearly operative—a condition not without significance, since it was during this period that very large gas reserves were committed to an interstate market.

After 1950, substantial changes occurred in field markets, some of which have been construed as monopolistic. Favored-nation clauses came into widespread use; contract price flexibility clauses became increasingly favorable to sellers; and a sharply rising price movement became evident in 1952. But it can hardly

be claimed that these changes were entirely the outcome of monopolistic influences. They could as readily have reflected an im-
proved seller bargaining position within a workably competitive
market context.

Supporting this possibility was the absence of any real evidence in the purchase contract data which indicated the existence
of any wide-ranging organized producer agreement to control
field prices. At best, a partial price leadership system within individual supply areas could have functioned through the use of
favored-nation clauses. Its effectiveness would have depended
upon seller adherence to a uniform favored-nation area. That such
a price leadership system actually functioned is sufficiently doubtful to require additional support and, if confirmed, would more
properly justify antitrust action than a detailed and far-reaching
field price regulation.

Nor did the purchase contract analysis give much support
to a contention that the machinery for a tacit but monopolistic
seller co-operation existed in the form of escalator clauses. These
devices, resulting in varying degrees of contract price flexibility,
had little monopolistic effect when considered separately, and they
were explicable as independent seller responses to field market
conditions. However, a mechanism evolving from a combination
of such practices with a long-term contractual commitment of
gas supplies could have had significant price effects. The system,
however, did not seem to have monopolistic origins, for the most
vital element in it—the long-term purchase contract—came from
the buyer's side of the market.

Considerable seller market power also assertedly arose from
large buyer exit-costs after a pipe line was committed to a particular supply source. But the market power accruing to a single
seller from this factor has been overstated, although the exit-costs
of withdrawing entirely from field markets has great importance
from another standpoint. While it is indisputable that "you can't
move a pipe line around like a garden hose," this scarcely defines
the supply options of most pipe lines with respect to any particular seller. Few pipe lines find it necessary to relocate or abandon

mainline facilities, and they can minimize the impact of exit-costs by diversifying purchases over many sellers.

Thus far, attention has been chiefly directed toward seller behavior, and little has been said about a competitive market structure. The latter, however, may be much more important, if competitive market conditions are to be a continuing possibility. The investigation of field markets disclosed the presence of numerous sellers capable of providing effective supply options to buyers. Such a structural condition certainly held true for the entire southwestern gas-producing region, as well as for the highly important Gulf Coast–East Texas market unit, and to a lesser degree it applied even within smaller submarkets. It was concluded that a structural condition existed which was capable of providing competitive price results.

Nevertheless, this structural potential may be impaired by the market imperfection of a long-term contractual commitment of gas reserves. Since it focuses new demands upon a diminishing amount of uncommitted gas reserves held by fewer sellers, this practice can exert a strong upward influence upon field prices. Not only does the contractual commitment of reserves prevent a reallocation of existing gas supplies with its restraining effect on price increases, but it also makes possible a distinctive monopolistic pressure upon field price levels.

For example, assuming a high degree of seller concentration among those holding uncommitted gas reserves, a monopolistic level of prices for such reserves could be established. If price redetermination devices were widespread, this monopolistic level of prices would be soon transmitted to previously committed gas supplies. Being "locked in" by long-term contractual commitments, these supplies could not be released to prevent further price rises. Conversely, if new buyers had the opportunity of bidding for their needs from a more widely held total gas supply, the market power accruing to those holding uncommitted gas would be effectively curtailed.

But the field price effects of long-term contracts and redetermination are not dependent upon a monopolistic control of uncommitted gas reserves; they are obtained, although with lesser force, even in the absence of such a monopolistic condition. In this case, new demands would still be focused upon uncommitted reserves, and the price levels set for them would still be transmitted to committed gas supplies.

Here, then, is one of the keys to understanding the field price problem. Long-term purchase contracts and the escalator of price redetermination can result in a level of field prices higher than that which would prevail in a competitive field market. The impact of these market imperfections has not always been clearly comprehended in the controversy over gas field monopoly. Yet their unrestrained operation could lead to field price levels unrelated to long-term demands for gas. Such field price distortions would not be easily corrected, and it is this possibility—even if its causes were not understood—which has undoubtedly motivated pipe-line and gas distributor support for field price regulation.

Regulatory intervention, short of fixing field prices, can be designed to mitigate substantially, if not resolve, the problem. The principle guiding that intervention would be the creation of conditions which permit as much of the total gas supplies as possible to be made available in the field market at any given time. In its simplest and strongest form, the proposed intervention would seek to eliminate any long-term contractual commitments of natural gas reserves.

Replacing these commitments would be an organized spot market for field gas, possibly under public supervision. A close approximation would be the use of very short-term contracts—perhaps for one- or two-year terms. With purchase arrangements of such short duration, price redetermination provisions would become unnecessary, and favored-nation clauses would not be particularly useful to sellers. In any case, such devices would be prohibited to the degree that they limit buyer access to gas supplies.

Since gas supplies sufficient to establish the economic feasibility of pipe-line facilities would no longer be assured through private contracts, a substitute would have to be provided. This need only take the form of a regulatory restraint on pipe-line overexpansion. The regulatory agent would continually ascertain whether or not total gas supplies were adequate to meet total pipe-line requirements for an accepted minimum time period. This period could be twenty years; it might be less, to take account of anticipated future additions to gas reserves.

Under such a system, a new pipe-line project or an expansion of existing facilities would be certificated only if the applicant or the regulatory agent could verify the availability of gas supplies necessary to establish its economic feasibility. Full implementation of the proposal might also require restraints on the withdrawal of gas supplies once they have been committed to a pipe-line market, as well as more complete regulatory knowledge regarding the amount of uncommitted gas reserves available at any given time.

A fundamental requirement for the above proposal is that a competitive market condition exist with respect to the total supply of gas. This appears capable of achievement. The structural potential for seller competition in field markets is high; strengthened by suitable antitrust enforcement action, it would minimize the probability of monopolistic seller agreement. Actually, the strongest monopolistic influence in the gas field stems from the possibility that a few sellers may increasingly dominate remaining uncommitted gas reserves. This likelihood can be almost entirely obviated by creating the market situation described.

The legislative implementation of such a proposal, however, would encounter strong opposition. It would lead to private losses, although in this respect the proposal is no different from other schemes which have been offered. Thus, some pipe lines hold relatively firm long-term contracts, negotiated during the period of low field prices. These buyers, and indirectly the gas distributors and the ultimate consumers in the market they serve, would sustain an economic injury. The producer under such contracts would, of course, benefit. On the other hand, some recent projects and their customers would probably gain by the pulling down of top field prices, and all would ultimately benefit, since future field price increases would be restrained.

Another solution to the field price problem which has been proposed is to institute some system of maximum price control for new purchases of gas reserves. In direct line with this has been the scheme of control included in one of the more recent legislative efforts to deal with the problem—the 1955 Harris-Fulbright Bill. While exempting independent producers from direct federal regulation, this legislation sought to give the Federal Power Commission authority to establish the maximum price for new gas supplies acquired by interstate pipe lines. This was to be accomplished indirectly by permitting the FPC to disallow as a pipe-line operating expense any part of the field price for such new purchases which was in excess of a "reasonable market price." This control was also to be applied to old purchase contracts whenever escalator clauses or contract price flexibility devices led to a price increase greater than a "reasonable market price."

In light of earlier analyses, this proposed legislation can be viewed as an attempt to prevent "unreasonable" prices from being established for uncommitted gas reserves and subsequently having these transmitted to old supplies by the operation of escalator clauses. Aside from the fact that its indirect, disallowance method of regulation was a serious deficiency, the legislation contained a major flaw. Its administration would have bogged down in the morass of finding a "reasonable market price," for the legislative architects plainly indicated that this was not to be based upon costs.

Regulation on such a standard would have meant no increase above existing top field price levels. Alternatively, it would have permitted continuous increases in the "reasonable market price" to make it conform with market prices established in new arm's-length transactions. However, such prices could readily have risen above competitive norms, since the underlying condition affecting their determination—the inability to bring demand to bear upon total gas supplies—would have been unchanged.

A final variable in the complex policy problem of field price regulation should be treated. Assuming that field price levels are always above competitive norms and that such levels are being transmitted to committed gas supplies, removal of the contractual hindrances to competitive adjustment—as proposed here—might not be sufficient. There is still the hindrance to adjustment presented by the large, long-lasting capital investments of pipe lines and distributors.

Here is the real "bite" of buyer exit-costs and the second key to the field price problem: the inability of pipe lines, distributors, and even ultimate consumers to leave the market when rising field prices destroy the economic feasibility of their facilities in the sense that full costs cannot be recovered. The costs of abandoning these facilities are so large that, unless the field price rose exceptionally high, the financial burden would be less if the facilities continued to operate.

As a consequence of such buyer immobilities, old gas supplies are not fully released, although some would be freed as buyers contracted their operations to minimize losses. The resulting field price level would be above a competitive norm—the price which would balance total demand with total gas supplies, assuming competitive behavior and structure among sellers, no contractual restraints, and all buyers with zero exit-costs. In short, once the field price structure is raised above long-term competitive levels, the exit-costs of buyers, which make them unable to withdraw entirely from the market, prevent an easy correction of the distortion.

It is readily seen from the above that the large immobilities and exit-costs of buyers could be used to justify the full-scale regulation of natural gas field prices—including the authority to order their reduction. It is to be noted, too, that this is a base for regulation which is completely independent of any monopoly condition among gas producers; and it has no connection with the scarcity return issue. Furthermore, field price regulation founded on this base would not infringe upon a gas producer claim for competitive returns. At least, it would not where these are defined as the returns which would be obtained in a market containing no cost restraints upon buyer exit. The problem, of course, is to devise a system of price regulation limited in its effects to a correction for buyer immobility.

In view of the importance of the buyer immobility argument for full-scale field price regulation, it would be well to restate it more fully. Thus, it would be claimed that the market practice of a long-term commitment of gas reserves to particular buyers—motivated by the rather unsuccessful efforts of individual pipe lines to hedge against the fact of immobility—has led to a price in excess of competitive norms. Removing contract restraints to adjustment would have a beneficial effect, but this would not be sufficient. The large investments of committed buyers prevent them from withdrawing entirely from a natural gas market—a choice many might accept if the cost of exit were zero. Consequently, the adjustment to a lower price is largely retarded. It would be concluded that an administrative regulation of natural gas field prices is necessary, in spite of a condition in which gas producers satisfy the criteria of competitive structure and behavior. The social objective would be to prevent gas producers in general from securing returns above competitive levels because of large exit-costs and to correct the inefficiencies of an imperfect market.

It should be pointed out that this argument for field price regulation is not supported by pointing to the economic distress of particular gas distributors or pipe lines, although these might be its main advocates. Even if field prices were set at a competitive level—as if exit-costs were nonexistent—such a price might still be so high that some buyers would be unable to cover this supply cost and the full costs of their existing facilities from any price they could charge final consumers. Field market demands of some purchasers are such that they may lead to a competitive field price which is uneconomical for other buyers. For example, pipe-line projects servicing Midwestern markets are probably able to pay field prices well beyond the limit of economic feasibility for many gas distributors and pipe lines serving markets on the Atlantic Seaboard.

Furthermore, the immobility argument for field price regulation cannot extend to the setting of prices below competitive norms in order to prevent losses to some committed buyers—buyers caught in the current of changing economic events. To do so subsidizes one private group at the expense of another. If this is to be an objective of field price regulation, it raises questions of public policy quite different from those concerned with securing competitive price results in the gas field.

The critical factor in deciding whether or not buyer immobility justifies field price regulation is the magnitude of the resulting differential above competitive norms. While little precise information is known or easily available on this question, there is considerable doubt that it would warrant full-scale field price regulation. In any case, devising the means of limiting field price control to this end would be extremely difficult. If contract restraints were removed, however, it is possible that an adjustment to competitive norms could occur to an extent that the social cost of further regulation to offset buyer immobility would be excessive relative to the gain therefrom. However, the uncertainties concerning this matter are great, and no easy judgment is possible.

To conclude, there are three distinguishable bases for seeking the public regulation of natural gas field prices:

1. to appropriate the scarcity returns or economic rents arising from natural limits upon gas supply.
2. to prevent monopoly returns from accruing to gas producers in field markets containing large elements of structural monopoly and much monopolistic behavior.
3. to prevent returns in excess of competitive norms from accruing to gas producers because of contract restraints or buyer immobilities.

With respect to scarcity returns, utility regulation of field prices on a cost basis may be a feasible but not an exclusive means of attaining that end. The social advisability of field price regulation for this purpose has not been considered in this study, although clarification of the other bases for regulation points up the need for a policy decision on this issue.

Concerning the second base for regulation, no general condition of monopoly could be found sufficient to warrant field price control. While undue concentration among uncommitted gas reserve holdings can create a significant monopolistic potential, the condition could be effectively neutralized if contractual restraints limiting access of buyers to total gas supplies were removed.

Contractual restraints are also important to the third base for regulation. In an otherwise competitive field market, they can operate to raise prices, as well as to retard downward price adjustment. Even without such restraints, large buyer exit-costs can lead to producer returns above competitive norms and financial losses for buyers because of delayed market adjustments. While the impact of buyer immobility is uncertain, nevertheless, it is judged that the elimination of contract restraints would go far in minimizing the need for price regulation on this ground. In general, if field price regulation is to be avoided, it is essential that contractually imposed barriers to market adjustment be removed.

Appendix

GAS SUPPLY AREA DEFINITIONS AND SOURCES OF DATA FOR
NATURAL GAS PURCHASE CONTRACTS SHOWN IN FIGURES I
THROUGH 8

I. GAS SUPPLY AREA DEFINITIONS

1. Panhandle-Hugoton gas supply area: the Panhandle gas field, located in northwestern Texas, and the Hugoton gas field, located in southwestern Kansas and the northwestern Panhandle portion of Oklahoma.

2. West Texas–Permian Basin gas supply area: western and southwestern Texas (Texas Railroad Commission District 8 and a portion of 7–C), as well as Lea and Eddy counties in southeastern New Mexico.

3. East Texas–North Louisiana gas supply area: the gas-producing fields of northern Louisiana, southwestern Arkansas, and eastern Texas (Texas R. R. Comm. Dist. 6).

4. Texas Gulf Coast gas supply area—Texas R. R. Comm. Dist. 2: the central area of the Texas Gulf Coast oil and gas producing region.

5. Texas Gulf Coast gas supply area—Texas R. R. Comm. Dist. 4: the southernmost portion of the Texas Gulf Coast oil and gas producing region.

6. Texas Gulf Coast gas supply area—Texas R. R. Comm. Dist. 3: the northern part of the Texas Gulf Coast oil and gas producing region.

7. Southwest Louisiana gas supply area: the western Louisiana Gulf Coast, including the following parishes—Beauregard, Allen, Evangeline, St. Landry, Calcasieu, Jefferson Davis, Acadia, Lafayette, St. Martin, Cameron, Vermilion, Iberia, and St. Mary.

8. Southeast Louisiana–Mississippi gas supply area: southeastern

Louisiana and southern Mississippi, including the Gwinville field, Mississippi.

9. San Juan–New Mexico gas supply area: the San Juan, Blanco, and Ignacio gas fields, as well as other fields in northwestern New Mexico and southwestern Colorado.

II. Sources of Data

The natural gas purchase contract data upon which figures 1 through 8 are based consist almost entirely of information reported to and initially compiled by the Federal Power Commission. A limited amount of contract data was obtained from various issues of Moody's *Public Utility Manual*.

Sources from which FPC natural gas purchase contract data have been obtained are as follows:

1. Contracts dated prior to 1947 (Kerr contracts): *96 Cong. Record 4022* (March 24, 1950).

2. Contracts dated 1947 to 1949 (Douglas contracts): *96 Cong. Record 3630* (March 20, 1950).

3. Contracts dated 1950 to 1952: Unpublished tabulations of natural gas purchase contracts, entitled "Data on Contracts Made by Interstate Pipe-Line Companies Since April 15, 1950, for the Purchase of Gas from Nonaffiliated Producers in or near Producing Fields" and "Data on Contracts Made by Interstate Pipe-Line Companies for the Purchase of Gas from Nonaffiliated Producers in or near Producing Fields, January 1, 1951 to January 1, 1953."[1]

4. Contracts dated 1953: Contract data supplied by the FPC and introduced into the record by Senator Paul H. Douglas of Illinois at *Hearings on S. 1853*, Committee on Interstate and Foreign Commerce, 84 Cong., 1 sess. (1955), 1595–1619. The tabular presentation is entitled "Data on Contracts Made by Interstate Pipe-Line Companies for the Purchase of Gas from Nonaffiliated Producers Based on Certificate Filings, January 1 to December 31, 1953."[2]

[1] These tabulations were prepared by the Federal Power Commission from the records filed with that agency and are identical in form with the 1953 FPC contract data noted in Item 4.

[2] A significant number of contracts recorded in this tabulation are dated before 1953, but they are not duplications of those found in the earlier compilations.

Selected Bibliography

Blachly, F. F., and M. E. Oatman. *Natural Gas and the Public Interest.* Washington, D. C.: Granite Press, 1947.

Boatwright, J. W. "Consumer Interest in Natural Gas Competition," reproduction of Statement on H. R. 4560 before the House Committee on Interstate and Foreign Commerce (84 Cong., 1 sess., 1955).

Cookenboo, L., Jr. *Competition in the Field Market for Natural Gas.* Houston: Rice Institute, 1958.

Douglas, Paul H. "The Case for the Consumer of Natural Gas," *Georgetown Law Journal,* Vol. XLIV (June, 1956).

————. "Federal Regulation of Independent Natural Gas Producers Is Essential," *Pub. Util. Fort.,* Vol. LVI (Oct. 13, 1955).

Edwards, C. D. *Maintaining Competition: Requisites of a Governmental Policy.* New York: McGraw-Hill, 1949.

Federal Power Commission. *Natural Gas Investigation, Docket G-580.* Washington, D. C.: U. S. Govt. Printing Office, 1948.

"Federal Price Control of Natural Gas Sold to Interstate Pipelines," *Yale Law Journal,* Vol. LIX (December, 1950).

Foster, R. L. "Natural-Gas Regulation from the Producers' Standpoint," *Georgetown Law Journal,* Vol. XLIV (June, 1956).

Francis, C. I. "Rate Regulation of Natural Gas Companies by the Federal Power Commission," *Law and Contemporary Problems,* Vol. XIX (Summer, 1954).

Gonzales, R. J. "Gas Prices Going Higher," *Gas Age,* Vol. CXIII (May 20, 1954).

Hardwicke, R. E. "Some Consequences of Fears by Independent Producers of Gas of Federal Regulation," *Law and Contemporary Problems,* Vol. XIX (Summer, 1954).

Holloway, W. J., Jr. "State Regulation of Minimum Field Gas Prices," *Okla. Law Rev.,* Vol. IV (1951).

Le Boeuf, R. J., Jr. "Chaos in the Natural Gas Industry from the

Distributor Viewpoint," *Georgetown Law Journal*, Vol. XLIV (June, 1956).

Lindahl, M. L. "Federal Regulation of Natural Gas Producers and Gatherers," American Economic Association *Papers and Proceedings—1955*. Menasha, Wisc., 1956.

McKie, J. W. *Regulation of Natural Gas*. Washington, D. C.: American Enterprise Association, 1957.

Miller, J. P. "Measures of Monopoly Power and Concentration: Their Economic Significance," *Business Concentration and Price Policy*. New York: National Bureau of Economic Research, 1955.

Neuner, Edward J. "Some Aspects of Natural Gas Regulation," Western Economic Association *Proceedings—1953 at Berkeley, California*. Salt Lake City: Univ. of Utah Press, 1954.

Pegrum, D. F. "Natural Gas Industry: An Economic Appraisal of Public Policy," *Land Economics*, Vol. XXIX (May, 1953).

Smith, C. W. "Producer Pricing Practices," *Gas Age*, Vol. CXVII (February 9, 1956).

Stigler, G. J. *The Theory of Price*. New York: Macmillan, 1952.

Stockton, J. R., R. C. Henshaw, and R. W. Graves. *Economics of Natural Gas in Texas*. Austin: Bureau of Business Research, Univ. of Texas, 1952.

Thompson, E. O. "The Railroad Commission of Texas, Oil and Gas Conservation Authority—the Legal Basis of its Operation," *Oil and Gas Compact Bulletin*, Vol. XV (June, 1956).

U. S. Congress

House. Committee on Interstate and Foreign Commerce, *Hearings on H. R. 4560, Exemption of Gas Producers*, Parts I and II (84 Cong., 1 sess., 1955).

House. Report No. 992 to accompany H. R. 6645 (84 Cong., 1 sess., 1955).

House. Committee on Interstate and Foreign Commerce, *Hearings on H. R. 79 and H. R. 1758, Natural Gas Act Amendments: Production and Gathering* (81 Cong., 1 sess., 1949).

House. Report No. 1140 to accompany H. R. 1758 (81 Cong., 1 sess., 1949).

Senate. Committee on Interstate and Foreign Commerce, *Hearings on S. 712, S. 1248, S. 1853, S. 1880, S. 1926, and S. 2001, Amendments to the Natural Gas Act* (84 Cong., 1 sess., 1955).

Senate. Committee on Interstate and Foreign Commerce, *Hear-*

ings on S. 1498, Amendments to the Natural Gas Act (81 Cong., 1 sess., 1949).

U. S. Temporary National Economic Committee, Monograph No. 36, Part I, *Report on Natural Gas and Natural Gas Pipelines in the U. S. A.* (1940).

Youngberg, J. C. *Natural Gas, America's Fastest Growing Industry.* San Francisco: Schwabacher-Frey Co., 1930.

Index

American Louisiana Pipe Line Co.: 76, 78, 99, 180, 188, 192–95
American Natural Gas Co.: 192
Appalachian gas fields: 74
Aqua Dulce field (Texas District 4): 161
Arkansas Louisiana Gas Co.: 137, 142
Athens field (La.): 135
Average contract price: 48–49, 153
Average wellhead value, gas: 43–44

Bayou Mallet field (La.): 193 n.
Bethany field (Texas): 135
Boatwright, John W.: 21, 22, 29, 81 n.
Boatwright study: 29
British-American Oil Producing Co.: 193 n.
Buyer dominance, pipe-line: 132, 133, 196, 198, 204
Buyer exit-costs: 235–36, 249, 282; as source of limited market power, 218; as argument for field price regulation, 286–89
Buyer immobility: 287; see also buyer exit-costs

Cameron field (La.): 193 n.
Carthage field (Texas): 72, 77, 89, 135, 138, 140, 144
Casinghead gas: 126
Chicago, Ill.: 115, 154
Chicago Corp.: 160
Chocolate Bayou field (Texas District 3): 169, 171, 176
Cities Service Gas Co.: 75, 117
Collective price leadership: 274; see also price leadership
Collusion, gas producers: price uniformity as test of, 132–33, 185–86, 260–61; problem of identification, 213, 255; possibility of loose cooperation, 261; assertions of in legislative hearings, 262, 268; as basis for prevalence of certain market practices, 270; evidence of, 278–79; conclusions concerning, 280, 282

Colorado Interstate Gas Co.: 73, 123
Columbia Gas System, Inc.: 76, 78, 191 n., 259 n.
Common carriers, gas pipe-line: 162, 175, 189
Communities of interest, gas producers and pipe lines: 263
Competition: criteria of, 211–12; market structure as standard of, 212, 238; seller behavior as standard of, 213; economic performance as standard of, 213–14, 216; as mechanism for income distribution and resource allocation, 214–16; determining the degree of, 217
Concentration, manufacturing: 243
Concentration, natural gas: reserve holdings, 16; measurement difficulties, 20–25; Boatwright study, 21–22, 29; field sales to interstate pipe lines, 26–34; intrastate field sales, 29; changes in, 30–34; within supply areas and submarkets, 35–40; as indicator of degree of market power, 239; uncommitted reserves, 240–41, 283; evaluation of, 242–45, 250; see also submarket concentration
Concentration, ratios: gas reserves of independent producers, 16, 18; independent producer sales to interstate pipe lines, 26, 34, 38; within gas supply areas and submarkets, 40; summary estimates, 240, 249
Concentration, seller: 5, 212, 238
Concerted seller action: 278; see also collusion, gas producers
Conservation, natural gas: 251–54; production allowables, 118; mini-

296

Index

mum field prices, 122; effect on availability of gas, 126; effect on field prices, 253

Consolidated Edison Co.: 81 n.

Continental Oil Co.: 184

Contract price flexibility: 51, 101, 104, 108–11, 153–54, 168, 195, 266

Contract renegotiation: 128, 144, 152–53

Contract restraints, gas field markets: 236, 288–89, 290; *see also* buyer exit-costs and policy proposal

Contract uniformity: *see* uniformity, price and contract conditions

Demand, postwar growth: 70–71, 74–75

Denver, Colo.: 115

Detroit, Mich.: 115, 192

Differential gas supply costs: 223–24; as source of market power, 219–20; relationship to differential rents, 220

Direct-distributor purchases: 78, 95 n., 151, 162, 174–75, 189, 203

Discontinuous supply function: 222–23

Distribution companies, as field market buyers: *see* direct-distributor purchases

Douglas, Paul Howard, Sen.: 9, 268 n., 292

Drainage, gas: 118

Dubach field (La.): 141

Durfee, James R.: 263 n.

East Haynesville field (La.): 135

East Mud Lake field (La.): 189 n.

East Texas–North Louisiana gas supply area: 72, 76, 77, 136; purchase contract data, 37, 54–55; sales concentration, 40; definition of, 48, 291; representative field prices, 63, 146–47; early commitment of gas reserves, 138; price variability, 138, 145; first appearance of third-party favored-nation clause, 140; variability in non-price contract conditions, 142; renegotiated contracts, 144

Effective contract term: definition of, 50; gas supply area patterns, 104–107; changes in duration, 122, 124

Ellis field (La.): 189 n.

El Paso Natural Gas Co.: 14, 24, 75, 89, 117, 120, 125, 127, 128

Entry restriction: 245; as basis for market power, 210; production quotas, 212

Equitable Gas Co.: 79, 151, 162

Erath field (La.): 191, 191 n.

Favored-nation clauses: 50 n., 96 n., 129; distributor objection, to 81 n.; definition of, 91; "triggering" of, 92 n., 95 n., 154, 175; purposes of, 93; price effects of, 95, 101–102; extent of use, 96–98; coverage area, 98–99, 140, 157, 187, 192, 195; use in various supply areas, 108–109, 124, 133, 139, 152–53, 157; buyer avoidance of, 155, 156, 171, 181, 187; exclusionary effect upon buyers, 167, 195 n.; as price offset, 168; as means of securing contract price flexibility, 191; as integral parts of price structure, 267; evaluation of as monopolistic practice, 267–68, 275, 279; asserted necessity that buyers accept, 268–69; evidence that higher price could offset, 269–70; prevalence not caused by seller agreement, 270; uniformity of coverage area as monopolistic test, 270; uniformity within coverage area of, 270, 271, 272; prevent buyer discrimination among sellers, 272; importance of coverage area, 273; monopolistic potential within gas supply areas, 273; explanation of absence in Panhandle-Hugoton gas supply area, 273–74; need not lead to uniformity in asking prices, 274–75

Federal Power Commission: *xvii*, 75, 158, 268, 269, 286, 292

Federal regulation, natural gas: *see* field price regulation

Federal Trade Commission: 244

Field market behavior: collusive uniformity as test of, 113, 185–86, 256; effect of pipe-line buyer dominance, 132–33, 196, 199; as competitive criterion, 212–13; difficulties in assessment of, 255; conclusions concerning, 260–61, 278–79, 281–82; *see also* price uniformity and collusion, gas producers

Field market imperfections: as basis for gas producer market power,

The Natural Gas Industry is set in eleven-point Linotype Janson
with two points of leading between the lines. The original Janson
type dates from about 1700 and is of Dutch origin, although some
sizes were cut in Germany. The original matrices have survived in
Germany and are now held by the Stempel Foundry in Frankfurt.

UNIVERSITY OF OKLAHOMA PRESS : NORMAN

DATE DUE